Contemporary Legal Issues in Africa

Olalekan Moyosore Lalude, editor

SULIS
ACADEMIC
PRESS

An Imprint of Sulis International Press
Los Angeles | Dallas | London

ISBN (print): 978-1-958139-33-2
ISBN (eBook): 978-1-958139-34-9

Published by Sulis Academic Press
An Imprint of Sulis International
Los Angeles | Dallas | London

www.sulisinternational.com

Contents

Acknowledgements

This book has been a journey of exploration, introspection, and collaboration. I am deeply grateful to everyone who has been instrumental in its creation. I extend my heartfelt appreciation to the individuals that have supported me throughout this endeavor. I would like to express my sincere gratitude to the scholars, whose research have inspired the pages of this book. Your rich and diverse experiences form the foundation of our shared narrative, and I hope that this work contributes to a deeper understanding of the contemporary legal issues facing the continent.

I would like to thank Dr. Alfred Kofi Ampadu Fofie, my Head of Department at the Faculty of Law at the Wisconsin International University College Kumasi Campus, Ghana, for his invaluable expertise and guidance in shaping the ideas that birthed this book. I would like to thank the authors whose insights have added depth and nuance to the exploration of complex issues, and I am grateful for the opportunity to learn from their studies.

I extend my appreciation to my family and friends for their unwavering support, understanding, and encouragement throughout the project. Their patience and belief in this project have been a source of strength and motivation. Finally, I would like to acknowledge the publishing team at Sulis Academic Press, whose dedication and professionalism have been instrumental in bringing this book to fruition. Thank you for your commitment to amplifying diverse voices and fostering a deeper understanding of the critical issues facing Africa today.

This book is a collective effort, and I am grateful to each person who has played a role, no matter how small, in bringing it

i

to existence. May the intellectual efforts invested in this book yield tremendous returns.

Introduction

Contemporary Legal Issues in Africa is a book in which scholars, legal practitioners, and researchers share their expertise and insights on various contemporary legal issues in Africa. The chapters critically analyze, discuss, and propose solutions to the legal challenges that are faced in Africa in the 21st century. The topics covered in this book are diverse and range from the influence of public sector corruption on the Nigerian oil sector to the challenges of good governance in West Africa. The authors that have contributed to this book have examined the legal frameworks for dispute resolution in the aviation industry, the emergence of new technology weapons during warfare in Africa, and the politics and challenges of state creation in Nigeria. They have also explored the environmental protection responsibilities in Nigeria from a human rights-based approach for effective implementation.

The first chapter of the book, 'The Influence of Public Sector Corruption on the Nigerian Oil Sector and the Effects,' by Professor Olusesan Oliyide and Sola Akinsanya, examined the impact of corruption on the Nigerian oil sector. The authors argued that corruption has had a significant impact on the Nigerian economy and has contributed to the country's underdevelopment. They further argued that the oil sector in Nigeria has been a double-edged sword, with high returns on one side and corruption on the other. Despite the Nigerian government and international organizations' efforts to combat corruption, the number of corruption cases continues to rise. While international organizations such as the World Bank and the IMF have provided support to Nigeria in developing better regulatory frameworks for finance, management of public funds, and procurement practices, there are still serious barriers to overcome. Nigeria's membership in the Extractive Industries Transparency Initiative (EITI) is a regional effort to promote transparency in payments made by oil, gas, mining, or other resource extraction corporations. However, the Nigerian government and other international organizations still face several difficulties in tackling corruption in the oil sector. The authors contend that these issues require sustained political will and strong institutions committed to transparency and accountability at all levels of the sector.

In Chapter two, 'Terra Nullius: Race and the Colonial Influence on International Environmental Law in Africa,' by Professor Ayoyemi Lawal-Arowolo and I, we explored the colonial influence on international environmental law in Africa. We argued that the colonial legacy has had a significant impact on the development of environmental law in Africa. Therefore there is need to retrace the steps of African environmental perspectives towards its earlier eco-centric stance. Professor Uwakwe Abugu and Rufus Adeoluwa Olodude, examined the legal frameworks for dispute resolution in the aviation industry. They suggest that the current legal frameworks are inadequate, and that there is need for an effective system that will ensure smooth dispute resolution in the aviation industry.

Dr King J. Nkum and Esther Sunday-Jock, explored the emergence of new technology weapons during warfare in Africa. They contend that the use of new technology weapons has significant implications for peace and security in Africa. They proposed that Africa is in need of prioritization in international governance platforms that deal with emerging technologies in peace and security. and that local regulations are necessary to protect civilians against the threats posed by these technologies, and Africa must be brought to the forefront of these discussions. An investigation into the implications of these technologies on peace and security on the continent is necessary to address these issues and ensure a more just and equitable future for Africa. The development of local regulations and policies will help to ensure that emerging technologies are used in a way that benefits the people of Africa and promotes peace and security. It is important that the international community works together to address these issues and to ensure that emerging technologies are used in a way that promotes peace and security in Africa.

Dr Joel Adelusi Adeyeye, examined the politics and challenges of state creation in Nigeria. He expressed that the current process of state creation in Nigeria is flawed and proposed that Nigeria should not create any new states over the next fifty years; instead, the current states should be strengthened to better serve the requirements of the nation's population. Fiscal federalism should be upheld, and the people should hold the government responsible for its financial operations. The federal government's authority must be transferred to the states and local government councils. State police should be permitted to operate in the same manner as other federating nations, such as the US and Australia. State and municipal governments should be in charge of road infrastructure and related issues. The revenue allocation system should be changed to provide state and local governments more money so they can carry out citizen-oriented activities. However, this should be closely watched to avoid office.

Nathal Kehinde Adegbite, explored the legal constraints in obtaining judicial dissolution of a statutory marriage in Nigeria. He argued that none of the three legally recognized marriages in Nigeria is superior or inferior to the other. The arguments the author presented in this chapter deserve serious consideration, as statutory marriage cannot be turned into a "cul de sac" for parties who enter into it in the name of protecting the marriage institution or keeping the sanctity of marriage, while the rules of exit in respect of the other types of marriage remain relaxed and less cumbersome. On the principles of equality and non-discrimination, reducing legal constraints of obtaining judicial dissolution of statutory marriage is a direction requiring both scholarly and legislative attention.

Ayobami Aluko, analyzed the environmental protection responsibilities in Nigeria from a human rights-based approach for effective implementation. The author maintained that the present legal framework and judicial activism have a positive influence on the implementation of the right to a healthy environment. Although there is still progress to be made, there is a progressive attitude towards the right to a healthy environment. Environmental protection responsibilities cannot be separated from good environmental governance in the quest for a healthy environment. Environmental governance generally relates to how and who decides, which often determines the type of decision made. The processes involved in conjunction with good governance precepts are important. Those involved in the process include the state, private sector, and civil society. According to Shelton, judicial oversight is necessary to protect the rights of those in marginalized and minority communities, who often bear a disproportionate burden of environmental harm. While it may not be desirable for the judiciary to delve into legislative decisions in environmental matters, a rights-based approach emphasizes the need for judicial oversight. The need to seek redress through courts in Nigeria is vivid, as the nation is fraught with balancing social, economic, cultural, and environmental imperatives.

Oreoluwa Omotayo Oduniyi, appraised the challenges of good governance in West Africa. Maintaining that Ghana's election success rate is a testament to the independence of its formal democratic institutions, which other West African states, including Nigeria, can learn from. And that the Election Commission, Judiciary, and Media are all independent and function seamlessly during and after an election cycle. Political actors must prioritize the democratic institutions of the country over their thirst for power. Any aggrieved party should seek redress in the courts rather than inciting violence and discrediting the entire election process. An election should not be a 'do-or-die' affair. Ghana's success is a model for other countries to follow, and it is essential to maintain the independence of democratic institutions to ensure free and fair elections.

Olalekan Moyosore Lalude, PhD
Faculty of Law, Wisconsin International University College,
Kumasi Campus
Ghana

The Influence of Public Sector Corruption on the Nigerian Oil Sector and the Effects

Olusesan Oluyide[1]
Nzeribe Abangwu[2]
Olusola Adesina[3]

Introduction

Economically and morally, corruption has serious costs which need to be deliberated on. It undermines public confidence in the integrity of governmental institutions and thus in the legitimacy of its actions. 'Economically,' public sector corruption intensifies the mal-distribution of funds because high-ranking bureaucrats shy away from pushing for policy changes that curb such behavior due to self-enrichment motive. They will not promote the adoption of rules and permits, but they shall encourage proliferation of rules and license procedures, hoping they get more ill-gotten gains through grease bribes. This chapter examined how corruption has had a profound influence on

[1]Professor of Law, Babcock University School of Law & Securities Ilishan-Remo, Ogun State.
[2]Senior Lecturer, Babcock University School of Law & Securities Ilishan-Remo, Ogun State.
[3]PhD Candidate, Babcock University School of Law & Securities Ilishan-Remo, Ogun State.

the oil sector in Nigeria, with far-reaching and detrimental effects on the country's economy and society. Nigeria, as a major oil producer, has experienced significant challenges due to corrupt practices within its public sector.

Public sector corruption worsens income inequality and perpetuates poverty because those reaping undue benefits of things like bribes, payoffs, and sweetheart deals are not typically in the lowest income bracket. Corruption has negative effects not only on GDP but also causes direct economic damage through exaction of extra-legal levies on businesses, raising the cost of doing business, and lowering the motivation to invest. In particular, "off book" payments for government projects are often much higher than the actual costs.[4] In addition, public sector corruption takes up a large chunk of the resources of small and medium business; in effect robbing Peter (the economy) to compensate for Paul (corrupt entities). Moreover, graft diverts national budget lines away from social benefits; in this regard, towards 'white elephant projects.'[5]

Nigeria's entrenched culture of corruption has resulted in a moral compass of its people taking an unfortunate nosedive over time. In the time past, corruption was depicted with terms which would make one cringe, but today it is disguised in more gentle terms, like 'the Nigerian Factor' and 'egunje,' while culprits of this act have had society's admiration due to their wealth and influence.[2] The economic effects of poor management, looting of public coffers and decay of civic value systems have brought disastrous long-term impacts in the coun-

---

[4]E. A. Owolabi, 'Corruption and Financial Crimes in Nigeria: Genesis, Trend and Consequences' (Central Bank of Nigeria Publications, 2007) <https://www.cbn.gov.ng/OUT/PUBLICATIONS/TRANSPARENCY/2007/TRANSPARENCY2007.PDF> accessed 1 September 2023.

[5]ibid

try's economy. Consequentially, this has caused mass poverty for every level of the population. In Nigeria, for example, GDP per capita had a steep drop from about U.S. $1,010.00 to about U.S. $300.00 only between the beginning of the 1980s and according to recent reliable polls, more than 70% of the nation lives below poverty, earning less than $1 a day.[6] Despite being now the sixth largest oil producing country in the world, Nigeria suffers from insufficient local refining capacity and therefore depends largely on importation of refined fuel products within the country. In fact, ironically enough, Indonesia, which is an oil abundant country, plans an MOU (memorandum of understanding) with the Nigerian Government to import oil products of Nigerian origin! It can be accounted for by the enormous ability of Indonesian crude refining its very own crude, which Nigeria does not have. It should as well be known that the higher value chain lays on the importation of refine product of petroleum as against the raw (uncertain) Crude. Corruption by itself, over time, became so endemic that it has created fertile ground for growth of all types of economic and organized crime to flourish. Nigeria remains an irredendist state in Africa, which is besmirched by the disgraceful title of being one of the most corrupt countries in the world.[7]

Corruption in the public sector often leads to the misallocation of oil revenue in Nigeria. Funds that should be invested in infrastructure development, education, and healthcare are siphoned off by corrupt officials or used for personal gain. This

---

[6]E. A. Owolabi, 'Corruption and Financial Crimes in Nigeria: Genesis, Trend and Consequences' (Central Bank of Nigeria Publications, 2007) <https://www.cbn.gov.ng/OUT/PUBLICATIONS/TRANSPARENCY/2007/TRANSPARENCY2007.PDF> accessed 1 September 2023
[7]ibid

misallocation stifles economic growth and development.[8] The influence of public sector corruption in the oil sector has resulted in substantial revenue losses for the Nigerian government.[9] Through various means, including bribery, embezzlement, and kickbacks, officials and stakeholders siphon off a significant portion of the revenue that should be going to the state.[10] This has dire consequences for public services and infrastructure. High levels of corruption in the public sector discourage foreign and domestic investments in Nigeria's oil industry.[11] The lack of transparency and accountability makes investors hesitant to engage in a sector riddled with corruption, hampering the country's ability to fully exploit its oil resources.

Public sector corruption has also exacerbated environmental problems in the oil sector.[12] Illicit activities such as illegal oil bunkering and lax enforcement of environmental regulations has led to oil spills, pollution, and long-term damage to the environment, affecting local communities and ecosystems. The unequal distribution of oil wealth due to corruption has con-

---

[8]DO Olayungbo, 'Effects of Oil Export Revenue on Economic Growth in Nigeria: A Time Varying Analysis of Resource Curse' (2019) 64 Resources Policy

[9]Olusola Joshua Olujobi, 'Nigeria's Upstream Petroleum Industry Anti-Corruption Legal Framework: The Necessity for Overhauling and Enrichment' 26(7) Journal of Money Laundering Control

[10]ibid

[11]Shang-Jin Wei, 'Corruption in Economic Development: Beneficial Grease, Minor Annoyance, or Major Obstacle?' (World Bank Group Policy Research Working Papers 25 June 2013) <https://elibrary.worldbank.org/doi/abs/10.1596/1813-9450-2048#:~:text=Corruption%20hinders%20economic%20development%20by,efficient%20but%20more%20manipulable%20public> accessed 1 September 2023

[12]Vincent Tawiah, Abdulrasheed Zakari and Rafael Alvarado, 'Effect of Corruption on Green Growth' (2023) Environment, Development and Sustainability

tributed to social inequality in Nigeria. While a select few benefit immensely, the majority of the population remains impoverished, leading to social unrest, crime, and political instability. Institutions responsible for regulating and overseeing the oil sector have been weakened.[13] This, in turn, perpetuates a cycle of corruption, as there is limited capacity to enforce anti-corruption measures effectively. Nigeria's reputation as a corrupt nation with a mismanaged oil sector has negative repercussions on its international standing. This can affect diplomatic relations, foreign aid, and the country's ability to attract investment and trade partners. Public sector corruption has had a detrimental influence on Nigeria's oil sector, resulting in revenue losses, environmental degradation, social inequality, and a weakened investment climate. Addressing corruption in the public sector is essential for Nigeria to harness its oil wealth for the benefit of its citizens and foster sustainable development. This chapter examined the extent of influence of public sector corruption.

Historical Overview of Public Sector Corruption in Nigeria's Oil Sector

The corruption in the natural resource extraction sector is persistent and deep-seated — most evidently in petroleum and geologic gas exploration and production, where substantial rents come to play. There is a whole range of corrupt behavior in here: from "launderers", from bribes and even facilitating financial terrorism. Consequently, individuals engaged in this sector face a significant and pressing challenge: — strategizing to reduce the dangerous exposure to being caught up in corrupt

---

[13]Olusola Joshua Olujobi, 'Deregulation of the Downstream Petroleum Industry: An Overview of The Legal Quandaries and Proposal For Improvement in Nigeria' (2021) 7(4) Heliyon

practices, whether within your own company or from doing business with third parties.[14]

Like many other sectors, oil & gas is not immune from the universal problem of corruption that has afflicted this sector as well as any others since oil was first discovered around Southern Nigeria. These efforts to investigate and rein in this problem can be seen since the 1950s at the reign of military dictator Olusegun Obasanjo. During this time, an investigative committee was set up to probe a missing sum of ₦2.8bn Naira that could not be traced from the Nigerian National Petroleum Corporation (NNPC). Afterward in 1979, when Shehu Shagari came into office, another panel was set up to investigate the disappearance of monies in the NNPC. But the reports of such probes did not satisfy the public opinion, for these reports only exposed names instead of filing charge- sheet against those named and those punished![15]

Moreover, the time of plenty for oil money saw billions siphoned off abroad, around $12.2billion — some of them still stolen. It was contained in reports submitted to the government by the panel headed by Dr Pius Okigbo, which in 1994 was set up at the instance of General Sani Abacha in response to the currency crisis then. Also, in 1998 and 1999, Chevron Nigeria Limited has been accused of complicity in tax evasion whereby it is said tax officers colluded with the Company resulting in an

---

[14]Chioma Barbara Achinike, 'Nigeria: Anti-Corruption Overview In The Oil And Gas Industry' (Mondaq, 13 December 2021) <https://www.mondaq.com/nigeria/white-collar-crime-anti-corruption--fraud/1130238/anti-corruption-overview-in-the-oil-and-gas-industry> accessed 10 September, 2023
[15]Chioma Barbara Achinike, 'Nigeria: Anti-Corruption Overview In The Oil And Gas Industry' (Mondaq, 13 December 2021) <https://www.mondaq.com/nigeria/white-collar-crime-anti-corruption--fraud/1130238/anti-corruption-overview-in-the-oil-and-gas-industry> accessed 10 September, 2023

alleged avoidance of about US$2.7 billion. The main contributors to these fraud cases were weaknesses (or lack) of comprehensive anti-corruption laws in the country.[16]

Funds earmarked for infrastructural developments at the center never got to their destinations due to corrupt officials who diverted them to personal accounts, leaving the populace in perpetual abject poverty even though Nigeria is the 8th largest producer of crude This is a factor because over the past several years, oil and gas corruption has been getting worse, partly as a result of crude oil prices going down and the considerable expenses that companies have had to make in the refining process. While increasing one's profit is inherent for all companies in the market, yet this downward course in O&G have fostered the use of unfair means, of which Bribing and Corruption is most prominent amongst! In 2011, two of the biggest names in the oil business — Royal Dutch Shell and Eni — had been accused of dodging $1.1 billion in governments revenues while drilling for oil (The Nigerian Government eventually lost to them on appeal). This was done by granting oil block OPL 245 to Malabu Oil and Gas Limited, a company allegedly belonging to Mr. Dan Etete, who at the material time was the Ministry of Petroleum. The powers to issue licenses and award contracts accorded to Ette were arbitrary and not guided by any rules, brewing clear violation of Nigeria's Corporate Governance Principles and also against the 1991 Code of Conduct Bureau and Tribunal Act. Clearly, current legal frameworks have not succeeded as deterrents. This particular scam saw individuals, companies (and a former petroleum minister) face criminal charges and prosecution overseas but an obvious lack of action or acknowledgement of corruption at home. Tackling corruption is a tough job, particularly in the complex maze of

---

[16]ibid

oil and gas, where large sums of money are needed for dealing with these challenges effectively.[17]

Public sector corruption works to amplify economic inequalities and poverty — usually those that profit from such corrupt practices aren't members of the poorer population in the first place. In the specific case of the Nigerian oil and gas sector, however, this lack of transparency has led to the gap between rich and poor growing ever larger, with serious destabilizing effect on society which is evident with increasing levels of militancy and political instability. It also exacerbated poverty as well as curtailed access to crucial public goods such as health care, education, transportation infrastructures, and communications networks at the expense of expensive "white elephants" or inferior infrastructures and legal systems. Clearly, fundamental needs, including lights and potable water, continue to go unmet, an illustration of how entire countries suffer under the weight of corruption and inept leadership.[18] In particular, the rebellion in the Niger Delta, one of Nigeria's regions with significant levels of oil production, is an example of how corrupt practices based on oil-related earning have a detrimental impact. Indeed, the intricate challenges posed by corruption in

---

[17]Chioma Barbara Achinike, 'Nigeria: Anti-Corruption Overview In The Oil And Gas Industry' (Mondaq, 13 December 2021) <https://www.mondaq.com/nigeria/white-collar-crime-anti-corruption--fraud/1130238/anti-corruption-overview-in-the-oil-and-gas-industry> accessed 10 September, 2023
[18]Salisu Ogbo Usman, 'The Opacity and Conduit of Corruption in the Nigeria Oil Sector: Beyond the Rhetoric of the Anti-Corruption Crusade'(2011) 13(2) Journal of Sustainable Development in Africa

Nigeria bear semblance to the concentric layers of an onion: underneath all masks lies an even nastier reality.[19]

Nigeria stands as one of sub-Saharan Africa's leading oil producer, boasting substantial reserves that surpass those of its neighboring countries.[20] Although it ranks as the 11th largest oil producer worldwide, Nigeria's significance on the global stage arises from several factors. These include the exceptional quality of its crude oil, its strategic accessibility to Western markets, ongoing opportunities for exploration, and its notable divergence from resource nationalization trends observed in other oil-producing nations.[21] Oil plays a central role in Nigeria's economy, contributing significantly to government revenues.[22] Paradoxically, Nigeria is internationally recognized as one of the most corrupt nations, and its oil sector is notorious for pervasive corruption. Due to the intricate and largely concealed nature of the oil industry's operations, it's challenging to

---

[19]Salisu Ogbo Usman, 'The Opacity and Conduit of Corruption in the Nigeria Oil Sector: Beyond the Rhetoric of the Anti-Corruption Crusade'(2011) 13(2) Journal of Sustainable Development in Africa

[20]Saifaddin Galal, 'Oil Production in Africa as of 2022, by Country' (Statista 22 September, 2023) <https://www.statista.com/statistics/1178514/main-oil-producing-countries-in-africa/#:~:text=Nigeria%20was%20the%20leading%20oil,above%2050%20million%20metric%20tons.>

[21]Alexandra Gillies, 'Reforming Corruption Out of Nigerian Oil? Part One: Mapping Corruption Risks in Oil Sector Governance' (Chr. Michelsen Institute 2009) <https://www.cmi.no/publications/3295-reforming-corruption-out-of-nigerian-oil-part-one> accessed 27 August, 2023

[22]Doris Dokua Sasu, 'Oil Industry in Nigeria - Statistics & Facts' (Statista, 29 June, 2023) <https://www.statista.com/topics/6914/oil-industry-in-nigeria/#topicOverview> accessed 27 August, 2023

precisely ascertain the how, when, and to what extent corruption occurs.[23]

The oil and gas industry remains the primary source of revenue for the Nigerian government and its citizens. Regrettably, instances of corruption are prevalent throughout the industry, spanning from oil and gas exploration to the refining and marketing of petroleum products. Given that the nation heavily relies on the oil and gas sector for sustainable development and national economic growth, the pervasive corruption within the industry has a cascading impact on all aspects of the country's socio-political economy. Numerous attempts have been undertaken by the federal government, industry management, and international organizations to root out corruption within the sector. However, the outcomes of these efforts often fall short of expectations. The battle against corruption in the industry, coupled with the capacity of stakeholders to uncover and expose acts of corruption, is crucial in deterring such malpractices.[24]

In this regard, the collaborative efforts of legal frameworks, such as anti-corruption agencies like the Economic and Financial Crimes Commission and the Independent Corrupt Practices and Other Related Offences Commission, along with the administrative framework provided by the Freedom of Information Act, which enables the press to report corruption cases without hindrance, are high-end tools for the resolution of cor-

---

[23] Alexandra Gillies, 'Reforming Corruption Out of Nigerian Oil? Part One: Mapping Corruption Risks in Oil Sector Governance' (Chr. Michelsen Institute 2009) <https://www.c-mi.no/publications/3295-reforming-corruption-out-of-nigerian-oil-part-one> accessed 27 August, 2023
[24] P.A. Donwa, C.O. Mgbame, O.M. Julius, 'Corruption in the Oil and Gas Industry: Implication for Economic Growth' 22 (2015) European Scientific Journal

ruption in the Nigerian oil sector. These combined efforts, involving the legislature, executive branch, and judiciary, are essential steps toward combating corruption effectively in the Nigerian oil and gas sector.[25] Given that the nation heavily relies on the oil and gas sector for sustainable development and national economic growth, the pervasive corruption within the industry has a cascading impact on all aspects of the country's socio-political economy.[26]

Public sector corruption infiltrates every facet of the industry, from the initial stages of oil and gas exploration to the subsequent processes of refining and marketing petroleum products.[27] The ramifications of this pervasive corruption are far-reaching and profoundly impactful, given the nation's heavy reliance on the oil and gas sector as a linchpin for sustainable development and national economic growth. Nigeria's socio-political economy, as a result, bears the brunt of this corrosive influence. Over the years, numerous attempts have been made by various stakeholders to address and combat the influence of public sector corruption within the oil and gas industry. These stakeholders include the federal government, industry management, and international organizations.[28] Regrettably, the

---

[25]ibid
[26]ibid
[27]Halimatu Muhammad Bande, 'Connivance in Criminality: Corruption and Corporate Social Responsibility in Nigeria's Oil Sector' in Steven Kayambazinthu Msosa, Shame Mugova, Courage Mlambo (eds) *Corporate Social Responsibility in Developing Countries: Challenges in the Extractive Industry* (Springer International Publishing, 2023)
[28]Anwar Shah, 'Combating Corruption in the Oil and Gas Sector' in Anwar Shah (ed) *Taxing Choices for Managing Natural Resources, the Environment, and Global Climate Change: Fiscal Systems Reform Perspectives* (Springer International Publishing 2023)

outcomes of these efforts have often fallen short of expectations. The battle against public sector corruption in the industry hinges on two critical factors. Firstly, there is the need for a robust framework and capacity among stakeholders to detect, investigate, and expose acts of corruption. Secondly, the collaborative efforts of legal and administrative structures must work in harmony to effectively combat this scourge. The Freedom of Information Bill, which grants the press the freedom to report on corruption cases without hindrance, provides an essential administrative framework. This legislative tool empowers the media to act as a watchdog, ensuring that corruption does not thrive in secrecy. The media plays a crucial role in shedding light on corruption and holding those responsible accountable.

The effectiveness of these measures hinges on a collaborative effort involving the legislative, executive, and judicial branches of government. This three-pronged approach ensures that anti-corruption efforts are not only comprehensive but also well-coordinated. The legislature enacts the necessary laws and regulations, the executive branch implements these measures, and the judiciary ensures that justice is served. Nigeria's oil and gas industry, as the backbone of the nation's revenue generation, faces the insidious challenge of corruption. However, the collective efforts of stakeholders, including anti-corruption agencies, legislative frameworks, and a vigilant media, offer hope for a brighter future. By working together and maintaining a steadfast commitment to combating corruption, Nigeria can mitigate the corrosive impact of corruption and pave the way for a more prosperous and equitable society.

Corruption Schemes in the Oil Sector

Corruption in the oil sector has been a perennial issue plaguing Nigeria, Africa's largest oil producer.[29] While the country possesses vast oil reserves that should drive economic development and prosperity, corruption schemes have hindered progress, resulting in massive losses of revenue, environmental degradation, and social inequality.[30] From bribery scandals, the case of public sector corruption in the Nigerian oil industry is an immense problem. In accordance with legal records, spanning the period from 2011 to 2015, Nigerian entrepreneurs Kolawole Akanni Aluko and Olajide Omokore, in concert with additional individuals, conspired to offer illicit inducements to Diezani Alison-Madueke, the former Minister for Petroleum Resources of Nigeria, who held authority over the nation's state-owned petroleum enterprise.[31] In exchange for these incentives, Alison-Madueke employed her influence to channel profitable petroleum contracts towards enterprises owned by Aluko and Omokore. The funds derived from these contracts,

---

[29]PA Donwa, CO Mgbame, OM Julius, 'Corruption in the Oil and Gas Industry: Implication for Economic Growth' (2015) 11 (22) European Scientific Journal

[30]Anga A Rosemary and Gomwalk O Bonmwa, 'Corruption and Economic Development in Nigeria: A Theoretical Review' (2014) 11(2) LWATI: A Journal of Contemporary Research

[31]Office of Public Affairs, 'Justice Department Recovers Over $53M in Profits Obtained from Corruption in the Nigerian Oil Industry' (Office of Public Affairs, US Department of Justice, 27 March, 2023) <https://www.justice.gov/opa/pr/justice-department-recovers-over-53m-profits-obtained-corruption-nigerian-oil-industry#:~:text=According%20to%20court%20documents%2C%20from,Nigeria's%20state-owned%20oil%20company.> accessed 14 August 2023

14

amounting to an excess of $100 million, were subsequently subjected to a money laundering scheme operating within the United States, facilitated by the procurement of various assets through discreet shell companies.[32]

These assets encompassed opulent real estate holdings situated in California and New York, as well as the acquisition of the Galactica Star, a superyacht spanning 65 meters in length. Additionally, the real estate holdings were leveraged as collateral for loans extended to Aluko and the shell corporations under his purview. As part of the asset forfeiture process, reimbursement was extended to the lien holders. The proclamation regarding these developments was articulated by Assistant Attorney General Kenneth A. Polite, Jr. of the Justice Department's Criminal Division, Assistant Director Luis Quesada of the FBI's Criminal Investigative Division, Assistant Director in Charge David Sundberg of the FBI Washington Field Office, and Chief Jim Lee of the IRS Criminal Investigation (IRS-CI). The investigations into these cases were conducted jointly by the FBI's International Corruption Squad within the Washing-

---

[32] Office of Public Affairs, 'Justice Department Recovers Over $53M in Profits Obtained from Corruption in the Nigerian Oil Industry' (Office of Public Affairs, US Department of Justice, 27 March, 2023) <https://www.justice.gov/opa/pr/justice-department-recovers-over-53m-profits-obtained-corruption-nigerian-oil-industry#:~:text=According%20to%20court%20documents%2C%20from,Nigeria's%20state-owned%20oil%20company.> accessed 14 August 2023

ton Field Office and the IRS-CI, with collaborative support from the FBI Los Angeles Field Office.[33]

Another problem caused by public sector corruption in the Nigerian oil sector is illegal-bunkering of oil.[34] The illicit trade in purloined petroleum, commonly referred to as "blood oil," presents a formidable challenge to the Nigerian state, manifesting deleterious effects on its economic stability and serving as a catalyst for the protracted insurgency prevailing within the Niger Delta region. Furthermore, this clandestine enterprise exerts a destabilizing influence on the security dynamics in the Gulf of Guinea and contributes to heightened volatility within the global energy markets. The precise quantification of daily oil theft in the Niger Delta remains elusive, with estimates ranging between 30,000 and 300,000 barrels. The cumulative economic detriment inflicted upon Nigeria as a result of unlawful oil bunkering during the period spanning from 2003 to 2008

---

[33]Office of Public Affairs, 'Justice Department Recovers Over $53M in Profits Obtained from Corruption in the Nigerian Oil Industry' (Office of Public Affairs, US Department of Justice, 27 March, 2023) <https://www.justice.gov/opa/pr/justice-department-recovers-over-53m-profits-obtained-corruption-nigerian-oil-industry#:~:text=According%20to%20court%20documents%2C%20from,Nigeria's%20state-owned%20oil%20company.> accessed 14 August 2023

[34]James Barnett, 'The Oil Thieves of Nigeria: How a Violent Conflict in the Resource-Rich Niger Delta has Wrought Ecological and Economic Devastation for a Generation' (News Lines Magazine, 26 January, 2023) <https://newlinesmag.com/reportage/the-oil-thieves-of-nigeria/#:~:text=While%20illegal%2C%20oil%20bunkering%20has,national%20security%20crisis%20for%20Nigeria.> accessed 14 August 2023

approximates a staggering sum of approximately US$100 billion.[35]

In light of these dire circumstances, it is incumbent upon the international community to assume a more proactive role in assisting Nigeria in navigating this intricate quandary. The endeavor to curtail blood oil activities must be concomitant with concerted actions aimed at combatting corruption, stemming the illicit importation of arms, and thwarting money laundering schemes. The conducive milieu fostering illegal oil bunkering is characterized by an amalgamation of factors encompassing elevated rates of unemployment among the youth demographic, the presence of armed ethnic militias, the ineffectiveness and corrupt disposition of law enforcement personnel, the complicity of government officials and politicians in shielding illicit operations, the complicity of corrupt oil company personnel, the existence of well-established international markets for stolen petroleum, and the overarching backdrop of endemic corruption.[36] The illicit oil bunkering enterprise can be segmented into three distinct categories, namely, small-scale pilferage tailored for the local market, large-scale tapping of pipelines to facilitate the filling of substantial tanker vessels earmarked for export, and the surreptitious extraction of crude oil in excess of the licensed allocation. The multifaceted array of stakeholders implicated in the illicit oil bunkering industry, spanning local youth, members of the Nigerian military and political elite, and foreign shipowners, engenders formidable

---

[35]Judith Burdin Asuni, 'Blood Oil in the Niger Delta' (United States Institute of Peace Special Report 2009)
[36]Joseph Ikechukwu Uduji, Elda Nduka Okolo-Obasi, and Simplice A Asongu, 'Cult violence in Nigeria and Corporate Social Responsibility In Oil-Producing Communities' (2023) 28(5) Local environment

challenges in attempting to unilaterally address this predicament.[37]

Prior endeavors undertaken by both the Nigerian government and the international community with the aim of curtailing illegal oil bunkering have yielded limited success in stemming the flow of blood oil. Corruption in Nigeria's oil sector is deeply entrenched in the political landscape. One of the key methods employed is the manipulation of political power. Powerful individuals, often in high-ranking government positions, conspire with oil companies to secure lucrative contracts and favorable policies in exchange for personal gain. These dealings, shrouded in secrecy, undermine the transparency and accountability required for equitable distribution of oil wealth. Rather than listing bribery and kickbacks as isolated points, it is important to understand them as integral components of corruption schemes. Corrupt officials and middlemen demand bribes and kickbacks from oil companies in exchange for access to oil blocks, licenses, and permits. These illicit payments distort the market, preventing fair competition and ensuring that the benefits of Nigeria's oil wealth are confined to a select few. Corruption thrives when the process of awarding contracts remains opaque. Rather than openly competing for projects, companies often collude with government officials to manipulate bidding processes. [38]

This collusion, which is facilitated by a lack of transparency, allows for inflated contract prices, substandard work, and the

---

[37]Judith Burdin Asuni, 'Blood Oil in the Niger Delta' (United States Institute of Peace Special Report 2009)
[38]ibid

embezzlement of funds.[39] The diversion and mismanagement of oil revenues represent another facet of corruption in Nigeria's oil sector.[40] Instead of these funds being used to benefit the entire nation, corrupt officials siphon off substantial amounts for personal enrichment. This diversion often occurs through fraudulent accounting practices and offshore accounts, making it challenging to trace and recover the stolen funds. Corruption in the oil sector is not limited to financial malfeasance. It extends to environmental degradation as well. Oil companies, in collusion with government officials, often neglect environmental regulations and safety standards in pursuit of higher profits.[41] This leads to oil spills, gas flaring, and other forms of environmental destruction, disproportionately affecting local communities. The absence of effective regulatory oversight exacerbates corruption schemes in the oil sector. Regulatory agencies tasked with monitoring and enforcing compliance are frequently understaffed, underfunded, or subject to political interference. This allows corrupt practices to persist unchecked.

The corruption schemes within Nigeria's oil sector are far-reaching and deeply ingrained in the nation's political and eco-

---

[39]NA Ozogu, OH Olabimtan, NC Chukwurah, MK Ukpong, DS Daniel, 'Effects and Causes of Illegal Crude Oil Bunkering in Nigeria: Case Study Niger Delta' (2023) 2(1) American Journal of IR 4.0 and Beyond (AJIRB)

[40]Marc-Antoine Pèrouse de Montclos, 'Oil Rent and Corruption: The Case of Nigeria' (Études de I' Ifri 2018)

[41]Kingsley E Ukhurebor and Others, 'Petroleum spills and the Communicative Response from Petroleum Agencies and Companies: Impact assessment from the Niger Delta Region of Nigeria' (2023) 15 The Extractive Industries and Society

nomic fabric.[42] Rather than listing these schemes in isolation, it is imperative to recognize them as interconnected elements of a broader issue. Addressing corruption in Nigeria's oil sector requires a multifaceted approach, including robust regulatory reforms, enhanced transparency, and a commitment to holding both public officials and private companies accountable. Only through these efforts can Nigeria unlock the true potential of its oil wealth for the benefit of all its citizens and mitigate the devastating impact of corruption on its society and environment.

Impact on Revenue Generation

In the heart of Nigeria's economic landscape, the oil and gas industry continue to reign supreme as the primary source of revenue for both the government and its citizens. It is a bittersweet truth, for amid the abundant promise of this industry, corruption has nestled itself from the very roots of oil and gas exploration to the intricate web of petroleum product refining and marketing.[43] The implications of this corrosive influence are far-reaching, as Nigeria's sustainable development and national economic growth hang precariously in the balance. The pervasive corruption within this vital sector casts a shadow that extends over all facets of the nation's socio-political economy. Despite valiant efforts mounted by the federal government, industry management, and international bodies to cleanse the industry of this nefarious stain, the outcomes thus far have fallen

---

[42]Ogbewere Bankole Ijewereme, 'Anatomy of Corruption in the Nigerian Public Sector: Theoretical Perspectives and Some Empirical Explanations' (2015) Sage Open
[43]Keith Panter-Brick (ed) *Soldiers and Oil: The Political Transformation of Nigeria* (Vol. 11 Taylor & Francis 2023)

disappointingly short of expectations. The battle against corruption within the sector hinges not only on these earnest endeavors, but also on the collective might of stakeholders, who must rise to the occasion in detecting and exposing these corrupt practices.[44]

Herein lies the linchpin of the anti-corruption crusade: the synergy of a robust legal framework, championed by agencies such as the Economic and Financial Crimes Commission and the Independent Corrupt Practices and Other Related Offences Commission, alongside the empowering administrative framework embodied by the Freedom of Information Act. These instruments empower the press to fearlessly report on cases of corruption without hindrance, while the pillars of Nigeria's governance – the legislature, executives, and the judiciary – must all rally behind the cause. In the spirit of reform, Donwa and others proposed a resolute stance against public looters. They advocated for thorough investigations into ill-gotten gains and the unwavering prosecution of those found guilty, ensuring that the stolen treasures are recouped to the full extent of their worth. It is, without a doubt, a challenging endeavor, but one that stands as a beacon of hope for a more transparent and just oil and gas industry in Nigeria.[45]

Public sector corruption often involves embezzlement and misappropriation of funds meant for public projects and services.[46] In the Nigerian oil sector, this diversion of funds away

---

[44]PA Donwa, CO Mgbame, OM Julius, 'Corruption in the Oil and Gas Industry: Implication for Economic Growth' (2015) 11 (22) European Scientific Journal
[45]ibid
[46]Ahmed Tanimu Mahmoud, 'Endemic Corruption in Nigeria's Public Service: Implication for Psycho-Criminal Assessment' (2023) 9(1) Research Journal of Criminal Policies and Social Studies

from essential infrastructure projects, education, healthcare, and other public services directly reduces the government's ability to generate revenue from taxes and other sources. When funds are siphoned off into private pockets, there is less money available for public investments that could drive economic growth. Public sector corruption can lead to underreporting of oil production volumes. Some actors within the industry may collude to understate the actual quantity of oil extracted and sold.[47] As a result, the government receives less revenue than it is entitled to from royalties and taxes based on production volumes.

In the corrupt Nigerian public sector system, companies operating in the oil sector may engage in bribery and offer kickbacks to government officials to secure favorable contracts or evade regulatory scrutiny.[48] These illicit transactions often involve reduced payments to the government for access to oil reserves or lax enforcement of environmental regulations. The revenue losses due to such underhanded deals are significant.[49] When officials are more concerned with personal gain than the public good, projects are delayed or substandard, leading to wasted resources. Inefficiencies in the oil sector translate into lost revenue opportunities, as projects may not be completed on time or may not yield their full economic potential.

Investor confidence in the Nigerian oil sector has plunged because of public sector corruption. Foreign investors are less

---

[47]Eddy Akpomera, 'International Crude Oil Theft: Elite Predatory Tendencies in Nigeria' (2015) 42(143) Review of African Political Economy

[48]Chioma Barbara Achinike, 'Nigeria: Anti-Corruption Overview In The Oil And Gas Industry' (Mondaq, 13 December 2021) <https://www.mondaq.com/nigeria/white-collar-crime-anti-corruption--fraud/1130238/anti-corruption-overview-in-the-oil-and-gas-industry> accessed 10 September, 2023

[49]ibid

likely to invest in a sector characterized by widespread corruption, fearing that their investments may be subject to extortion or arbitrary government actions.[50] Reduced foreign direct investment means missed opportunities for revenue generation, job creation, and technology transfer. There is a negative influence of public sector corruption in the misallocation of resources, including oil revenues. Funds that should be reinvested in the oil sector to improve infrastructure, enhance production efficiency, and explore new reserves are instead squandered or diverted for personal gain. This misallocation of resources diminishes the sector's long-term revenue potential.[51] Public sector corruption in the Nigerian oil sector contributes to broader economic stagnation. When funds that should be reinvested in the economy are stolen or misappropriated, the overall economic growth is slowed. A stagnant economy generates fewer opportunities for revenue generation through taxes, job creation, and increased economic activity. Public sector corruption in the Nigerian oil sector has a cascading effect on revenue generation. It not only directly depletes the government's coffers but also erodes the sector's efficiency, investor confidence, and economic growth, all of which are critical factors for sustainable revenue generation and economic development. Addressing corruption in the sector is essential for Nigeria to harness the full revenue potential of its oil resources.

---

[50]Uchechukwu Nwoke, Chinwe Martha Ekwelem, and Henrietta Chibugo Agbowo-Egbo, 'Curbing Corruption and Promoting a More Efficient Corporate Governance Regime in Nigeria' (2023) 30(2) Journal of Financial Crime

[51]Gustavo Anríquez, William Foster and Jorge Ortega, 'Rural and Agricultural Subsidies in Latin America: Development costs of Misallocated Public Resources' (2020) 38(1) Development Policy Review

Resource Misallocation and Infrastructure Deficit

Donwa and others found unequivocally that corruption levels in Nigeria exert a profoundly significant influence on economic growth. It is evident that the presence of corruption impedes the nation's economic advancement. They argued that rapid economic growth necessitates a resolute stance of zero tolerance towards corruption.[52] Donwa and others concluded that, despite the commendable efforts put forth by bodies such as the ICPC and EFCC, corruption continues to plague Nigeria's economy. As a forward-looking recommendation, Donwa and others advocated for comprehensive investigations into all instances of public misappropriation. Those found guilty must be subjected to legal prosecution, and the ill-gotten gain in the Nigerian oil sector, endowed with vast reserves and potential, has long been a critical component of the nation's economy. However, despite its enormous promise, this sector grapples with a persistent challenge: resource misallocation.[53] Resource misallocation in the Nigerian oil sector refers to the inefficient allocation of financial, human, and technological resources within the industry. It manifests in various forms.

The misallocation of capital resources is rampant in the sector. Funds that should be invested in infrastructure development, exploration, and technology enhancement are often diverted for non-productive purposes or, worse, siphoned off through corrupt practices. The oil sector demands continuous technological advancements to improve extraction efficiency, environmental sustainability, and safety. However, resource

---

[52]P.A. Donwa, CO Mgbame, OM Julius, 'Corruption in the Oil and Gas Industry: Implication for Economic Growth' (2015) 11 (22) European Scientific Journal
[53]ibid

misallocation often leads to insufficient investment in research and technology, hindering progress. Adequate human resources are crucial for the sector's success. Resource misallocation results in insufficient investment in workforce training and development, leading to a lack of skilled professionals. The infrastructure deficit within the Nigerian oil sector is a stark reality that exacerbates resource misallocation.

Nigeria, despite being a major oil producer, relies heavily on imported refined petroleum products due to a lack of domestic refining capacity.[54] This deficit not only drains foreign exchange reserves but also impedes the sector's growth. The country's transportation infrastructure for moving crude oil from production sites to refineries or export terminals is often dilapidated and insufficient. This leads to production bottlenecks and increases costs.[55] The oil sector's activities have a significant impact on the environment. The infrastructure deficit in terms of environmentally friendly technologies and practices contributes to pollution and degradation, leading to social and economic costs. Resource misallocation and infrastructure deficits hinder the sector's growth potential, resulting in economic stagnation. This affects government revenue, foreign direct investment, and employment opportunities. The lack of investment in eco-friendly infrastructure exacerbates environmental degradation, leading to health problems and additional costs for environmental remediation.[56]

---

[54]Khalid Siddig and others, 'Impacts of Removing Fuel Import Subsidies in Nigeria on Poverty' (2014) 69 Energy Policy
[55]ibid
[56]Busayo Victor Osuntuyi and Hooi Hooi Lean, 'Economic Growth, Energy Consumption And Environmental Degradation Nexus In Heterogeneous Countries: Does Education Matter?' (2022) 34(1) Environmental Sciences Europe

The inadequate refining capacity necessitates the importation of refined petroleum products, depleting foreign reserves and contributing to the country's trade deficit.[57] Resource misallocation leads to inefficiency and waste, reducing the sector's profitability and long-term sustainability. Resource misallocation and infrastructure deficits in the Nigerian oil sector are intertwined challenges that hinder economic growth and environmental sustainability. Addressing these issues requires a concerted effort by the government, industry stakeholders, and international partners. By implementing transparent resource allocation, prioritizing technology and infrastructure development, and investing in human capital, Nigeria can unlock the full potential of its oil sector and foster long-term economic growth.

Foreign Investment and Investor Deterrence

Corruption has been around for ages in the oil business in Nigeria, scaring away both internal and external financiers and limiting growth and technical progress of the sector. Nigeria, as an oil-rich country, has seen a fair share of booms and crashes with her oil industry. These booms — most notably, the boom of the 1970s — brought large amounts of money into Nigeria (if properly managed, which it was not), and the potential for real development. But the poor handling of this windfall has actually morphed it into a curse instead of the blessing it could have been. Moreover, corruption is deeply ingrained in diverse sectors of the Nigerian economy, where bribery is common. Bureaucrats serve in government offices as factories producing

[57] A Ogbuigwe, 'Refining in Nigeria: History, Challenges and Prospects' (2018) 8 Applied Petrochemical Research

bribes in Nigeria, with even the legislative branches deeply involved in corruption.

Olujobi showed that corruption flourishes when anti-corruption laws are not enforced effectively and when political leaders lack the commitment to implement measures. Additionally, he emphasized that the inefficiency of anti-corruption agencies, in Nigeria can be attributed to the federal government's lack of determination to fight corruption, insufficient funding and a lenient approach towards enforcing anti-corruption laws, in the country.[58]

Corruption has indeed posed an obstacle to the growth and technological advancement of Nigeria's oil industry, impacting both domestic investments. Nigeria, being rich in resources and having oil reserves, has faced challenges due to corruption.[59] The presence of corruption undermines the confidence of investors, making them hesitant to invest sums of money in Nigeria's oil sector.[60] The uncertainty surrounding practices such as bribery and embezzlement discourages long-term commitments. Moreover, corruption often leads to the misallocation of resources within the oil industry in Nigeria, diverting funds that were meant for infrastructure development, technological progress and environmental protection. As a result, the

---

[58]Olusola Joshua Olujobi, 'Nigeria's Upstream Petroleum Industry Anti-Corruption Legal Framework: The Necessity for Overhauling and Enrichment' (2021) 26(7) Journal of Money Laundering Control

[59]Gian Marco Moisé, 'Corruption in the Oil Sector: A Systematic Review and Critique of the Literature' (2020) 7(1) The Extractive Industries and Society

[60]Cordelia Onyinyechi Omodero, 'Effect of Corruption on Foreign Direct Investment Inflows in Nigeria' (2019) 29(2) Studia Universitatis Vasile Goldiş, Arad-Seria Ştiinţe Economice

industry's potential, for growth and modernization, is restricted.[61]

Nigeria's global reputation as one of the world's most corrupt nations, much of which is linked to oil-related scandals of military rule. The basic idea of what the Obasanjo government was trying to establish, was a break away from the past, where there had been widespread corruption in governance. Should these initiatives come to fruition, they will likely lure new capital into non-oil industries—which in turn could spur further GDP expansion and help underprivileged populations. Preventing further grafts and regaining public trust is essential in addressing public anxiety about the sharing of oil revenue. Greater transparency around how the Government collects and disburses oil revenues is perhaps one of the most important steps toward limiting corruption, building trust in the Government. Hard as it might be, it is worth pointing out that the British authorities have set up an 'Extractive Industries Transparency Initiative' (EITI) supposedly meant to bring about greater openness in the oil industry. This could provide valuable back-up help.[62]

Corruption has indeed played the role of an important impediment for foreign and domestic investment in Nigeria's Oil Industry, which resulted in hindrance to growth and development of its technology. Nigeria is richly endowed with natural resources, especially in oil reserves, and this has been a major

---

[61]Rabah Arezki and Markus Brückner , 'Oil Rents, Corruption, and State Stability: Evidence From Panel Data Regressions' (International Monetary Fund, Working Paper WP/09/267 2009)
[62]Michael L. Ross, 'Nigeria's Oil Sector and the Poor' (Prepared for the UK Department for International Development "Nigeria: Drivers of Change" program 2003) <http://www.sscnet.ucla.edu/polisci/faculty/ross/papers/other/NigeriaOil.pdf> accessed 24 August, 2023

setback to its growth in the sector due to corrupt practices. Corruption erodes investor confidence. With such perception of high corruption risk in the oil sector, foreign and domestic investors alike would be discouraged from injecting significant capital into the Nigerian petroleum industry. Unpredictability in corruption such as bribery and misappropriation of funds may deter long-term investment. Misallocation of resources occurs frequently in the oil sector due to corruption. Meant for infrastructural development, techno advancement and environment protection, these moneys diverted to the black money market, thereby curtained in growth and modernization in this trade. Bureaucratic corruption can be seen through delays in approvals and permits, where officials will ask for bribes to push paperwork through the system. This both adds to the cost of doing business and slows down timelines for technological advancements.

Lack of transparency in procurement procedures and revenue management further inhibits private sector involvement.[63] They are worried that their deals will get rewritten, that the 'law' won't actually protect them from getting robbed. The corruption may reduce productivity in the oil industry as well. Contracts may be granted to favored companies on the merits of their political connections rather than technical expertise, leading to less-than-optimal extractive processes. And corruption can result in the failure to protect the environment, where regulators may look the other way on pollution, as long as some cash is being paid. It may also lead to oil spills, environmental

---

[63]Andrew Bauer, 'Subnational Oil, Gas and Mineral Revenue Management' (Revenue Watch Institute Briefing The Revenue Watch Institute. Disponible 2013) <en: http://www. resourcegovernance. org/sites/default/files/RWI_Sub_Oil_Gas_Mgmt_EN_ rev1. Pdf> accessed 25 Ausgust.

damage, and other unsustainable practices that repel socially responsible investors.

Level playing field due to corruption in the industry discourages innovation within industry. Companies that are dishonest might not have the motivation to invest in advanced technology or to adopt good standards, as they would not see any benefit from doing so. In a corrupt business environment, businesses may be exposed to legal and reputational risks. International regulatory and anticorruption laws apply to them, which may lead to penalties or the perception of corruption may negatively impact their brand and reputation. Steps towards ending corruption include the setting up of anti-corrupt institutions, and promoting greater openness about revenues through transparency measures. Nevertheless, slow progress continues to be evident in this sector, where corruption retains a significant foothold.

Environmental Consequences

Corruption in the oil industry, whereby individuals abuse their positions to profit personally from oil extraction, has resulted in major environmental harm; including but not limited to oil spills, pollution and habitat destruction, that largely impacts the local population.[64] Inadequate oversight by regulatory bodies, due to corruption, will eventually create hazardous conditions. Consequently, companies may opt for cost-cutting measures, resulting in equipment malfunctions, poor upkeep, as well as shoddy procedures — the risk of oil spills rises accordingly.

Oil leak spells disaster for surrounding neighborhoods. They pollute water sources, harm aquatic creatures, and reduce the quality of planted crops. Many coastal communities that have

[64]ibid

long relied on small-scale subsistence fishing or other forms of farming struggle to recover when what they have built up over generations is suddenly wiped away. In addition, the potential contact with oil and its poisonous parts is dangerous for the local people.

Corruption can also lead to lax enforcement of environmental laws, leaving people unprotected. This may result in emissions of pollutants, including heavy metals during oil extraction and processing, which contributes to air and water pollution.[65]

Pollution from the oil industry affects the health and well-being of communities in close proximity leading to respiratory problems, skin diseases and more. Impure water sources can lead to numerous health issues when used for drinking, cooking or bathing. In addition to this environmental damage, air pollution also damages farm crops and exacerbates problems of the local economy. The consequences of corruption, then, are a free pass to rape the earth with little to no resistance from governmental organizations and regulatory bodies such as the International Oil Pollution Compensation Funds (IOPC funds) in places like Nigeria where oil spills have destabilized ecosystems and endangered biodiversity. Communities often live off healthy ecosystems, be it agriculture, hunting, or cultural practices. Ecosystem degradation could cause disruptions to these livelihoods, causing hunger and poverty. This could mean the destruction of traditional ecological knowledge, culture and spirituality.

---

[65]ibid

Global Reputation and Diplomatic Relations

The corruption in Nigeria's oil industry has had a serious dent to its reputation abroad. Nigeria, as one of Africa's largest oil producers and a significant player in the global energy market, has faced several consequences due to corruption within this vital sector. Nigeria's oil sector has gotten such bad publicity that this image of endemic corruption is attached to its name.[66] Nigeria typically ranks low on transparency and high on corruption indices amongst international organizations and bodies. Such perception has its effect not only on relationships between the government of the country, but also between foreign governments, enterprises, and investors. This corruption deters foreign investment in the petroleum sector. Multinational corporations, which hold significant influence over the oil sector, might not want to put their money into a country with rampant corruption. The low FDI inflows can potentially stifle Nigeria's economic prowess as a frontline developing economy and its quest for economic growth and diversification.

Oil is one of the largest sources of revenue for the Government of Nigeria. Public sector corruption results in loss of public revenue, thus hampering the government's ability to spend on roads, schools, hospitals and other essential areas. Hence, the growth and eradication of poverty in Nigerian is impeded. It has been established, for instance, that corruption in the oil sector contributed to the security problems of oil theft and militancy in the Niger Delta. This not only hampers the nation's oil production; this also adds to to insecurity that discourages foreign direct investments in the country as well tarnishes the na-

---

[66]Nicholas Shaxson, 'Oil, Corruption and the Resource Curse' (2007) 83(6) International Affairs

tion's name internationally.[67] Nigeria as an important oil producer may have influence on the world market and energy security due to its internal problems. The fear of Nigeria being unable to manage its stable oil production has reverberations across the global energy market.

Anti-Corruption Efforts and Challenges

More corrupt governments will also generally receive less foreign aid and support. Corruption can turn off donors: When there is corruption, the donor nations and international organizations might not want to disperse money to such countries. It could even add more pressure on Nigeria's ability to deal with the range of social and economic issues facing each state in particular. Corruption of these fuels contributes to ecosystem destruction and social instability. The international spotlight has shone on oil spill accidents as well as the poisoning of communities from those affected. Such an approach can be bad for PR-wise — not the least due to countries concerned about environmentally and human right issues getting riled up. Managing oil revenues transparently is an important issue to international actors. Several transparency efforts — including EITI countries that publish company-by-company reconciliations of tax payments with government receipts — have drawn attention to both the lack of transparency about who benefits from oil, gas and mining and how governments use these revenues. There is the question of how these reforms reflect on Nigeria's regional and global performance.

---

[67]Al Chukwuma Okoli and Francis Okpaleke, 'Banditry and Crisis of Public Safety in Nigeria: Issues in National Security Strategies' (2014) 10(4) European Scientific Journal

The high returns from the oil sector are making it difficult combating corruption in Nigeria, as corruption cases continue to increase over time. As the Nigerian government and international bodies attempt to tackle this situation, multiple actions have been deployed, but there remain serious barriers. Support from international organizations including the World Bank and the IMF has assisted Nigeria in developing better regulatory frameworks for finance, management of public funds, and procurement practices. Nigeria is part of regional efforts including membership in the Extractive Industries Transparency Initiative (EITI – an intergovernmental body to promote transparency in payments made by oil, gas, mining, or other resource extraction corporations. Consequently, though the Nigerian government and other international organizations have intensified their efforts to tackle Corruption in Oil Sector, but they still face several difficulties. These issues need sustained political will and strong institutions committed to transparency and accountability at all levels of the sector. Moreover, transitioning to other sectors will also lessen the need for petrodollars to compensate those who would otherwise be impoverished and unemployed by non-corrupt economic practices.

Terra Nullius: Race and the Colonial Influence on International Environmental Law in Africa

Olalekan Moyosore Lalude, PhD[1]
Ayoyemi Lawal-Arowolo, PhD[2]

Introduction

There are several dimensions to the discussion on international environmental law and environmental justice in Africa, and one dimension is on race, colonialism and their imperialistic connotations. The subject of race is one that cannot be dissociated from the colonial experience. Colonialism fostered racial and cultural imperialism in Africa. It also ensured an exploitative approach to the environment and corrupted the evolution of the international environmental law system, as it ensured that colonialists plundered natural resources without care for the environment nor the communities where the resources were found. Colonialism was primarily about racial, economic and

[1]Lecturer, Faculty of Law, Wisconsin International University College, Ghana.
[2]Professor of Law, Faculty of Law, Babcock University School of Law and Security Studies, Nigeria.

cultural advantage without responsibility for the consequences of its impacts. Thus, Atiles-Osoria wrote:

The exploitation of natural resources and the extraction of wealth (in mineral, human, energy and biological terms), the destruction of the environment and related epistemologies, have traditionally been considered as primary manifestations of colonialism.[3]

Colonialism left a legacy of damaging perceptions of the environment in Africa, and it put the continent in perpetual subordination, leaving its politics and environment vulnerable. The role of race in the colonialist exploitation of Africa and its environment was in the support of a narrative that the colonisers brought modernity and enlightenment to Africa. Afagla argued, using George Lamming's Natives of my person as a point of reference, that the exposition on the motives behind colonialism diminishes its flimsy façade of philanthropic enlightenment of colonised peoples to a repugnant mission.[4] The postcolonial agency is a concept of resistance by colonised people.

There have been many sociological and literary works that document the exercise of postcolonial agency. One of such books was Chinua Achebe's Things Fall Apart. Postcolonial agency in the context of the African environment, and of the resistance of racial imperialism, has roots in the consciousness of dispossessing cultural and spiritual posturing of the colonisers. Colonialism sought to own so as to conform human and natural resources for the benefit of the coloniser. Hence, to en-

---

[3] José M. Atiles-Osoria, 'Environmental Colonialism, Criminalization and Resistance: Puerto Rican Mobilizations for Environmental Justice in the 21st Century' (2014) 6(6) RCCS Annual Review 7.

[4] Kodjo Afagla, 'Shattering the Civilizing Claims of Colonialism: George Lamming's Natives of My Person' (2015) 3(1) Revue du CAMES

sure an enduring system of exploitation, the coloniser ensured that cultural integration was substituted for cultural domination. Swati Parashar and Michael Schulz argued that the influence of colonialism is far-reaching on the colonised.[5]

The whole system of ideological foundations, conceptual frameworks and methodological orientations are deeply influenced by Western epistemological systems.[6] The vulnerability induced by the under-appreciation of the postcolonial agency prevents Africa from providing solutions to its own environmental problems. The history of the postcolonial resistance of the colonised people in the struggle for land and the redemption of its essence has been well captured in literary texts. *Weep Not*, Child by Ngugi wa Thiong'o is a leading text that aptly presents the postcolonial conflict for ancestral land. In the book, the importance of land to the Gikuyu was well represented in the words:

Any man who had land was considered rich. If a man had plenty of money, many motor cars but no land, he could never be counted as rich. A man who went with tattered clothes but had at least an acre of red earth was better off than the man with money.[7]

The significance of land to the Gikuyu in *Weep Not, Child* is representative of the conception of land in many precolonial African cultural contexts, it was an assertion of the connection with the earth which fuelled many attempts at resistance.

---

[5]Swati Parashar and Michael Schulz 'Colonial Legacies, Postcolonial "Selfhood" and the (Un)Doing Of Africa' (2021) Third World Quarterly 3
[6]ibid
[7]Ngugi wa Thiong'o, *Weep Not, Child,* (Heinemann 1964)

Racial Privilege, Colonialism and Environmental Justice

Environmental justice in Africa is defined by a colonial history, exploitation through the exercise of racial privilege and a voicelessness in the global power dynamics of environmental politics. Racial privilege in the context of environmental justice in Africa is a creation of cultural imperialism and colonialism. The danger of racial privilege to the realisation of environmental justice in Africa is that it ensures that the colonialist structure under which the international environmental law system was formed persists, and thus, eventually denying Africa indigenous legal solutions that would address African environmental problems.

Colonialism has transcended the original reference, where occupation and control of a territory means economic and political power. It has become an evolved process of control that allows a continual domination of a region or regions through structures that exert both economic, political and social influence at a global level. Colonialism does not just have a literal meaning, since it has become sustained by the circumstances of its legacies. Colonialism poses a threat to the international system because its ghost haunts the states where it was once practiced. In Africa, territories carved up in error by colonialists have resulted in boundary disputes. The impact of colonialism and value imposition on international environmental law is significant and informs the concern on Africa's plight as regards environmental justice. The developmental processes of the international environmental law system took place in the temporal atmosphere of colonialism and cultural imperialism.[8]

---

[8]Sundyha Pahuja, *Decolonising International Law: Development, Economic Growth and the Politics of Universality.* (Cambridge University Press 2011)

One of the instruments that highlighted the anthropocentric spirit of international environmental law instruments within a colonial context was the 1900 London Convention, Designed to Ensure the Conservation of Various Species of Wild Animals in Africa That Are Useful to Man or Inoffensive. Since the primary purpose of colonialism in Africa was the exploitation of natural resources, as shown by the 1884 Scramble for Africa, the tendency towards the conservation of natural resources for future use was necessary. The current anthropocentric nature of many international environmental law instruments is still driven by the kind of worldview that empowered colonialism.

The worldview that the exploitation of the environment cannot be done away with, thereby substituting reckless exploitation with responsible exploitation, brought about the use of the word 'conservation.' There is a careful distinction between 'conservation' and 'preservation'. The National Geographic encyclopedia, conservation and preservation refer to the protection of the environment, but they differ in their trajectory of purpose. While preservation aims for the protection of the environment from the destructive impact of human activities. Conservation aspires to the protection of the environment 'through the responsible use of natural resources.[9] The colonial approach to environmental protection was conservationist. The agreement between colonial powers to protect nature in Africa, in the form of the 1933 London Convention Relative to the Preservation of Fauna and Flora in Their Natural State, was defined by its approach towards responsible exploitation.

It allowed the exploitation of nature under special permissions. There had been a relentless exploitation of the African

---

[9]National Geographic, 'Preservation' (National Geographic Resource Library: Encyclopedic Entry 2021) < https://www.nationalgeographic.org/encyclopedia/preservation/> accessed 11 May 2021

environment, albeit, the colonial powers had ensured the making of norms both at domestic and regional levels to lessen the negative influence of environmental exploitation. These norms, however, were limited to specifically target certain natural resources and were oriented towards responsible exploitation.[10] The influence of racial privilege on the discourse on environmental justice in Africa is resonated by colonialist narratives and the inferential posturing of the international environmental law history and its purposes.

A Disquisition on Race and the Environment

Race has had an impact on environmental justice as far back as colonial times, but the discourse has been far more concentrated on societies where issues of racial justice have been stark in their severity. Environmental justice was forged in the fires of racial adversity. This is because in modern history, the greatest discriminations have been perpetrated through race. These discriminations have not been limited to persons but have been extended to the environment. Environmental justice evolved from the racially divisive expression of 'us' and 'them' concretising racial segregation through geographical boundaries and the establishment of different standards for environmental risks, even though environmental justice is beyond race, as it involves fairness and the significant engagement of all people, 'regardless of race, color, national origin, or income, with respect to the development, implementation, and enforcement of

---

[10]Ogolla Bondi, 'Environmental Law in Africa: Status and Trends' (1995) 23 International Business Lawyer

environmental laws, regulations, and policies.'[11] The subject of race has been notoriously prominent in the historical impropriety of varying the value to human life. The privilege of race in environmental justice ensures that by virtue of the distribution of global GDP per capita, Sub-Saharan Africa is at the bottom rung of the ladder. [12] The implication of Africa's material poverty is that it is left more vulnerable to environmental abuse and injustice. It also implies that Africa suffers the most of the problems presented by climate change, as it has little financial resources to combat the environmental crisis.

In his description of racialised practices within the colonial territories, George Steinmetz noted: 'Racialised practices ranged from formally segregated cities and mandatory forced labour to bans on mixed marriage.'[13] In the colonial African territories, there was a forced perception of Europeans and Western values that ensured that they were considered superior in their interactions with the natives.[14] The perception of racial superiority was to subdue the postcolonial agency and to implement the psychology of dependence. Jemima Pierre argued that Africa is a racialised construction and that the African people have been the protagonists in the modern construction of

---

[11]Hilmi S Salem, 'No Sustainable Development in the Lack of Environmental Justice' (2019) 12(3) Environmental Justice
[12]Aaron O'Neill, 'Gross Domestic Product (GDP) Per Capita in Selected Global Regions 2019' (Statista, 21 March 2021) <https://www.statista.com/statistics/256413/gross-domestic-product-per-capita-in-selected-global-regions/> accessed 13 May, 2021
[13]ibid
[14]Vincent Khapoya, *The African Experience* (4th edn Routledge 2012)

race.[15] The creation of artificial boundaries and the colonial legacies of Europe in Africa define the continent and its present problems. The African environment under the colonial order was primed for the sustenance of its exploitation. French ties with its former African colonies that had been based on the resource needs of France has seen to French foreign policy leaning towards Africa.[16] The exploitative nature of colonialism left a damaging legacy of environmental abuse and a culture of resource exploitation. This is more so that many colonial practices in Africa have not been transformed several decades after the independence of African states, but have been grafted into institutional processes.

Environmental Racism

Environmental racism is the type of structural racism that causes people of color to be disproportionately affected by policies and practices that necessitate them to live close to places with toxic waste like landfills, sewage works, mines, power stations and other such locations that pose a risk to their health or safety.[17] Environmental racism is the deliberate placement of toxic

---

[15]Jemima Pierre, 'Structure, Project, Process: Anthropology, Colonialism, and Race in Africa' (2018) 96 Journal of Anthropological Sciences

[16]IJ Benneyworth, 'The Ongoing Relationship Between France and its Former African Colonies' (E-INTERNATIONAL RELATIONS, 11 June, 20110) <https://www.e-ir.info/2011/06/11/the-ongoing-relationship-between-france-and-its-former-african-colonies/> accessed 13 May, 2021

[17]Peter Beech, 'What is Environmental Racism?' (World Economic Forum, June 2020) <https://www.weforum.org/agenda/2020/07/what-is-environmental-racism-pollution-covid-systemic/> accessed 28 July, 2021

waste sites, landfills, incinerators and industries that pollute the environment in communities of people of color.[18] In a broader context, environmental racism poses a significant risk to the poorest countries in the world, most of which are in Africa.[19] Besides the inefficient environmental policymaking in many African countries, the flow of plastics to Africa is contributing to the buildup of an immense environmental crisis. There has been a consistent dumping of electronic products in Africa, this alone accounts for a significant share of the environmental risk that Africa is exposed to.[20]

Environmental racism emerged from structural racism[21], and it is one of the creations of racial imperialism. Asides other factors, environmental racism is one of the greatest challenges to environmental justice in the world. Environmental racism has existed as long as racial imperialism has been at the heart of colonialism, but its use emerged from the American justice movement that began in the 1980s.[22] In the study of environ-

---

[18]Irwin Weintraub, 'Fighting Environmental Racism: a Selected Annotated Bibliography' (1994) 1(1) Electronic Green Journal < https://escholarship.org/content/qt1qx663rf/qt1qx663rf.pdf?t=q9ns0m> accessed 28 July, 2021

[19]Oliver Reynolds, 'The Poorest Countries in the World' (Focus Economics: Economic Forecasts from the World Leading Economists, 18 February, 2021) <https://www.focus-economics.com/blog/the-poorest-countries-in-the-world> accessed 28 July, 2021

[20]UN Environment, 'Africa Waste Management Outlook: Summary for Decision Makers' (UN Environment) <https://wedoc-s.unep.org/bitstream/handle/20.500.11822/25515/Africa_W-MO_Summary.pdf?sequence=1&isAllowed=y> accessed 28 July, 2021

[21]Sheree Henderson, 'Environmental Racism and the Contamination of Black Lives' (2021) 25 Journal of African American Studies

[22]Thom Davies, 'Clean and White: A History of Environmental Racism in the United States' (2017) Ethnic and Racial Studies

mental racism, the American experience is important as it gives a better idea of the concept and how the United States has helped perpetuate a global economic system that is less committed to environmental justice in the Global South, especially Africa where global carbon emissions have been at its lowest. Since the Jeffersonian Era in an 18th century America that saw the state bifurcated along two psychological positions: racial imperialism that assumed only whiteness could confer personhood and liberalism that considered the humanity of black bodies, racial anxiety has often defined US social policy.

This racial anxiety, which Zimring wrote that Thomas Jefferson embodied in his book Clean and White: A History of Environmental Racism in the United States,[23] has often plagued the American identity and defines the meta-narrative of American environmental relations. Thom Davies has argued that environmental racism dates far back in America.[24] The growth of environmental justice as a system of demand against environmental racism grew and broadened in the 20th century to cover instances of environmental inequity on a global scale, at this point, it evolved to frame 'A pattern of injustices that disproportionately exposed minority and low-income communities to toxic hazards.'[25] In the case of Africa, it was mired in the racist reductionism of colonialism. The perception of Africa by European historians was towards undermining its representations. For instance, Hegel had argued hundreds of years ago thus:

Africa has no historical interest of its own, for we find its inhabitants living in barbarism and savagery.... From the earli-

---

[23]Carl Zimring, *Clean and White: a History of Environmental Racism in the United States* (New York University Press 2016)
[24]Thom Davies, 'Clean and White: A History of Environmental Racism in the United States' (2017) Ethnic and Racial Studies
[25]Stella M Capek, The Environmental Justice Frame (Sage Publications Inc 2021)

est historical times, Africa has remained cutoff from all contacts with the rest of the world; it is the land of gold, forever pressing it upon itself, and the land of childhood, removed from the light of self-conscious history and wrapped in the dark mantle of night. Its isolation is not just a result of its tropical nature, but an essential consequence of its geographical nature. It is still unexplored, and has no connections whatsoever with Europe.... In this main portion of Africa, history is, in fact, out of the question.[26]

Following in his footsteps, Hugh Trevor-Roper, at the University of Oxford had said: 'Perhaps in the future, there will be some African history to teach. But at the present there is none: there is only the history of Europeans in Africa. The rest is darkness... And darkness is not a subject of history.'[27] The reductionist description of these scholars of African history showed that whatever interest Europe had in Africa was toward the exploitation of its natural resources, a dismissal of its people as a subhuman race incapable of developing its own civilisation. The Hegelian position on Africa that undermined the life and civilisations of several African tribes from the Songhai to the Nok, from the Benin Empire to the Ashanti Empire, was one of the damaging descriptions that has framed Africa in a picture that made it suitable as a recipient for the products of racism.

Colonial exploitation stemming from environmental racism is perpetrated on the assumption that the native inhabitants are inferior and as such, their needs come second to that of the coloniser. In analysing the concept of exploitation, Nagtzaam

---

[26]Bryant P Shaw, 'Africa in World History: A Teaching Conference' (Airforce Academy Colorado Springs, Colorado, 25-26 April, 1986)

[27]Hugh Trevor-Roper, The Rise of Christian Europe (1st edn Thames & Hudson 1966)

and others, observed that the concept has received little attention as against the ideas of 'conservation' and 'preservation'.[28] However, Wertheimer has opined that exploitation takes place when 'A takes unfair advantage of B.'[29] The consensus of several analyses on the idea of exploitation is that it is a problematic interaction among parties.[30] Fergusona and Vrousalis argued that there are ethical issues to exploitation. According to them, exploitation personifies and usually boosts social and economic injustices.[31] Exploitation is enabled where there is a power imbalance between parties. Its perpetration often continues where opportunities are extended for it. In the case of colonialism, exploitation existed for economic reasons. Those that partitioned Africa saw it as an opportunity to exploit a seemingly uncharted terrain. Kalu and Falola argue that Africa is still plagued by exploitation and that the only difference is the beneficiaries of exploitation.[32]

The challenge of Africa, in proceeding from a system of exploitation that continually keeps it from developing as it should, is rooted in the establishment of ill-suited structures of governance and identity that had been forced on by colonialism. Understanding that colonialism, as a system to subdue and exploit, is responsible for the devastating exploitation of the

---

[28]Gerry Nagtzaam, Evan Van Hook and Douglas Guilfoyle, *International Environmental Law: A Case Study Analysis* (Routledge 2020)

[29]Alan Wertheimer *Exploitation* (Princeton University Press 1996)

[30]Benjamin Fergusona and Nicholas Vrousalis, 'Exploitation and the Social Economy' (2019) 77(2) Review of Social Economy

[31]ibid

[32]Kenneth Kalu and Toyin Falola, 'Introduction: Exploitation, Colonialism and Postcolonial Misrule in Africa' in Kenneth Kalu and Toyin Falola (eds) *Exploitation, Colonialism and Postcolonial Misrule in Africa* (Palgrave Macmillan 2019)

earth's resources,[33] is an indication of how the African environment still bears scars from colonial exploitation, added to that is the burden of the global markets and their structural inequities through which Africa must deal with the rest of the world.

Racial Privilege

Racial privilege and its tendency to affect environmental justice evolved from discussions on racial influence on environmental issues. Many studies, including historical accounts, have demonstrated that environmental racism can be a motive for environmental injustice.[34] Andrews argued that imperialism is still thriving, and it now exists in a situation in which the United States and not Europe is leading Western dominion.[35] It is also not a coincidence that environmental racism was primarily a subject of racially motivated American environmental conflict in the 1970s and 1980s. Environmental racism embodies the likelihood that toxic waste facilities would be sited in

---

[33]Joseph McQuade, 'Earth Day: Colonialism's Role in the Overexploitation of Natural Resources' (The Conversation, 18 April, 2019) <https://theconversation.com/earth-day-colonialisms-role-in-the-overexploitation-of-natural-resources-113995> accessed 15 May 2021

[34]See Lynn E Blais, 'Environmental Racism Considered' (1996) 75(1) North Carolina Law Review 75; Judy Logan, Liberty and Environmental Justice for All: An Empirical Approach to Environmental Racism' (2018) 53(4) Wake Forest Law Review 739; Idna G Castellon,'Cancer Alley and the Fight Against Environmental Racism' (2021) 32(1) Villanova Environmental Law Journal 15

[35]Kehinde Andrews, *The Age of New Empire: How Racism and Colonialism Still Rule the World* (Public Affairs 2020)

48

places where people of colour live than in white populated areas.[36]

In Africa, racial privilege is more pronounced because of the damage that colonialism wreaked on African self-perception, cultural and environmental consciousness. One of the casualties of colonialism in Africa is animism. Animism, according to Berkes, is the 'belief in spiritual beings.'[37] African animism ensured that there was respect for nature. The belief that spirits inhabited natural things like trees allowed for the preservation of forests, in the conviction that they signified some spiritual essence. The relationship with nature in pre-colonial Africa was one that was moderated by a spiritual consciousness. The spiritual role that forests served was that of a cathedral where people could worship. It also served as a huge resource for traditional pharmacy.[38] The biodiversity of trees provided an endless range of cures to almost all known ailments and was the school where traditional herbalism was learnt. It is still believed in Africa that there is no disease in Africa whose cure eludes what can be yielded from plants in the forests.

The notion of a spiritual essence helped with maintaining a healthy space between human technology and ecological habitats. Oluseye and others have criticised the condescension with which traditional animism is treated with. They argue that the

---

[36]Steve Vanderheiden, 'Environmental Racism' in Deen K Chatterjee (ed), *Encyclopedia of Global Justice* (Springer: Dordrecht 2011)

[37]Fikret Berkes, 'Religious Traditions and Biodiversity' (2nd edn Encyclopedia of Biodiversity: ScienceDirect, 2013) <https://www.sciencedirect.com/topics/social-sciences/animism> accessed 8 April 2021

[38]Walter Fam Nkwi, 'The Sacred Forest and the Mythical Python: Ecology, Conservation, and Sustainability in Kom, Cameroon, c.1700-200' (2017) 11(2) Journal of Global Initiatives: Policy, Pedagogy, Perspective

conception of traditional animism as paganistic and primitive is a disarticulation of the concept. They further claimed that animism is closely tied to nature.[39] Colonialism brought a disruption to the perception of nature in Africa. Since the aim of colonialism was to exploit the resources of the colonial subjects, colonialism introduced an exploitative approach towards nature. As a consequence, many forests that used to be cathedrals, have given way to many economically exploitative practices like logging and real estate development. Ancient trees have been hewn, and exotic animals have been exterminated through forest fires started by humans. The language of environmental exploitation has become normalized today in Africa, with natural resources taking the centre stage in human interaction with the environment. Environmental justice in Africa is a casualty of colonialism and the imperialistic assertion of racial privilege. From the economic exploitation of Africa that brought about the destruction of many forests on the continent, to toxic waste pollution, trophy hunting of rare species and environmentally dangerous experimentation, there have been protestations by nature which has seen some devastating effects on rural life.

Racial privilege is the status acquired by those regarded as white or Caucasians due to the color of their skin. Peggy McIntosh described white privilege as a corollary of racism.[40] She further argued that white privilege tends to be an evasive and fugitive subject. This perhaps is in relation to its diverse mani-

---

[39] Abiodun Babatunde Oluwaseye, Senayon Olaloluwa and Charles Ogbulogo, 'Ecocentrism: Locating the Animist Figurings in Remi Raji's *Sea of My Mind'* (2020) SAGE Open
[40] Peggy McIntosh, 'White Privilege: Unpacking the Invisible Backpack' (*University of Michigan Social Research: Kirkwood Community College*, 8 September 2020) <https://guides.kirkwood.edu/privilege/race> accessed 15 October, 2020

festations and the denial of its existence by many of the people who wield it.[41] The possession of racial privilege is a result of the dominance that has been attributed to whiteness. This comes from economic and political dominance. From internal dominance of white people in western societies to the extension of hegemonic power at the international level, white privilege has grown for decades to assume a silent but intimidating presence in the interaction between those who possess this privilege and those who do not.[42]

Anthropocentrism

In environmental ethics, anthropocentricism refers to the worldview that value can only be derived from humanity. It further connotes that all other life forms should exist only for human use.[43] This would mean that the earth's biosphere value is determined by its utility to humans.[44] Anthropocentrism has defined much of the way humanity has treated the planet and considered its own ontology long before the study of this worldview. The word first appeared in the 1860s, at the time Darwin's theory of evolution was generating a popular debate on the place of humanity as the prime of creation.[45]

---

[41]ibid
[42]L. Taylor Phillips and Brian S. Lowery, 'Herd Invisibility: The Psychology of Racial Privilege' (2018) 27(3) Current Directions in Psychological Science
[43]Helen Kopnina, Haydn Washington, Bron Taylor, John J Piccolo, 'Anthropocentrism: More than Just a Misunderstood Problem' (2018) 31 Journal of Agricultural and Environmental Ethics
[44]Gerry Nagtzaam, Evan Van Hook and Douglas Guilfoyle, *International Environmental Law: A Case Study Analysis* (Routledge 2020)
[45]ibid

Anthropocentrism has deep roots in the Abrahamic religions, as many of the teachings place humanity as the central figure to many prophesies. The centrality of humans to religious teachings in the Abrahamic religions often places so much emphasis on human ontology that the human environment only features to accentuate human spirituality. In Christianity, there is the emphasis on the primacy of humanity. In the book of Genesis Chapter 1 Verse 26 it is written:

And God said, let us make man in our image after our likeness and let them have dominion over the fish of the sea, and over the fowl of the air, and over the cattle and over all the earth, and over every creeping thing that creepeth upon the earth.[46]

The creation of man as told by the Christian Bible puts humanity as a god in a material space. The superintendence of humanity in the Christian story of creation aligns with the anthropocentric view that every life form on earth outside of man derives its value as a thing of use for the benefit of humanity. In the Qur'an, God brought Adam before the angels and asked that they prostrate before him, they obeyed, and his superiority was affirmed.[47] These anthropocentric views of the Abrahamic religions have informed doctrinal practices for a long time and has influenced the relationship between humanity and its environment. This was even reflected in 17th century philosophical thinking, as René Descartes wrote in his *Discours de la méth-*

---

[46]The Holy Bible (King James James Version)
[47]Haleema Sadia, Syed Naeem Badshah, Karim dad, Janas Khan, Nasrullah, Saqib Shahzad, 'The Creation of Man in the Bible and the Quran' (2012) 2(6) International Journal of Asian Social Science

ode that animals have no souls and are creatures that operate only by their biological wiring.[48]

Immanuel Kant's epistemological position framed his anthropocentric approach to philosophical enquiry, his entire philosophy even relied on universal human reason.[49] Christianity influenced the philosophical thought of 17th century Europe, and perhaps was the reason why anthropocentrism was the driving force of European colonialism. Even Wittgenstein attempted to show that the concept of necessity is anthropocentric.[50] Another dimension to anthropocentrism is the Cornucopian philosophy that contends claims that the earth's resources are not infinite and that the human population, if unchecked, will grow beyond what the earth can support. Cornucopian philosophers are of the conviction that the argument that resources are not infinite or that the earth has a limit to the human population it can support are either overstated or that by the time there is ever a challenge of scarcity of resources, there would be such technology that would help resolve the problems.[51]

The assumptions that Cornucopian philosophy bear regarding the earth has helped in the reckless exploitation of nature. Against scientific presentation of the earth's steady decline and the increasing toxicity caused by human civilisation without the exploration of means to creating a balance between indus-

---

[48]Desmond Osford, Uneasy Anthropocentrism: Cartesianism and the Ethics of Species Differentiation in Seventeenth Century France' (2010) 30(3/4) JAC

[49]Tsaiyi Wu, 'A Dream of a Stone: The Ethics of De-anthropocentrism' (2020) 3 Open Philosophy

[50]Cornel West, 'Philosophy and the Afro-American Experience' (1977) 9 (2/3) The Philosophical Forum

[51]Sarah Boslaugh, 'Anthropocentrism' (Encyclopedia Britannica 11 January, 2016) <https://www.britannica.com/topic/anthropocentrism> accessed 16 May, 2021

trialisation and ecological wellbeing. Through centuries the earth has seen the disappearance of species and threat to biodiversity, through anthropocentric solutions to rectifying the relationship between humanity and the environment, there is yet to be a clear direction how to tackle the urgency of climate change. Behind European colonialism was an anthropocentric willpower that merged with Eurocentrism. European Colonialism of Africa meant there had to be a hierarchy of anthropocentric considerations.

The white colonial officer over the native subject. Livia Gershon wrote about how the legal concept of *terra nullius* (no man's land) defined European colonialism and still is at the heart of conservation. The hierarchy of anthropocentric considerations that highlighted European colonialism showed in the way the colonial powers used the concept of *terra nullius* to take over lands that had earlier accommodated native subjects.[52] This was the spirit behind the Scramble for Africa, and it was the psychology that saw Africa as a means to an economic end. The influence of European anthropocentrism and its destructive adoption of the terra nullius concept in colonising Africa is immense on modern African approach to environmental management. This plays out in the weak response of African governments to the effects of illegal mining on the local population. It also defines intra-communal relations and perception of resource-rich lands. Anthropocentrism has evolved within contexts, and sometimes it is exclusive in its agenda for a racial order.

The exploitative practices of big corporations have put a strain on the African resource market for a long time, with sup-

---

[52]Livia Gershon, 'How Conservation Is Shaped by Settler Colonialism' (JSTOR Daily 31 January, 2020) <https://daily.jstor.org/how-conservation-is-shaped-by-settler-colonialism/> accessed 16 May, 2021

ply trying to rack up considerable profit where prices have been affected by the devaluation of currencies and the competition of alternative markets. The emergence of an anthropocentric view towards the apprehension of problems presented by climate change resulted from an age-long tradition of seeing the earth as a resource pool for the benefit of humanity. There is a possibility that proffered anthropocentric solutions to environmental problems are expected to strike a balance between capitalist aspirations and conservationist prescriptions.

Ecocentrism

Ecocentrism is the ethical perception that all life-forms and ecosystems, including their abiotic parts, have an intrinsic value.[53] Ecocentrism's recognition by the deep ecological movement was in the 1970s.[54] It was descriptive of the position that humans do not possess a moral priority over the rest of nature. Ecocentrism relies on the ontological question of essence. That the essence of an ecosystem is for the interaction between species, an interaction that should be balanced, devoid of an intrusive attitude. The notion of nature in the natural sciences, whose paradigms and its anthropocentric underpinnings are the reason for the modern industrial civilisation, considers nature

---

[53]Haydn Washington, Bron Taylor, Helen Kopnina, Paul Cryer and John J Piccolo, 'Why Ecocentrism is the Key Pathway to Sustainability' (2017) 1(1) The Ecological Citizen
[54]Gerry Nagtzaam, Evan Van Hook and Douglas Guilfoyle, *International Environmental Law: A Case Study Analysis* (Routledge 2020)

as a function of the activities of humans only.[55] Ecocentrism gives a balanced coverage of the ethical entitlement of all species. Biological diversity has been under siege, with the measured outcomes alarming in what they portend. The challenge might partly be the lack of political will in tackling the problem stemming from an anthropocentric ethical system and the kind of moral argument engaged in the cause of modern conservation.[56]

The 1970s was a time that saw the rise of environmental ethical reflection in academic discourse.[57] This was a time many African states have become independent and which saw many of these states looking to develop industrially. It was also a time when anthropocentric exploitation of natural resources was considered the way towards economic development. Today, the advocacy for a shift towards an ecocentric view in regard to the attitude towards nature has been largely frustrated by capitalist considerations across the world. This often exists in weighing the economic profits of land use over the preservation of the ecosystem. An instance is the deforestation of the Amazon Forest in Brazil, putting profit above nature preservation.

In Africa, an economically exploitative attitude towards the environment resulted from the loss of an ecocentric value sys-

---

[55]Freya Mathews, 'Environmental Philosophy' in Graham Oppy and NN Trakakis (eds), *History of Philosophy in Australia and New Zealand* (Springer Link 2014)
Dejan Donev, 'Ecocentrism or the Attempt to Leave Antropocentricity' (2019) Trivent Publishing
[56]Bron Taylor, Guillaume Chapron, Helen Kopnina, Ewa Orlikowska, Joe Gray, and John J Piccolo, 'The Need For Ecocentrism In Biodiversity Conservation' (2020) 34(5) Conservation Biology
[57]David Molina-Motos, 'Ecophilosophical Principles for an Ecocentric Environmental Education' (2019) Education Sciences

tem that defined African spirituality and relationship with nature. Before colonialism, the animist tendency of African traditional religion inspired an ecocentric behaviour towards nature. Even today, in the West African country of Senegal, there is still an animist dimension to spirituality.[58] For instance, in Senegal, the use of animal totemism is a significant aspect of religion. In Southeastern Nigeria, the worship of deities through animals is quite common. Some animals are regarded to be sacred. This is not just limited to animals, trees and plants too sometimes are regarded to be spiritually linked to an ancestral power or to a spirit entity.[59] Sometimes the life of humans is considered to have a spiritual link with that of animals. An instance is the belief of a family in a clan in Ezioha, a village in Southeastern Nigeria, that a specie of monkeys called *Utobo* are a connection to their ancestors and as such should not be hunted or eaten.[60]

In Eha-Amufu, another village in Southeastern Nigeria, it is believed that a spirit called *Ebe* is in charge of the fishes of the river in that community. It is considered that the big fishes in the river represent the people of substance in that community, while the small fishes are representative of people of small means. It is forbidden to fish in the river.[61] Animal and nature totemism in the traditional religion of the African people was a thing that uniquely defined the precolonial perspective of the

---

[58]Peter Balonon-Rosen, 'Out of this World: An Ethnographic Study of Mystics, Spirits, and Animist Practices in Senegal' (2013) Independent Study Project (ISP) Collection. 1511 <https://digitalcollections.sit.edu/isp_collection/1511> accessed 19 May, 2021
[59]Vitalis Nwashindu & Nkemjika Chimee Ihediwa, 'Totemism in Igbo land and the Challenges of the 21st Century' (2014-2015) 7-8 Bassey Andah Journal
[60]ibid
[61]ibid

African people. Many literary texts document the sacredness and spirituality ascribed to trees, plants and animals. In Achebe's Arrow of God, there is a myth among the Igbo people that *Idemili* as a male god of the sky owned a sacred python.[62] The association of the python with *Idemili* among the Igbo people is a myth with huge influence even on modern perception of the big snake.

Among the Yoruba, the sacredness of trees is an aspect of the spirituality of the traditional beliefs. There is a mythological conviction that trees harbour spirits. The *Iroko* tree, a tree that is believed by the Yorubas to be the inhabitation of a powerful spirit and thus cannot be hewed down without the performance of rituals.[63] These animist beliefs that spanned across African communities are evidence of the ecocentric nature of precolonial African spirituality and its reverence of nature. The relegation of traditional beliefs by the colonial influence has changed the African relationship with the environment. It has replaced veneration with wanton destruction for profit. The definition of civilisation from a colonial perspective included the invasion of nature and hailed concrete jungles over natural sanctuaries.

The hunting of elephants for their tusks and the aspiration to satisfy an international market for exotic animals marked the significance of colonialism and its expression of imperial pow-

---

[62]Isidore Diala, 'Medidating Mythology, Mollifying Women: Achebe's Anhills of the Savannah' (2004) 30(2-3) Ufahamu: A Journal of African Studies,
[63]Thorogood, 'The Iroko's Indomitable Role in African Culture' (Thorogood Timber Merchants, 2021) <https://www.thorogood.co.uk/the-irokos-indomitable-role-in-african-culture/> accessed 19 May, 2021

er.[64] While colonialism mocked the animist view of the African traditional religion, there is a new interest in animism and how it can change the present relationship between humans and nature. Animist ecology for instance proposes that every relation with the earth is defined by respect.[65] This approach towards the relationship with nature has far-reaching implications for the current regime of international environmental law. It would mean the entire decolonization of the system and stronger efforts in the protection of indigenous people.

Principle of Ecological Unity

One of the points that makes environmental justice worthy of global concern is that pollution oftentimes does not respect artificial boundaries, nor even natural boundaries. Its impact is felt as far as its magnitude. This is why environmental justice is not just a problem of the world's poorest and most economically vulnerable but a problem of the entire world, since environmental problems could be transboundary. With the environment, there is only one human destiny, and this is the result of however nature responds to human abuse.

There has been emphasis on how the earth is humanity's only home, and this has been the logic employed in anthropocentrically defined conservation efforts. Ecological unity is premised on the indivisibility and the singleness of nature. This principle

---

[64]Marianna Syzczyygielska, 'Elephant Ivory, Zoos, and Extinction in the Age of Imperialism (1870s-1940a)' (Max-Planck-Institut für Wissenschaftsgeschichte 5 July, 2019) <https://www.mpiwg-berlin.mpg.de/feature-story/elephant-ivory-zoos-and-extinction-age-imperialism-1870s-1940s> accessed 19 May, 2021

[65]Graham Harvey, 'Animism and Ecology: Participating in the World Community' (2019) 3 The Ecological Citizen

has been deployed against acts against the realisation of environmental justice. The principle of ecological unity is explained further in the Brundtland Report, and it is clear in the concerns expressed:

The Earth is one, but the world is not. We all depend on one biosphere for sustaining our lives. Yet each community, each country, strives for survival and prosperity with little regard for its impact on others. Some consume the Earth's resources at a rate that would leave little for future generations. Others, many more in number, consume far too little and live with the prospect of hunger, squalor, disease, and early death.[66]

It is recognised that the earth is one indivisible entity, even if the world might be split across many political and social aspirations, yet it is necessary that the whole world consider that the earth needs to be treated with care and responsibility. In the *Crown Zellerbach*[67] case, LaForest J. noted in his dissenting judgment that pollution control was just a part of the great global challenge of environmental management.[68] Pollution, which can be in the form of an environmental disruption through the illegal dumping of toxic waste or the experimentation of dangerous material, has proven to have fallout effects that could trail back to the polluter.

The reasoning behind ecological unity is that if responsibility to the environment and to nature is taken seriously, it would be to the benefit of the entire humanity. The Brundtland Report, that emphasizes on how ecological unity shows that the human destiny is a common one, points out that the rate of globalization demonstrates the extent to which humans were bound by

---

[66]United Nations, 'Report of the World Commission on Environment and Development: Our Common Future' (Oxford University Press 1987)
[67]*R. v. Crown Zellerbach Canada Ltd.*, [1988] 1 SCR 401
[68]ibid

economy and ecology.[69] Ecological unity allows that even problems such as the growing income inequality across the world be considered a global challenge, since income inequality inspires undocumented migration and causes insecurity through its tremendous capacity to displace populations. To implement the principle of ecological unity would be to ensure that the prescriptions to environmental justice capture the peculiar challenges of communities across the world.

Interdependence of Species

Human activity has undermined the structure of life on earth. It has been argued that there is a constant interaction between organisms and ecological networks.[70] This interaction forms the basis for the biological food chain. Microscopic organisms are quite essential to the food chain, such that from the micro-organic decomposers that allow the soil to process nutrients beneficial for plant growth to the complex interaction of symbiotism, the structure of organic interdependency assures that ecological unity should define how humans engage nature. Environmental science has shown the extent of destruction that human activity has wreaked on nature. The Exxon Valdez oil spill that occurred in 1989 polluted the ecosystem with around 11 million gallons of crude oil in Prince William Sound. This oil spill caused the death of wildlife and made the ecosystem toxic

---

[69]United Nations, 'Report of the World Commission on Environment and Development: Our Common Future' (Oxford University Press 1987)

[70]Carlos J Melián, Blake Matthews, Cecilia S de Andreazzi, Jorge P Rodríguez, Luke J Harmon, and Miguel A Fortuna, 'Deciphering the Interdependence between Ecological and Evolutionary Networks' (2018) Trends in Ecology & Evolution

to invertebrates and microscopic organisms that were important to the biological workings of the ecosystem. This led to severe after-effects that lingered for years after the oil spill.[71]

Humans depend on other organisms for their survival, and reckless acts against nature undermine the balance that ensure the smooth-running of ecosystems. Reckless ecosystem altering activities also have devastating effects on the marine ecology. For instance, the effect of climate change is significant for plankton, an important microorganism in the marine food web.[72] The 1992 Convention for Biological Diversity, which symbolizes the practicality of the legalization of the ecocentric paradigm, noted in its preamble that there should not be a postponement of strategies and actions to prevent the risk of the significant reduction or of losing biodiversity as a result of not having full scientific certainty.[73]

This translates that there should be an urgency that should be assumed in the protection of biological diversity, which is the foundation for the interdependency of species. The ecocentric instrument provides that the protection and sustainable use of biological diversity should be based on cooperation amongst states.[74] This is in acknowledgment that without the cooperation of states there can be no effective protection and sustainable use of biological diversity, since ecological unity makes environmental intervention the responsibility of a multilateral effort rather than a unilateral one. Ecological unity and the interdependence of species are concepts that justify environmen-

---

[71]Alaska's Ecology, 'Human Impacts on Ecosystems' (Alaska's Ecology 2001)
[72]Walker Smith, Deborah Steinberg, Deborah Bronk and Kam Tang, 'Marine Plankton Food Webs and Climate Change' (Virginia Institute of Marine Science, October 2008)
[73]UN Convention on Biological Diversity [1992] Preamble
[74]UN Convention on Biological Diversity [1992] art. 5

tal justice. The ecocentric paradigm provides an opportunity to achieve environmental justice and to have a better ethical perspective on the environment. It also allows an altruistic and meaningful perspective on the issue of environmental benefits. The ecocentric paradigm is a medium through which the decolonization of the international environmental law system can be executed, and it is also the path through which Africa can reinvent itself and align its environmental needs with its future.

Freedom from Ecological Destruction

The place of human rights in environmental protection is quite essential, since ecological protection often have positive effects on humans. Understanding how significant anthropocentric activities can be on the environment, the Stockholm Declaration recognised the human role in the environment as both a part of the biotic community and as an active agent of environmental change who has much to benefit from the environment, physically, intellectually, spiritually, morally and socially. It also acknowledged the importance of the natural and man-made environment to humans through its centrality to human rights and wellbeing.[75] The Stockholm Declaration went on to provide a solid ground for the interaction between human rights and environmental protection when it stated that humans have the right to freedom, equality and good conditions of living in a viable environment that supports human wellbeing and dignity.[76]

The freedom from ecological destruction entails that people should be able to enjoy the benefits of living in a safe environ-

---

[75]Stockholm Declaration on the United Nations Conference on the Human Environment [1972] A_CON-48_INF-5_Rev.1
[76]Ibid principle 1

ment that supports their livelihoods and dignity, away from ravaging poverty and ill-health induced by a poor environment. Ecological destruction is a process that goes beyond the direct anthropocentric interference with ecosystems. At the heart of ecological destruction are economic ventures, corporations and powerful external interests that have sustained environmental exploitation in vulnerable states in the developing world. There are other factors that cause ecological destruction. One of these factors could be developmental. In Congo, it was found that things, such as infrastructure extension; roads, settlement and industrial needs could bring about deforestation in the Congo Basin, which is the 'second largest contiguous block of forest in the world.'[77] In Africa, it is not often considered that infrastructural development should not be haphazard; hence there is often no plan for natural sanctuaries. From an environmental justice standpoint, ecological destruction in Africa has been piecemeal.

Colonialism was the foundation for an ecologically destructive system of exploitation that has continued, sustained by the inequities in global environmental relations. The vice-hold of colonialist structures and the rigidity of their nature towards a restructuring has maintained economic systems in Africa that creates wealth for a few people against the realisation of environmental justice. Poverty allows for environmental exploitation, and since Africa has a very high level of income inequality, environmental exploitation is sustained by colonial structures that have restricted political and economic development. In Congo, environmental exploitation takes the place of mineral mining. Dowling found that in Congo, the vicious vestiges of

---

[77]Carole Megevand, 'Deforestation Trends in the Congo Basin: Reconciling Economic Growth and Forest Protection' (World Bank 2013)

colonial oppression has established a long-lasting pattern.[78] He argued that the global capitalist system exploits the lapses in the African policy framework that has been long entrenched by colonialism in the African governmental structures.[79]

There is a perpetual frustration of the right to freedom from ecological destruction in Africa because the African socio-economic structure has been framed by colonialism to support environmental classism and thereby ensure that communities remain poor and without access to environmental justice. Masron found that there is a connection between poverty and environmental degradation.[80] The role that immense poverty has in ecological destruction is in the pressure of growing populations who have to engage the environment in unsustainable ways. The use of wood for fuel, hunting animals in the wild and the improper siting of waste dumps are ecologically destructive practices in communities with low socio-economic status.

Land degradation has severe consequences for climate change, and it results to the economic vulnerability of many people, especially in states that are fragile.[81] Climate change has impacted Africa tremendously because of how it has created more social inequities and increased conflicts. For Africa, progressing through the systemic challenges allowing ecological destruction, which was created by oppressive colonialism and its turbulent political history, to reign in the deepening divide of its people along social classes, would involve a con-

---

[78]Owen Dowling, 'The Political Economy of Super-Exploitation in Congolese Mineral Mining' (Peter Peckard Memorial Prize, Cambridge University, 2020)
[79]ibid
[80]Tajul Ariffin Masron, 'Does Poverty Cause Environmental Degradation? Evidence from Developing Countries' (2019) 23(1) Journal of Poverty
[81]Isabel Kempf, 'Poverty and the Environment/Climate Change' (UNDP-UNEP Poverty-Environment Initiative 2015)

certed attempt at establishing cooperative legal and political efforts amongst African states.

Environmental Perspectives and Racial Values

Environmental perspectives can be framed by racial values. Racial values are distinctive social preferences that are informed by racial traditions. Bezerra and others stated that the process of assigning values to some groups can be adopted as a means for the determination of distinguishing factors between in-group and out-group.[82] The social construction of race and the biases and prejudices that are consequent of racial designation have environmental backlash. Structural racism and racial exclusion have had destructive effects on the environment. There has been a trove of research reports that prove that blacks, in the context of the United States, have been excluded from nature, they keep away from it, and would rather incline towards urban areas and well-developed spaces.[83] This finding mirrors a prevailing aversion for nature to developed landscapes in many parts of Africa.

Asides the colonial re-orientation on the emphasis of value on urbanisation above nature, there is an ugly interpretation of that emphasis on value, and which is that nature has little role to play in the urbanisation process. This was reflected in a re-

---

[82]Samuel Lincoln Bezerra, Tiago Jesse Souza de Lima, Luana Elayne Cunha de Souza, Aline Lima-Nunes, Leoncio Camino, 'Racial Prejudice and Social Values: How I perceive Others and Myself' (2017) 22(2) Psico-USF Braganca Paulista
[83]Dorceta E Taylor, 'Connectedness to Nature and Landscape Preferences Among College Students' (2018) 11(3) Environmental Justice

port that showed that in many African cities, especially in the poorer ones, there is usually small space left for greenery. The report further stated that spaces left for public parks, recreational areas, greenways, waterways and such kinds of places that are open for general use is below 1 million square mile per inhabitant in cities across Africa, like Luanda, Cairo and Alexandria.[84] The green space in Dakar, Senegal shrunk by 34 percent between 1988 and 2008 as reported by the World Bank in 2009.[85]

Addis Ababa, Ethiopia, has favoured the hewing down of trees to create more spaces for housing.[86] Lagos, Nigeria's most populated city, spots an almost treeless landscape as it has lost a significant part of its forests[87] and has poor environmental management practices as part of its expansion plans. In countries like the United States, black alienation from nature may be more economic than cultural; however, economically driven values usually are pushed further by deeper social factors. In the case of Africa, colonial values that had sustained economic exploitation had also ensured that there was less regard for the preservation of nature. In Africa today, the idea of preservation that had been a part of African tradition as a result of ancient religious practices has now been considered Western

---

[84]Roland White, Jane Turpie and Gwyneth Letley, *Greening Africa's Cities: Enhancing the relationship between Urbanization, Environmental Assets and Ecosystem Services* (World Bank 2017)
[85]ibid
[86]ibid
[87]Fola Babalola, 'What to Consider Before Mass Planting of Trees in Nigeria's Lagos State' (The Conversation, 2 June, 2020) <https://www.google.com/amp/what-to-consider-before-before-mass-planting-of-trees-in-nigerias-lagos-state-137634> accessed 19 May, 2021

and replaced with an ecologically destructive aspiration to build cities that would exclude nature.

Decolonising International Environmental Law

International environmental law (IEL) has developed through a colonial history, it has also thrived in the time-framed sphere alongside the global problem of racism. The discourse of IEL has often excluded the problem of environmental injustice, not until recently when the racial problems in the American society necessitated a need to consider a paradigm shift in the way environmental concerns are viewed. As has earlier been discussed, the history of IEL in Africa had often been about resources rather than about the protection of both the indigenous people, their ways and their environments. IEL institutions developed in the political climate that colonialism had established.[88] Castro asserts that there is an obvious dimension of domination that IEL possesses in its nature.[89] He further argued that this nature of IEL makes it quite a challenge since IEL is supposed to be progressive.[90]

In the development of IEL, issues relating to the historically engaging problems of racial and social domination have often appeared negligible. The discussion centering on the environment as a common resource pool for humanity has often assumed that equality and fair access to the benefits of the environment are constant variables that attend the long-standing reality of the human condition. Anthropocentrism, being the traditional approach to IEL, has regarded the major challenge of the environment as one in which humans constantly exploit

---

[88]Douglas de Castro, 'The Colonial Aspects of the International Environmental Law – Treaties as Promoters of Continuous Structural Violence' (October 11 2017) Groningen Journal of International Law
[89]ibid
[90]ibid

the environment and the consequences suffered by a collective human destiny. Over the years, IEL had failed to address environmental issues from efforts to understand inequality and its effects on the environment until recently. In 2003, Boyce argued that there are winners in the economic activities that have led to the degradation of the environment.[91] And that there are three possibilities; the first being that there might be no losers yet, since the losers would be people of the future. The second, that there could be losers, who might not know what extent they are losing. And in the third, that the possible losers are aware that they are losing, but are powerless in resisting the costs that have been put on them.[92]

With the emergence of studies in environmental justice, it is clear that there have been losers for a long time, and these losers have always been in plain sight, sometimes not aware of the damage that they have been caused since sometimes to lose to environmental degradation often mean that a people must exist in some kind of powerlessness either an economic, social or political kind. In the case of the black community in the United States, where the environmental justice movement started, it was both racial discrimination and socio-economic powerlessness. In the case of Africa, colonialism set the continent for decades of losing to economic profiteers of its environment.

The colonial framework in which IEL found itself ensured that it was desensitized to the plight of those who were losing in the race to exploit the environment. The decolonization of IEL is a process that must allow a reflection on the costs for the world's most vulnerable populations. It is a process that must

---

[91]James K Boyce, 'Inequality and Environmental Protection' (2003) Political Economy Research Institute: University of Massachusetts Amherst Working Paper Number 52
[92]ibid

invest in principles that provide for the reparation of environmental injustices and should develop a deeper sensitivity to the plight of minorities. IEL must transition along the line of an equitable treatment of the issues resulting from North-South environmental relations. This is because there is a tendency for regions of the Global South, like Africa, to suffer the detrimental effects of economic activities engaged by countries of the Global North.

Critical Race Theory in Context

Environmental justice has exposed the racial and socio-economic aspects of climate change and environmental pollution. The role of racial identity and the attendant social distinctions in the discourse of environmental justice are emphasised when structural racism decides who suffers more from the actions of others. Critical Race Theory (CRT) is essential in framing the challenges of environmental justice not just at the community or national level, but in a global arena. CRT is an intellectual movement that explores the concept of white supremacy, in a bid to understand how it is sustained and recycled within a system of cultural legal and political dynamics, basically in an American context.[93] Outside the American society, CRT offers insight to a more complex racial politics at the international level. White supremacy is a racial phenomenon that has proved its own existence in human history, from the Aryanism that inspired the Nazis during the Second World War to the imperial-

---

[93]Antonio Tomas De La Garza and Kent A Ono, 'Critical Race Theory' in Klaus Bruhn Jensen and Robert T. Craig (eds), Jefferson D Pooley and Eric W Rothenbuhler (assoc eds) *The International Encyclopedia of Communication Theory and Philosophy* (John Wiley & Sons, Inc 2016)

ist claims of colonialists. In the 19th Century, scholars in Europe were consumed by the promise of racial supremacy. For instance, Arthur de Gobineau in 1855 argued about cognitive differences between races, and that civilisations fall when there is a corruption of racial purity.[94]

He further asserted that the white race was superior to others.[95] This position was no different from the works of European historians like Hugh Trevor-Roper, with imperialistic conclusions on the African continent. While CRT has been claimed to be part of a research tradition that has come a long way from the time of WEB Du Bois, Frantz Fanon, Angela Davies, Audre Lorde, Gloria Anzaldúa and Cherríe Moraga, it presents itself distinctly as an approach that began in legal studies and aspires to be a tool for social and political change.[96] In a broader context, CRT provides a particularly strong emphasis on the complex issues of race in a global environmental justice agenda. In a consideration of the operation of CRT in an international context, it is agreed that there is need for a further examination of economic status and national origin.[97] In this work, CRT is necessary in the examination of the damage that

---

[94]Arthur de Gobineau, The Inequality of the Human Races (3rd edn, Ostara Publications 2016)
[95]ibid
[96]Antonio Tomas De La Garza and Kent A Ono, 'Critical Race Theory' in Klaus Bruhn Jensen and Robert T. Craig (eds), Jefferson D Pooley and Eric W Rothenbuhler (assoc eds) *The International Encyclopedia of Communication Theory and Philosophy* (John Wiley & Sons, Inc, 2016)
[97]Jennifer Willet, 'Infusing Critical Race Theory into Environmental Justice: Lessons from Nevada' (Society for Social Work and Research, 22nd Annual Conference-Achieving Equal Opportunity, Equity and Justice) <https://sswr.confex.com/sswr/2018/webprogram/Paper2563.html> accessed 21 June, 2021

colonialism wreaked on the African environment through its claims to racial and cultural imperialism.

CRT enables a critical look at the continued operation of colonialism and its legacies that has ensured that Africa's growth is locked in a constant battle with the ghosts from its past. Colonialism, as earlier argued, has roots locked into a foundation of racial superiority, and this was quite demonstrated through its structures in Africa. Asides colonialism's guiding principle of exploitation, it was further sustained through dangerous structures that have continued to endure. These dangerous structures have allowed a kind of economic and environmental oppression that put pressure on the African environment. It has brought about a metaphoric situation where Africa feeds its resources into an insatiable abyss.

The consequences have been environmental pollution, deeply entrenched poverty and child labor. For instance, Nigeria's oil exploitation dates back to the colonial era. Where the monopolization of the industry by Shell British Petroleum had been made possible by its ties to the colonial power.[98] The activities of Shell in post-independence Nigeria saw an impoverished Niger Delta, where oil spills ruined the agricultural and fishing prospects of communities in oil-laden creeks. Colonialism also strengthened dictatorships in post-independent African states.[99] The autocratic power structures favored easy collusion to exploit the African environment of resources. One attempt to immortalize colonialism is the argument that is made in its de-

---

[98]Jêdrzerj George Frymas, Matthias P Beck and Kamel Mellahi, 'Maintaining Corporate Dominance after Decolonization: the 'First Mover Advantage' of Shell BP in Nigeria' (2000) 85 Review of African Political Economy
[99]Nic Cheeseman and Jonathan Fisher, *Authoritarian Africa: Repression, Resistance and the Power of Ideas (African World Histories)* (OUP USA 2019)

fense. That the colonies must have been put on a path of development through self-governance and an improved standard of living.[100] In 2011, David Cameron said in a speech to the Conservative Party Conference, 'Britain did not rule the waves with armbands on.'[101] This was in appreciation of a British Empire that dealt ruthlessly with its colonies. The argument that Africa benefitted from colonialism is weak in many ways, particularly in the context of environmental justice in Africa. It justifies the exploitative practice that has now become a standard for African governments, to think about economic development not in the productivity of the human population, but in the exploitation of the environment.

Postcolonialism

The discussion of racial privilege and environmental justice in the context of Africa as much as it concerns colonialism demands that there be a theoretical grounding in postcolonialism. This is because the study of colonial impact cannot be complete without engaging the narrative of the resistance to it. Postcolonialism is the aspect of contemporary theory that makes an inquiry into, and builds propositions relating to the cultural and political effect of European conquest upon colo-

---

[100]Bruce Gilley, 'The Case for Colonialism' (2017) Third World Quarterly
[101]See Nicholas Watt, 'David Cameron speech: let's show the world some fight' (*The Guardian,* 5 October 2011) https://www.theguardian.com/politics/2011/oct/05/david-cameron-speech-show-world-fight>accessed 21 June, 2021

nized societies, and the types of responses they make.[102] Post-colonialism has come a long way in its development, and it appears that there is a normalization of colonialism into a subject that exclusively describes the relationship between the Western Empire and their colonies.[103] Beyond just making an investigation and building propositions of the cultural and political effect of colonialism and its resistance, postcolonialism covers the consequence of colonialism. The resistance of colonized societies in their quest for autonomy is important in the study of environmental justice on the continent, as this provides a foundation for future conflict of purposes.

History has shown that the structural violence against Africa, in the form of colonialism, was not the case of the Western colonizers on one part and the colonized societies on the other, there were collusions of benefit that sustained colonialism and ensured that the post-independent politics of the region were dominated by the Africans who colluded with them. Racial privilege in the postcolonial discourse ensured a leverage of power and influence that distinguished actors in the colonial world. In Kochar and Khan's environmental postcolonialism, there is a description of the extent to which colonialism devastated the African environment. It explains that colonialism was

---

[102]Bill Ashcroft, 'A Convivial Critical Democracy: Postcolonial Studies in the Twenty-First Century' in Bill Ashcroft, Ranjini Mendis, Juli McGonegal, and Arun Murkherjee (eds) *Literature for Our Times: Postcolonial Studies in the Twenty-First Century* (Brill 2012)

[103]Monika Albrecht, 'Multidirectional perspectives on imperial and colonial pasts and the neocolonial present' in Bill Ashcroft, Ranjini Mendis, Juli McGonegal, and Arun Murkherjee (eds) *Literature for Our Times: Postcolonial Studies in the Twenty-First Century* (Brill 2012)

driven by greed, such that it never made provisions nor bothered with developing the human and non-human subjects.[104]

Kochar and Khan argued that the prime target of colonialism was land. This explains the Scramble for Africa, and why there are conflicts motivated by land in parts of Africa, as there has been an alteration of the natural boundaries.[105] Colonialism created artificial borders and brought incompatible peoples together in countries that have continued to witness unrest and political warring. Kochar and Khan further made an important claim that there is a blurring of material distinction between identity and land.[106] This is true when there is a consideration of the fact that culture and traditions that inform collective identity could be environmentally expedient. The postcolonial relevance of resistance in an environmental justice discourse is pertinent especially upon the assertion that colonialism is not over; it has only receded into the shadows where it wields a dangerous influence on the socio-environmental relations with Africa.

The challenges of environmental justice in Africa are concretely rooted in the damage that colonialism wreaked on the human and non-human subjects. In the human subjects, it brought about the corruption of the existing value for the environment. There was no doubt that the prevailing practice in precolonial African societies helped preserve the environment and acknowledged the sanctity of the land. In post-independent Africa, the environment is seen in what it could yield for human profit and exploited relentlessly. Colonialism's effect on the non-human subject was the commercialization of the conti-

---

[104]Shubhanku Kochar and Anjum Khan (eds) *Environmental Postcolonialism: A Literary Response* (Rowman & Littlefield 2021)
[105]ibid
[106]ibid

nent and its reduction into a source of profit for the colonialists. Furthermore, the anthropocentric boundaries of conservation that keeps shifting to accommodate the realities of the economic activities of the developed world was a function of colonialism, as colonialism introduced the practice of invasive exploitation.

The role of race in the sustenance of colonialism was in its creation of its privilege by conditioning the minds of colonial subjects to accept its unequal distinction. Therefore, a white man in the eyes of the colonial subject became imperial and distinguished because of the psychological conditioning that the colonialist was not to be questioned. The effect of this on environmental justice in Africa is pervasive and yet to be resolved. It is the same effect that has made the ecocentric perception of land in Africa seem anti-development. It has created a distortion in the notion of development. Environmental justice in Africa today is critically affected by the development pattern created by colonialism. Poverty created by colonial exploitation in the form of underpriced natural resources and by retained colonial trusteeship of state assets has been a powerful impediment in advancing environmental justice in Africa. To unbundle these challenges for environmental justice in Africa, there must be a review of current colonial ties and their effect on the African environment.

African states must explore grounds that would bring about a balance in economic relations with the West. Many African states would have to reassess their development pattern and its effect on the environment and on vulnerable people in Africa. In realigning with its environmentally benevolent past, Africa must integrate only eco-friendly developmental solutions and encourage investment through policies that are mindful of the environment. There is also the problem of government-supported urban gentrification in many African states that seem to push environmental burdens on vulnerable people. African cities should take into consideration that a common environment is the burden of the collective, and a transfer of the burden would only lead to a future where stockpiled environmental burdens would create more overwhelming challenges for the continent.

Examination of International Legal Frameworks for Dispute Resolution in the Aviation Industry

Uwakwe Abugu[1]
Rufus Adeoluwa Olodude[2]

Introduction

Aviation, encompassing all aspects of mechanical flight and the aircraft industry, operates within the intricate landscape of international disputes. Recognizing the inherent complexities, established international frameworks were instituted to regulate the aviation sector and facilitate dispute resolution among industry stakeholders. However, given the magnitude of conflicts inherent to aviation, the current framework has proven insufficient. This chapter comprehensively examines the effectiveness and limitations of the prevailing international legal framework governing the aviation dispute. The chapter identifies a significant deficiency within the current international framework: a

---

[1]Professor of Medical Law & Ethics, University of Abuja, Abuja, Email: uwakwe.abugu@uniabuja.edu.ng.
[2]PhD Candidate, University of Abuja, Abuja, Email: adeoluwaolodude@gmail.com.

notable absence of robust enforcement mechanisms required to achieve desired outcomes. To address this issue, we propose a thorough review of international aviation regulations, coupled with the implementation of a fortified framework equipped with enhanced enforcement capabilities. Such an initiative promises to foster a more conducive environment for global aviation transactions, ultimately benefiting stakeholders worldwide. It ensures equitable and effective regulation within the aviation sector, aligning with the evolving dynamics of this critical global industry.

In the dynamic realm of international aviation, disputes are an inevitable part of the landscape. Even though there are considerable frameworks in place, aviation causes a number of disputes and disagreements.[3] However, the said dispute in the air transport services may either be solved through peaceful means or by coercion. In some instances, states may resort to political or legal settlements, or may request the intervention of the International Civil Aviation Organization (ICAO) Council.[4] From contractual conflicts to safety concerns, resolving issues efficiently is vital. This study delves into exploring how aviation disputes are addressed within the framework of international law. This study aims to provide a comprehensive understanding of the historical development of aviation dispute resolution, from its early days to the present. There shall also be an evaluation of the effectiveness of existing mechanisms in addressing contemporary aviation challenges. As aviation continues to connect the world, understanding the mechanisms behind dispute resolution is crucial.

---

[3]Z Jeremic, 'Dispute Resolution in International Civil Aviation' (Master's Dissertation, Institute of Air and Space Law McGill University 1996)
[4]ibid

It is pertinent to situate this chapter among other related literatures that have attempted delving into this discuss earlier. Kaul[5] Kaul in his paper analyzed the Chicago convention's achievements and shortcomings, highlighting its legal form and detailed articles. However, he noted that the ICAO Council's role in settling disputes between contracting states has been mixed, with many being settled informally and not being noticed. Notable disputes settled by the Council under Articles 84 and 85 include the India-Pakistan dispute, the US-Cuba dispute, and the US-EU dispute. He further stated that the Chicago Convention, which established the International Civil Aviation Organization (ICAO), has seen only three major amendments in its 66-year existence. Kerkonian and Raju in their article[6] explore the concept of the Chicago Convention, a multilateral treaty that addresses international civil aviation. The treaty, signed around the end of World War II, extended territorial sovereignty to include airspace above a state's physical territory. Since then, the concept of sovereignty has applied, requiring explicit permission for a state to travel over a territory through its airspace. He is of the view that the Chicago Convention reinforces state sovereignty over airspace through provisions such as requiring special permission before operating international air services through another state's airspace.

Malhotra discusses the laws governing the aviation industry and the principle of bilateral air transport agreements. He high-

---

[5]Sanat Kaul, 'Chicago Convention Revisited: Review of Chicago Convention and Bilateralism in Air Services' (Scribd) <https://www.scribd.com/document/300831060/Chicago-Convention> accessed July 20, 2022
[6]AD Kerkonian and N Raju, 'The Legal Challenges of International Suborbital Flights: A Bilateral Solution' (2020) 85 Journal of Air Law & Commerce <https://scholar.smu.edu/jalc/vol85/iss3/1> accessed March 10, 2022

lights the need for countries to relate bilaterally in the air sector, leading to the need for bilateral air service agreements. The first bilateral air transport agreement was signed in 1946 between the United States and the United Kingdom. Malhotra discusses the various forums for Aviation Dispute Resolution, including the International Civil Aviation Organization (ICAO), International Court of Justice (ICJ), Shanghai International Aviation Court of Arbitration (SIACA), and American Arbitration Association. He believes that arbitration is an exponentially growing dispute resolution mechanism, as it plays a crucial role in managing disputes in global industries.[7] However, the major drawback of arbitration is the difficulty of enforcing awards, as the other party may find loopholes to stop enforcement, leading to appeals to state courts. Additionally, the recognition and enforcement of foreign seated awards vary among different laws, which delays dispute resolution and fails to achieve desired results. The European legal framework for air navigation services was analyzed, focusing on regulatory and enforcement competencies of the European Civil Aviation Conference (ECAC, EUROCONTROL) and the European Community.

Malhotra further differentiates cross-border provision of air navigation services from other types. He distinguishes between sovereignty and jurisdiction in international law, stating that sovereignty refers to the legal personality of a state, while jurisdiction refers to specific aspects of the state's rights, claims, liberties, and powers.[8] The Chicago Convention acknowledges that every state has complete and exclusive sovereignty over airspace above its territory. The study concludes that the

---

[7]VS Malhotra, 'Arbitration in the Aviation Industry' (iPleaders 2021) <https://blog.ipleaders.in/arbitration-aviation-industry/#The_Civil_Aviation_Requirements>accessed May 7, 2022
[8]ibid

Chicago Convention is open for adherence by states, including those not members of the United Nations or associated states.

Li-Juan explores the Warsaw and Montreal Conventions and their impact on consumer protection and passenger protection in the US and EU. She highlights the inadequacies of relying on international conventions for a harmonized solution for flight delay claims. He focuses on advanced aviation markets like the US and EU, as well as emerging markets like Mainland China and Taiwan. He noted that the Warsaw Convention was drafted to avoid financial crises for air carriers in case of aircraft crashes. It aimed to standardize elements such as removing conflicts, creating internationally recognized documentation, prescribing a limitation period for claims, resolving jurisdictional questions, and imposing strict limits on carriers' liability. The liability rules established by the Convention favored air carriers to promote investment in the commercial air transport industry.[9] Article 23 nullifies abusive provisions in contracts of carriage, while Article 32 renders contractual provisions infringing on the Convention's rules concerning the choice of law and court jurisdiction null and void. From the above, it could be gleaned that there is no comprehensive analysis of the international legal framework on aviation dispute.

---

[9] J Li-Juan, 'Remedies for Passengers for Flight Delays Caused By Force Majeure: Perspectives from Taiwan for a Harmonized Solution' (Institute of Air and Space Law McGill University, Montreal 2006) < http//4198b82-7aab-4965-bb30-4b1058b24776.> accessed March 7, 2022.

International Frameworks

Paris Convention 1919

The Paris Convention 1919 is the first international Aviation Convention in the history of multilateral agreement among countries in the world, and especially in Europe, where the state members to the convention were from. The idea of a convention which was first birthed from a meeting organized by France, inviting other European Nations to make regulations on civil Aviation on May 10, 1910, shortly after a record of mass German planes landing in the French territory, could not reach the goal of signing such Convention, until after the first world war, and the eventual reconvening of Paris Peace Conference on October 13, 1919.[10] The signatory to this convention on that day included: The United States of America, Belgium, Bolivia, Brazil, The British Empire, China, Cuba, Ecuador, France, Greece, Guatemala, Haiti, The Hedjaz, Honduras, Italy, Japan, Liberia, Nicaragua, Panama, Peru, Poland, Portugal, Romania, the Serb-Croat-Slovene State, Siam, Czechoslovakia and Uruguay.

Furthermore, the convention establishes an International Commission for Air Navigation, a permanent commission placed under the aegis of the defunct League of Nations.[11] The purpose of this commission is similar to that of the present International Civil Aviation Organization and was saddled with the responsibility to receive proposals from or to make proposals to any of the contracting States for the modification or amendment of the provisions of the present Convention, to notify changes adopted on the convention, to oversee the registra-

---

[10]JC Cooper, 'The International Air Navigation Conference, Paris 1910' (1952) 19(2) Journal of Air Law and Commerce
[11]Paris Convention 1919, Article 34

tion of National carriers and national aircrafts as provided in Article 9 of the Convention, to validate certificate of airworthiness and licenses of competency issued to aircrafts in contracting states, to collect and communicate to the contracting States information of every kind concerning international air navigation; even information on telegraphy, meteorology and medical science which may be of interest to air navigation, and to examine questions from member states submitted in regard to inter territorial air navigation[12].

Dispute Resolution Mechanism

It is important to note, nevertheless, that the major highlight of this Convention under this discourse is its Aviation dispute resolution technique, especially the promotion of alternative dispute resolution mechanisms. The convention provides that in the case of a disagreement between two or more States relating to the interpretation of its provisions, the question in dispute shall be determined by the Permanent Court of International Justice to be established by the League of Nations. However, until its establishment, such disagreements are to be resolved primarily by arbitration.[13] Such disagreement to be resolved by arbitration would however not include disagreement relating to the technical regulations annexed to the present Convention, which is to be settled by the decision of the International Commission for Air Navigation by a majority of votes.[14] It is important to state that settling a dispute through casting of vote can be counter-productive as such decision will be subject rather than objective. Hence, there is a need to establish a veritable framework for technical regulations.

---

[12]Paris Convention 1919, Article 34 (a)-(g)
[13]Paris Convention 1919, Article 37
[14]Paris convention 1919, Para 4, Article 37

Examining the Arbitration framework in the convention, it is noteworthy to appraise the level of freedom awarded to the two in appointing an arbitrator and the reduced influence of the International Commission to the barest minimum. The two parties themselves, are expected to appoint a third-party arbitrator who is to settle the dispute, and where the parties are unable to reach a consensus as to the same choice of arbitrator, they may each nominate arbitrators who in their own stead would decide on the umpire between them. If this also fails, the parties are still allowed each to name a third State, and the third State so named shall proceed to designate the umpire, by agreement or by each proposing a name and then determining the choice by lot[15]. Following the consensual approach of the arbitration framework, it is therefore no surprise that the convention also deems the decision of the arbitration absolute and final in resolving such form of dispute within its jurisdiction[16].

The United Nation Charter

The United Nation Charter 1945 is the foundation treaty of the United Nations as an International Organization after the end of the second world war. The convention which was first signed in 1945 in San Francisco, California, United states by the big six China, France, the United Kingdom, United states, the Soviet Union and China, alongside forty-six other signatories, now has 193 member states as parties to the Convention,

---

[15]Paris Convention, 1919, Article 37,
[16]Paris Convention, 1919, Para 5, Article 37

hence, increasing its overreaching effect as an International Instrument.[17]

According to the objective of the Preamble of the Charter, the United Nation Charter serve as an instrument reflecting the consent of diverse nations across the world to ensure world peace and avoid the scourge of war in the coming generations. The charter seeks to reaffirm faith in fundamental human rights, in the dignity and worth of the human person, in the equal rights of men and women and of nations large and small, and to establish conditions under which justice and respect for the obligations arising from treaties and other sources of international law can be maintained, promoting social progress and better standards of life in larger freedom. Furthermore, it encourages seeking the practice of tolerance and togetherness among nations and to unite the strength of all to maintain national peace and security.[18] In the light of this objective, the Charter of the United Nations therefore provides for a dispute resolution mechanism among member states, to apprehend disputes for peaceful settlement before it develops to an armed conflict.

Dispute Resolution Mechanism

Examining the dispute resolution framework under this treaty, the United Nations Charter promotes the use of Alternative Dispute Resolution as a first-hand mechanism in resolving inter member state disputes before approaching the International Court of Justice. Article 33(1) and (2) of the Charter, in Chap-

---

[17]United Nations, '1945: The San Francisco Conference' (United Nations 26 August 2015) www.un.org. Accessed 10 October, 2022.
[18]See also Article 1, Charter of United Nations 1945

ter IV under the heading 'Pacific Settlement of Disputes' provides that:

1) The parties to any dispute, the continuance of which is likely to endanger the maintenance of international peace and security, shall, first of all, seek a solution by negotiation, enquiry, mediation, conciliation, arbitration, judicial settlement, resort to regional agencies or arrangements, or other peaceful means of their own choice.

2) The Security Council shall, when it deems necessary, call upon the parties to settle their dispute by such means.

Howbeit, where the two parties have exhausted the option of alternative dispute resolution exhaustively, that is either by enquiry, mediation, conciliation, or arbitration, but nevertheless unable to sufficiently resolve the dispute, the parties are required to bring the subject of the dispute to the attention of the General Assembly or the Security council. On the note of such report, the General Assembly or the Security Council will in situations where such a dispute could lead to a breach of international peace in turn make recommendations to the parties involved, including a possible reference of such dispute to the International Court of Justice established in Article 92, of the Charter.

It is important to note, that while the Charter of the United Nations does not expressly as a sui generis international instrument governing the practice of Civil Aviation, the medium of dispute resolution provided in the charter can, nevertheless, be applied in the settlement of international Civil Aviation dispute between contracting states to the charter. Moreover, the United Nations Condition for Aircraft Charter Agreement[19] which lays down the principle of aircraft charter agreement of the United Nations, as a good model for air charter agreement

---

[19]Hereinafter UNCACA

by other states, also provides for alternative dispute resolution in resolving aviation dispute. The Condition provides that parties in a charter agreement shall use their best effort in settling any dispute or claim arising from a charter agreement or its breach, termination or invalidity amicably through conciliation in accordance with the Conciliation Rules of The United Nations Commission on International Trade Law (UNCITRAL) or such other means agreed by the parties in writing[20]. Also, where such is not settled with sixty days (60) under the previous condition, the parties are required to require such dispute to arbitration under the UNICITRAL Arbitration Rules.[21]

Hague Convention 1899

The Hague Conventions of 1899 is one of the series of international treaties and declarations negotiated at the international peace conferences in The Hague, Netherlands. It was the first attempt at creating a multilateral framework for keeping world peace, and also for regulating the prosecutions of war as well as conducts of warfare. According to Micheal Haas[22] the Hague convention came from a proposal on 24 August 1898 by Russian Tsar Nicholas II. Nicholas and Count Mikhail Nikolayevich Muravyov, his foreign minister, were instrumental in initiating the conference on 18th of May 1899. The conference which had 34 rulers present including the President of United states, the German Emperor, King of Prussia; His Majesty the Emperor of Austria, King of Bohemia, etc., enacted three treaties for the prosecution of war and the settle-

---

[20], UNCACA, Article 16.1
[21]UNCACA, Article 62
[22]M Haas, 'International Human Rights: A Comprehensive Introduction' (Routledge Publications 2008)

ment of discord among party nations which are: The Convention for the Pacific Settlement of International Dispute 1899, The Convention in Respect to the Laws and Customs of War on Land, and Convention for the Adaptation to Maritime Warfare of the Principles of the Geneva Convention of 22 August 1864. For the purpose of the discussion in view, more interest will be avered to examining the dispute resolution framework of the first convention, which is the Convention for the Pacific Settlement of International Dispute.[23]

Dispute Resolution Mechanism

To start with, it is pertinent to note that the Hague Convention I of 1899 on dispute settlement only employs Alternative Dispute Resolution mechanisms as it believes that the employment of legal courts is within the exclusive Sovereignty of each party states. Moreover, alternative dispute resolution and the reference of dispute to be addressed using them are friendly gestures from parties involved and the best efforts in the friendly settlement of an international dispute. Therefore, the convention discourages the use of force in relations to disputes between state, and requires the signatory power to instead employ the Pacific settlement of international dispute by Mediation, Enquiry and Arbitration.[24]

In serious disagreements, before an appeal to arms, signatory parties are required to have recourse to good office and mediation, the mediator being one of the signatory parties neutral or indifferent to the subject of discord between the parties.[25] The duty of the mediator under the convention is to reconcile opposing claims and appease the feelings of resentment between

[23]Hereinafter 'Hague Convention I, 1899'
[24]Hague Convention I, 1899, Article 1
[25]Hague Convention I, 1899, Article 3

the two parties[26]. More also, the mediator's decision are non-binding but rather in form of advice to both parties which can be accepted or rejected.[27] Therefore, where both parties reject the recommendations of the mediator, its duties and role in the dispute resolution comes to an end, and other medium of resolution must be employed.[28] Furthermore, the commencement of a mediation process or acceptance of mediation unless by an agreement is not expected under the convention to be a ground *suo motu* in the suspension of hostilities.[29] While mediation is on, parties may continue its preparation for hostilities and may conduct hostilities against the other party. This, obviously, was one of the Achilles heels of the convention and the reason it failed in averting the first world war of 1914.

Furthermore, where mediation fails, signatory parties are required to create a commission of enquiry to look into the object of hostilities, and facilitate a solution to the differences harboured by both parties as provided in Article 32 of the Convention, by means of impartial and conscientious investigation.[30] The commission of enquiry is expected to be impartial and constituted with membership from all parties in the hostilities. Most importantly, the commission must hear the sides of both parties in the hostilities without prejudice, or favour. After a thorough investigation into the cause of the hostilities, the body is required to make reports to both parties, suggesting ways of resolving the hostilities amicably.[31] However, just like in mediation, the reports of the committees are not binding and can be rejected by both parties.[32]

----

[26]Hague Convention I, 1899, Article 4
[27]Hague Convention I, 1899, Article 6,
[28]Hague Convention I, 1899, Article 5
[29]Hague Convention I, 1899, Article 7
[30]Hague Convention I, 1899, Article 9
[31]Hague Convention I, 1899, Article 13
[32]Hague Convention I, 1899, Article 14,

The apex dispute resolution mechanism by the body after the two methods espoused above would be Arbitration. Infact, the convention referred to this mechanism as the most effective and the most equitable where diplomacy fails in dispute of a legal nature, requiring the interpretation or application of International Convention or agreements.[33] The supremacy of Arbitration as a medium of dispute resolution would also come in the consensual submission of the parties to its awards, as they are required by state signatories to be indicated in their treaties or by express stipulation in their agreements.[34] To this end, the convention therefore established the Permanent Court of Arbitration and saddled it with the jurisdiction to hear all arbitration cases, unless the parties agree otherwise to special tribunals of their own.[35]

The Permanent court of Arbitration under the Convention plays a similar role to the International Court of Justice in the novel Charter of the United Nations. Just like the latter, the decision of the former is binding and final, and is jointly enforced by signatory parties to the convention against a defaulting party through sanctions or joint military actions.[36] More also, the composition of the arbitration court is one that advocates equal representation as state parties are allowed to nominate four members each to the arbitration panel; persons with known competence in International Law, and with the highest reputation and morals.[37] They are appointed for six years and in overseeing an arbitration tribunal often elect the sole umpire among themselves to give a decision.

---

[33]Hague Convention I, 1899, Article 15
[34]Hague Convention I, 1899, Article 18
[35]Hague Convention I, 1899, Article 21
[36]Hague Convention I, 1899, Article 46
[37]Hague Convention I, 1899, Article 23

One appraisal of the arbitration system in the Hague Convention, important to note, would be its relative seating flexibility. Under the convention, the International Bureau, which is also the channel of the communications relative to the meeting of the court, as well as the Permanent Arbitration Court itself are seated in Hague. However, the convention allows parties by consensus to request the sitting of the arbitration court in other locations which matches their convenience, or in cases of war, peaceable areas proximate to them.[38]

The Convention on Damage by Foreign Aircraft to the Third Parties on the Surface (ICAO) 1952

The Convention on Damage by Foreign Aircraft to the Third Parties on the Surface (1952)[39] is a convention signed at Rome by Five contracting states on 7th October 1952, with the purpose of ensuring adequate compensation to persons who suffer damage caused on the surface by foreign aircraft, while limiting in a reasonable manner the extent of the liabilities incurred for such damage in order not to completely hinder the development of international civil air transportation. As provided in Article 1 of the Convention, it provides for compensation to any person who suffers damages on the surface, upon proof of such damages from an aircraft in flight or by any person or anything falling from it, such damages also being a direct consequence of the incident giving rise to the damage.

Also, for the purpose of providing compensation for damages done, the convention holds the operator or the registered owner of the aircraft liable for damages done by their aircraft[40]. However, in certain cases, this liability might be shifted to another person, especially in the situation of a charter agreement or rent, where the operator or the registered owner is out of exclu-

---

[38]Hague Convention I, 1899, Article 25,
[39]Hereinafter CDFATPS (ICAO) 1952.
[40]CDFATPS (ICAO) 1952, Article 2

sive ownership or control of the aircraft for a period of more than fourteen days.[41] Nevertheless, it is pertinent to note that the exception rule on suspension of ownership is not in itself absolute. Therefore, if a person makes use of an aircraft without the consent of the person entitled to its navigational control, the owner, unless he proves that he has exercised due care to prevent such use, shall be jointly and severally liable with the unlawful user for damage giving a right to compensation.[42]

In action for damages, the claimant is at first expected to file his action within two years from the day of the incident,[43] at a court within the jurisdiction of the contracting states to the Convention, where the damage occurred.[44] The parties may however agree or in interest of justice without prejudice to the claimant allow such action to be instituted at any of the contracting states to the convention. More also, the parties may also result in arbitration instead of court proceedings, but such must also be within the jurisdiction or seated in a contracting state territory.[45]

Furthermore, in the execution of court judgement, the convention provides for an outraging effect of a court judgement in a contracting state to be executed outside the territory of such state, provided it conforms with the laws of the other state being either a Contracting State where the judgment debtor has his residence or principal place of business or, a territory where the judgement debtor has assets not being a contracting state provided that the assets available in the state where the judge-

---

[41]CDFATPS (ICAO) 1952, Article 3
[42]CDFATPS (ICAO) 1952, Article 4
[43]CDFATPS (ICAO) 1952, Article 21
[44]CDFATPS (ICAO) 1952, Article 20
[45]Ibid.

ment is pronounced, and the contracting state are not sufficient.[46]

It is important to note, nevertheless, that in the execution of a judgment given by a court in a contracting state, adequate notice of six months must have been given to the aircraft owner, a duration from the date of incidence, in order to afford him the privilege of defending himself appropriately[47]. Where this is not obliged with, the claimant may find it difficult to enforce the judgment given by the court, since the court may stay the execution of its judgement in circumstances where the judgment was given by default and the defendant did not acquire knowledge of the proceedings in sufficient time to act upon it. Other grounds that may also facilitate the stay of execution in a judgment includes: where the defendant was not given a fair and adequate opportunity to defend his interests, the judgment is in respect of a cause of action which had already, as between the same parties, formed the subject of a judgment or an arbitral award which, under the law of the State where execution is sought, is recognized as final and conclusive; or where the judgment has been obtained by fraud of any of the parties; or the right to enforce the judgment is not vested in the person by whom the application for execution is made.[48]

Rules of Procedure for the Settlement of Differences

The Rules of Procedure for the Settlement of Dispute[49] is a procedural rule for the settlement of civil Aviation disputes en-

---

[46]CDFATPS (ICAO) 1952, Article 20(4)
[47]CDFATPS (ICAO) 1952, Article 19
[48]CDFATPS (ICAO) 1952, Article 20(9)
[49]Hereinafter ICAO RPSD 1975

acted by the International Civil Aviation Organization. The Rules are set to govern the settlement of disagreements between Contracting States which are referred to the Council, on the interpretation or application of the Convention on International Civil Aviation, otherwise known as the Chicago Convention, and its Annexes (Articles 84 to 88 of the Convention).[50] Also, the rules are to be applied in resolving disagreement between two or more Contracting States relating to the interpretation or application of the International Air Services Transit Agreement and of the International Air Transport Agreement between it.[51]

Dispute Resolution Mechanism

To start with, the ICAO RPSD provides for parties to the dispute to attempt negotiation and other alternative dispute resolution medium before referring their dispute to the council. As a matter of fact, in filing an action under this procedural instrument is required that parties show that negotiations have been attempted in resolving the impasse, and have, in fact, broken down.[52] Alongside that, the applicant is expected to file an application and a memorial containing essential details of the applicant, the statement of fact, statements of law, etc.[53]

After receiving the application of the applicant, the Secretary General is thereby required to forward a notice of receipt to the applicant, and also notify the other parties to the instrument as well as the members of the council.[54] The respondent is also forwarded a copy of the Application by the Secretary General

---

[50]ICAO RPSD 1975, Article 1(1)(a)
[51]ICAO RPSD 1975, Article 1(1)(b)
[52]ICAO RPSD 1975, Article 2(g)
[53]ICAO RPSD 1975, Article 3(2)(b)
[54]ICAO RPSD, 1975, Article 3

and invited to forward a counter memorial to the applicant's arguments, wherefore he may also lay a counter-claim.[55] Furthermore, after the receipt of the respondent's counter-claim, the Council shall decide whether at that stage the parties should be invited to enter into direct negotiations for a second time as provided in Article 14(1) of the ICAO RPSD. According to the afore cited article:

The Council may, at any time during the proceedings and prior to the meeting at which the decision is rendered as provided in Article 15 (4), invite the parties to the dispute to engage in direct negotiations, if the Council deems that the possibilities of settling the dispute or narrowing the issues through negotiations have not been exhausted.

Therefore, in the situation, where the parties accept the invitation to negotiate, the Council may set a time-limit for the completion of such negotiations, during which other proceedings on the merits with the ICAO shall be suspended.[56] Also, subject to the consent of the parties concerned, the Council may render any assistance likely to further the negotiations, including the designation of an individual or a group of individuals to act as conciliator during the negotiations[57]. Finally, any solution agreed through negotiations shall be recorded by Council. If no solution is found, the parties shall so report to Council and the suspended proceedings will be resumed.[58] At the recommencement of the proceeding on merit, the ICAO may hear arguments from both parties, receive evidence, ask questions, seek expert opinions and even conduct investigations into the merit of the case on its own account[59]. The posi-

---

[55]ICAO RPSD, 1975, Article 4(1)
[56]ICAO RPSD, 1975, Article 14(2)
[57]ICAO RPSD, 1975, Article 14(3)
[58]ICAO RPSD, 1975, Article 14(4)
[59]ICAO RPSD, 1975, Article 8

tion of the ICAO is rather inquisitor rather than an indifferent umpire in an adversarial tribunal. More also, at the conclusion of arguments by both parties, and diligent examination of the case on its merit by the ICAO, a binding decision would be given by the body. The decision of the Council shall be rendered at a meeting of the Council called for that purpose, to be held as soon as practicable after the close of the proceedings, to discuss the enforcement of such decision[60].

It is pertinent to note, however, that even after negotiation fails the second time, any time before the decision of the council is given, the parties involved might choose to discontinue the case by an application from the applicant and seek to have it resolved by personal negotiation.[61] Also, while the decision to the ICAO is intended to be binding, and a default of such could be accompanied by sanctions, and the disengagement from certain privileges, the decision of the council may be appealed within sixty days (60) of its delivery by putting the Secretary General on Notice pursuant to Article 84 of the Chicago Convention[62]. Finally, it is also pertinent to note that the principle of estoppel also applies to decisions given by the ICAO on a state party or Privy of such state to an agreement under discord; therefore, it is provided by the ICAO RPSD that State which is a party to the particular instrument, the interpretation or application of which has been made the subject of a dispute under these Rules, and which is directly affected by the dispute, has the right to intervene in the proceedings. The state party privy must also accept that its right to be joined in the proceeding shall transcribe to an undertaking to abide by the decision of the Council as the other parties, without attempting

---

[60]ICAO RPSD, 1975, Article 15
[61]ICAO RPSD, 1975, Article 17
[62]ICAO RPSD, 1975, Article 18

a refiling of complaint on the same subject matter with the council[63].

Madrid Convention of Air Navigation, 1926

The Madrid Convention of Air Navigation of 1926 is one of the earliest forms of international civil aviation agreement that established a legal framework for the regulation and resolution of international civil aviation disputes before the second world war. It similarly referred to as the Ibero-American Convention and modelled after the Paris Convention on Air Navigation[64]. It was signed by the member states on the 1st of November 1926 at Madrid, and member states to the convention includes several countries such as the United States, the United Kingdom, and France[65]. The convention is referred to as one of the most remarkable agreements on Civil Aviation and the development of International Law on Civil Aviation before the formation of the Chicago Convention of 1944, which now serves as the Modal Multilateral Convention on Air Navigation for most countries around the world[66]. Nevertheless, the Madrid Convention of Air Navigation remains one of the most important agreements in the field of civil aviation law, and provides a remarkable framework for the Resolution of Civil Aviation dispute, most of which though are modelled after the provision of the Paris Conference, are still being referred to today.

---

[63]ICAO RPSD, 1975, Article 19(1)

[64]Wenceslas J Wagner, 'International Air Transportation as Affected by State Sovereignty' (Etablissements Emile Bruylant 1970)

[65]Ibid.

[66]Welch Pogue, Airline Deregulation, Before and After: What Next? 16 (Lindbergh Memorial Lecture 1991)

Dispute Resolution Mechanism

Without further ado, the dispute resolution mechanism of the convention, which is the crux of this appraisal, is similarly fashioned to that obtainable in the Havana Convention 1928, and the Paris Conference before it[67]. The convention provided for the resolution of disputes related to civil aviation through diplomatic channels, especially providing that parties should, at first instance of the dispute, exhaust all medium of negotiating an agreement for the resolution between themselves[68]. Also, parties could negotiate the settlement of their dispute with the aid of a Mediator appointed from another member state who is not a party to the dispute, but a party to the convention[69]. Nevertheless, in the case of an impasse in negotiation, the Convention recognizes the Jurisdiction of the International Court of Justice or the Permanent Court of Justice, thence permitting the referral of the disputes to it for resolution[70].

In conclusion, the Madrid Convention of Air Navigation of 1926 established a comprehensive legal framework for the regulation and resolution of international civil aviation disputes, which is premised on the principle of diplomacy and amiable settlements.

---

[67]Cooper (n.2)
[68]Ibid.
[69]Ibero-American Convention Relating to Aerial Navigation (Madrid, 1926) Article 18
[70]Ibero-American Convention Relating to Aerial Navigation (Madrid, 1926) Article 23

The Convention on International Civil Aviation (The Chicago Convention, 1944) and its annexes

The International Aviation Convention 1944,[71] also known as the Chicago Convention, is a multilateral aviation agreement between state parties to govern the Aviation relations among them as sovereign entities. It is also jeered to develop a framework for civil aviation operation between these states, such that fosters development, preserve friendship, and promotes understanding. More also, the Convention aims as a matter of international peace to avoid friction in Civil Aviation relations among member states. On this note, while it guarantees the Sovereignty of each member state over its airspace[72], it also creates a corresponding framework of right and obligations to guide the operation of interstate civil Aviation, that is, for instance while member states get a right of passage through the territory of another member state for both scheduled and non-scheduled flight,[73] they are in turn expected to seek the approval of the member state for landing at the designated airport, and also subjected to compliance with the local legislation of such state in compliance to air regulation, custom and immigration clearances[74].

Aside from the main convention, it is pertinent to note that the Chicago Convention is joined by a total of 19 annexes. These annexes cover a wide range of topics related to civil aviation, including airworthiness, air traffic control, aviation security, and the investigation of accidents. Each annex provides additional guidance and standards for the implementation of

---

[71]Hereinafter "Chicago Convention 1944"
[72]Chicago Convention, 1944, Article 1
[73]Chicago Convention, 1944, Article 5 & 6
[74]Chicago Convention, 1944, Article 6, 10 & 13

the convention's provisions. The annexes are regularly updated and revised by the International Civil Aviation Organization (ICAO) to ensure that they remain current and relevant to the changing needs of the global aviation community.

A brief list of the annexes includes: Annex 1 - Personnel Licensing: Standards for the licensing of flight crews, air traffic controllers, and other aviation personnel; Annex 2 - Rules of the Air: Standardized rules and procedures for the operation of aircraft in international airspace; Annex 3 - Meteorological Service for International Air Navigation: Standards for the provision of meteorological services to the aviation community, Annex 4 - Aeronautical Charts: Standards for the production and distribution of aeronautical charts and related materials, Annex 5 - Units of Measurement to be Used in Air and Ground Operations: Standards for the use of units of measurement in aviation, Annex 6 - Operation of Aircraft: Standards for the safe operation of aircraft, including airworthiness, maintenance, and operating procedures, et cetera.

Furthermore, the modal convention creates an international regulatory body for the administration of Interstate civil Aviation among parties to the Convention- the International Civil Aviation Organization. This body is majorly made up of an Assembly and a Council, as well as other sub administrative bodies created to implement its functions under the Convention which includes: ensuring the safe and orderly growth of international civil aviation throughout the world, encouraging the development of airways, airports, and air navigation facilities for international civil aviation, prohibiting discrimination of states in civil Aviation operation, and most importantly among other, ensuring that the rights of contracting States are fully respected and that every contracting State has a fair opportunity to operate international airlines.[75]

Dispute Resolution Mechanism

According to this Convention, disputes between member parties are expected to first be approached for settlement by both parties via negotiation. As a matter of fact, in referring the dispute to the ICAO, it is expected that the applicant submits proofs that negotiation had been attempted by bother parties to resolve the dispute but had irrevocably failed. Where negotiation, however, fails, the parties may refer the dispute to the ICAO by application of any of the state concerned in the disagreement for the decision of the council. Furthermore, the rules and procedure for the determination of disputes by the ICAO are formulated by the body pursuant to its powers in Article 49(d) of the Convention and may also be amended by it. As of the time of this writing, examining the dispute settlement framework of the ICAO under the Chicago Convention 1944, the rules of procedure for the settlement of dispute by the ICAO is the ICAO Rules for the Settlement of Differences 1975.

Disputes referred to the Council, after hearing both sides, as well as taking evidence and testimonies from experts and its own enquiries, are decided by the majority voting decision of its members, excluding the parties to the disputes. Once a decision has been given, it is expected that parties to the dispute complies with the decision or appeal such decision with 60 days' notice to the ICAO to an Arbitral Tribunal or the ICJ[76]. Where the parties to the dispute are such that do not accept the Jurisdiction of the ICJ; however, the parties are expected to ap-

---

[75]Chicago Convention 1944, Article 44 (a-f)
[76]Ibid.

point an arbitrator or the choice of the arbitral Tribunal to hear their appeal. Nevertheless, in a situation where both parties are unable to agree to an arbitrator or an arbitrator Tribunal, the President of the Council may make an appointment of arbitrators to hear the appeal on behalf of the state, requesting the arbitrators to consensually pick an umpire among themselves. Also, where the arbitrators are unable to consensually make such appointment, the President of the Council may appoint an umpire himself among the arbitrators to hear the appeal, and together they shall jointly constitute an arbitral Tribunal. On the other hand, the group of arbitrators is at liberty to formulate their own rules of procedure, and are to give their decisions by majority vote. More also, the decisions of the arbitral tribunal, just like the ICJ on Aviation dispute is provided to be final and binding.[77]

In conclusion, it is important to note that the ICAO in the resolution of civil Aviation disputes prefers amicable settlement among parties in such a way that leaves no grievances. This is the rationale behind the open option clause of the ICAO to allow parties at any point in time to suspend the dispute referred to it for determination, and seek to enter into conciliation or negotiation[78]. As a matter of fact, the ICAO itself is obliged to assist the parties to seek the application of alternative dispute resolution mediums to their dispute any time before giving its decision.[79] Once its decision has been given, however, it is ultimate and binding unless appealed. Delinquent airlines to the decision could be at the risk of restrained operations in con-

---

[77]Articles 86, Chicago Convention 1944.
[78]Article 17, ICAO Rules and Procedure for the Settlement of Differences, 1975.
[79]Article 14, ICAO Rules and Procedure for the Settlement of Differences, 1975.

tracting states[80], or flying across a contracting state, while a delinquent contracting state could also stand the risk of losing its voting powers at the Assembly[81].

The Charter of Organization of African Unity

The Charter of Organization of African Unity is a charter among African countries signed on the 25th of May 1963 at Addis Ababa Ethiopia to create a United African front and establish a multilateral body for the unity of the region. According to the objective of the charter, it aims to provide freedom, equality, justice and dignity to the African race, to harness the human and natural resources of the region for the total advancement of its people, and to create a common determination that promote understanding among states in the spirit of brotherhood which transcends ethnic and national differences. The charter also aims to maintain peace in the region, and bring about progress to the African states who have fought hard to regain their freedom from the colonialist.

Nevertheless, it is pertinent to note that while the charter was signed by 33 member states at the time of its creation, and witnessed some quantum of success while it subsisted, however since 9th July 2002, the charter has ceased to exist under this name or form, but rather has passed down the spirit of its provisions to the new Constitutive Act of the African Union which birthed the African Union. The new Constitutive Act of the African Union was signed by 53 African states in 2002, including Nigeria, bringing an end to the era of the Organization of African Union.

---

[80]Article 87, Chicago Convention 1944.
[81]Chicago Convention 1944, Article 87,

Dispute Resolution Mechanism

An overview of the Charter of the Organization of African Union 1963 on its dispute resolution mechanism shows a similar admiration for alternative dispute resolution by the regional body, in similar fashion to the United Nations. In Article XIX of the charter, member States pledges to the charter to settle all disputes among themselves by peaceful means that is Mediation, Arbitration and Conciliation. On this end, the Charter established a Commission of Mediation, Conciliation and Arbitration, the composition of which and conditions of service was defined by a separate protocol approved by the Assembly of Heads of State and Government, one forming an integral part of the present Charter. The incorporation of this clause in the charter was undoubtedly one of the reasons why most of the conflicts apprehended by the organization were able to be settled amicably. For instance, in the Moroccan-Algeria Boundary crisis of 1964-65, the Moroccan invasion of Algerian territory, was resolved amicably by mediation through the OAU mediators which was set up by the Organization's Council of Ministers as an ad hoc commission, comprising Ethiopia, Côte d'Ivoire, Mali, Nigeria, Senegal, Sudan and Tanzania (then Tanganyika).[82]

In the same vein, the Constitutive Act of the African Union also successively provides for Mediation and alternative dispute resolution in resolving dispute among member states to the Treaty. According to Article 4(3) of the Treaty, the Union and its members are expected to function on the principle of peaceful resolution of conflicts among member states of the union by appropriate means to be recommended by the Assem-

---

[82]African Union & ACCORD, *African Union Mediation Handbook*, (African Centre for the Constructive Resolution of Disputes (ACCORD) publication, Revised Edition 2014)

bly, such means including mediation, good offices, and enquiry.[83]

Therefore, flowing from the provisions of this treaty, it is therefore expected that disputes between members of the African Union on Civil Aviation will have to be resolved via alternative dispute resolution methods first. Also, while the Constitutive Act does not expressly provide for Civil Aviation dispute, and in fact not a sui generis treaty to the subject matter, it is argued that the intentions of the Constitutive Act are reflective Yamoussoukro Decision, one widely adopted by members of the African Union on the subject of liberalized airspace and civil aviation. According to the decision, If any dispute arises between States Parties relating to the interpretation or application of this Decision (the Yamoussoukro Decision), the States Parties concerned shall in the first place endeavor to settle the dispute by negotiation.[84]

Conclusion

Following the examination of this study, it is reiterated that international cooperation and legal framework is important for best practices in the industry. This will undoubtedly guide the way forward in ensuring that aviation disputes are addressed promptly and fairly, safeguarding the industry's integrity, and enabling it to continue connecting the world. The mechanisms for resolving disputes are not just a matter of legal procedure but are crucial to maintaining safety, security and sustainability of a global industry that transcends borders. In this light, a workable framework should be put in place for its easy enforcement and implementation.

---

[83]African Union Peace and Security Council Protocol, Article 6
[84]Yamoussoukro Decision, Article 8.1

An Examination of the Emergence of New Technology Weapons During Warfare in Africa: Implications for Peace and Security

King J. Nkum, PhD[1]
Esther Jock Sunday[2]

Introduction

Technology has played a significant role in shaping civilization and global peace, dividing the rich, poor, and nations. It has improved lives but also destroyed moral fibers. The military has entered a digital phase with artificial intelligence, smartphones, social media, big data, robotics, and the internet. However, efforts to monitor technology through policies and regulations and ethical codes of conduct are insufficient for a responsible digital future. Other attempts, such as shaping technologies, are often too late and slow to keep up with technological advancements. Legal professionals also struggle to keep up

---

[1]Senior Lecturer/Deputy Dean of Law, Taraba State University –
Nigeria. Email: kingjamesnkum@gmail.com.
[2]Lecturer, Department of Public Law, Taraba State University –
Nigeria. Email: estherjock@yahoo.com.

with data analysis, the internet, and cloud technology, leading to countries trying to regulate tomorrow's technology with legal prescripts from the past.

Africa has adopted the Fourth Industrial Revolution, embracing emerging technologies that may disrupt sectors and society. For instance, drones have improved healthcare in Rwanda by delivering blood in remote areas. Other technologies being researched and tested include mixed reality, Augmented Reality, VR, 5G, AI, and Blockchain. Africa is also engaged in technological research and development, with countries like Nigeria and Ethiopia having thriving AI hubs. Google has its own AI hub in Ghana, and the UN has an AI center, the UN Global Pulse lab, in Kampala. This demonstrates Africa's commitment to technological advancements and its potential impact on the continent.[3]

Emerging technologies, such as AI, have been used to persecute, monitor, and target minorities, as well as specific groups during disinformation operations during elections. Security literature has begun to explore the implications of these technologies at state and institutional levels, but less so among the population.[4] South Africa is a prime example of a country that is embracing technology, particularly drones, despite the rapid development of technology. The South African military has only invested in drones less than three years ago, primarily for border patrolling. Artificial Intelligence (AI) is also being inte-

---

[3]Denise Garcia,'Lethal Artificial Intelligence and Change: The Future of International Peace and Security' (2018) (20) 2 International Studies Review, 334–41 <https://doi.org/10.1093/isr/viy029> Accessed 12 October 2023.

[4]Daniele Rotolo, Hicks Diana and Ben Martin, 'What is an Emerging Technology?' (2015) 44(10) Research Policy, 1827–43 <http://www.sciencedirect.com/science/article/pii/S0048733315001031> accessed 12 October 2023

grated into the South African military, which could potentially increase the use of force while reducing the risk to soldiers. AI not only alters the soldier's fighting style, but also their identity, impacting military recruitment and the relationship between the military and society it defends. This is particularly important in South Africa, where the military has a history of being used as an instrument of power to further apartheid and suppress freedom fighter ideologies. Despite understanding the military's role in a democratic society, South African society still has little trust in the military, and the apartheid wounds caused by the military are not yet healed.

Artificial intelligence and technology like drones can be disruptive due to their attributes and interactions with specific users. This can raise ethical and moral concerns, impacting justice, well-being, human autonomy, and social disruption. AI has become an academic discipline attracting students from various fields, but there is limited literature on its impact on African values and ethics. Despite the growing body of literature on emerging technologies in relation to peace and security, little is known about their implications for peace and conflict dynamics, particularly in Africa.

This chapter explores significant trends and the implications of emerging technologies for peace and conflict in Africa. The paper aims to answer questions about the challenges of emerging technology in African military values and ethics, and which African values are likely to be impacted by it. The research uses qualitative methodology and a literature study of primary and secondary sources to gather information. The paper concludes by reflecting on the potential challenges of emerging technology in the African military on African values and ethics.

Legal Framework

Generally, armed conflict is regulated by the rules of International Humanitarian Law (IHL) which are applicable and enforceable on all nation states during the situation of armed conflict. The major legal framework on the use of New Technology Weapons during the situation of warfare or armed conflict. The means and method of warfare are guided by the rules of International Conventions, particularly, Articles 35 (1-3)[5] which states as follows:

1. In any armed conflict, the right of the Parties to the conflict to choose methods or means of warfare is not unlimited.

2. It is prohibited to employ weapons, projectiles and material and methods of warfare of a nature to cause superfluous injury or unnecessary suffering.

3. It is prohibited to employ methods or means of warfare which are intended, or may be expected, to cause widespread, long-term and severe damage to the natural environment.

Although the above article is meant to control the use of New Technology Weapons during warfare in other to protect victims, it is sad to state that the use of new technology weapons has come to stay in the civilized world and will gradually find its place into Africa.

Furthermore, Article 36[6] In the study, development, acquisition or adoption of a new weapon, means or method of warfare, a High Contracting Party is under an obligation to determine whether its employment would, in some or all circumstances,

---

[5]Additional Protocol 1,1949 Geneva Convention.
[6]Ibid

be prohibited by this Protocol or by any other rule of international law applicable to the High Contracting Party, which requires states to conduct legal reviews of all new weapons, means and methods of warfare in order to determine whether their use is prohibited by international law. In other words, this provision requires nation States to determine whether the employment of a new weapon, means or method of warfare that it studies, develops, acquires or adopts in some or all circumstances, be prohibited by the rules of international law.

In Africa today, there is no specific legislation at the moment regarding the use of New Technology Weapons. However, it is no secret that that States like Nigeria has signed the Treaty on the Prohibition of Nuclear Weapons (TPNW) to the UN secretary-general on 20 February 2021 confirming that it does not own, possess, or control nuclear weapons, has never done so, and does not host any other state's nuclear weapons on its territory[7] Although South Africa between the period of 1940s-1990s during the apartheid government engaged in research and development of weapons of mass destruction but, however, decides to end the nuclear program which could have made South Africa the only African country to achieve a nuclear weapon capability and voluntarily relinquish it In 1993, as well as its biological, chemical, and ballistic missile programs.[8] Even though South Africa is an arms-producing country that has developed highly automated active protection weapon systems for tanks.

The emergence of the use of New Technology Weapons in Africa as seen in the above legal framework requires an urgent

---

[7]In accordance with Article 2 of the Treaty on the Prohibition of Nuclear Weapons.
[8]http://www.nti.org> countries>south Africa. Accessed on 10th November,2023

need for domestic legislations, especially for its implications on peace and security.

Moral and Ethical Issues in New Technology Weapons (Drones)

The morality of drones is a complex issue, with arguments about their morality and immorality. While drones offer benefits to militaries, they fail to meet the ethical conditions of justified military force, as they require no courage, willingness to sacrifice, respect for wounded or enemy, and personal humility. They also reduce soldiers' direct interaction with the enemy and reduce their understanding of war. Drone operators are expected to make ethical decisions that comply with the laws of war and *Jus in Bello*, but using drones in battle may require less humility, virtues, or self-awareness. Some argue that drones make war human by enabling greater precision and less collateral damage, but this only holds true if viewed from the perspective of the enemy and innocent civilians. Drones could potentially be used in war, but their ethical implications are debated. While shooting a regular soldier on the battlefield with ground troops or manned aircraft is similar, drones can be used if the mission could be completed using manned vehicles without problems. The main objection to drones is the issue of proportionality, as they can create fear and distrust within society. African people may be afraid to help victims of drone attacks, leading to distrust in communities. This trust deficit was evident during apartheid times when communities were turned into police, leading to some being killed by the same police. However, from the just war theory perspective, drones could meet the criteria of just cause, not the criteria of last resort. Drones promote the use of force without going into a full-scale war, and bureaucracies may not be concerned about moral problems. Anti-war advocates argue that drones make war easy, as people do not experience the horrors of war and are not personally affected.[9] Throughout history, people have witnessed the deaths or injuries of those who experienced war. In 2011, former US President Obama used drones to remove Libyan President Muammar Gaddafi from power, claiming he did not require congressional authorization due to the lack of sustained conflict. This approach could be applied to South Africa, where drones could be used to target the South African people. Without international regulatory frameworks like the United Nations, civilians will continue to suffer in wars with impunity. It is crucial to hold governments ethically accountable for the senseless killing of innocent civilians.[10]

From an ethical point perspective, technology presents moral dilemmas that society faces daily, affecting various aspects of life, including foreign policies, human rights, medical technologies, and wars. Addressing these ethical issues is challenging, as it requires analyzing facts and considering values. A number of approaches to values have been developed by philosophers to address moral concerns:

Fact-based: Facts often provide what is, not what ought to be.

Value-based: Values can guide decision-making and guide moral decisions.

---

[9]See Robert M Taylor, 'Ethical Principles and Concepts in Medicine' in James L. Bernat and H. Richard Beresford (eds) *Handbook of Clinical Neurology* (Elsevier 2013) <https://www.researchgate.net/publication/258250395_Chapter_1_Ethical_principles_and_concepts_in_medicine> Accessed 26 September, 2023

[10]C Stephen, 'The Problems of Duty and Loyalty' (2009) 8 Journal of Military Ethics, 110

Value-based: Values can guide moral decisions and guide moral decisions.

Addressing moral dilemmas through various approaches is crucial for societal progress.

The Rights Approach is a moral philosophy that emphasizes respect for human dignity and the right to freely choose our lives. It is based on the United Nations' Universal Declaration of Human Rights and requires individuals to recognize their legal rights and duties in each situation. When faced with competing interests or rights, individuals must prioritize the one that best safeguards or guarantees that interest. For example, the South African Constitution grants everyone the right to freedom of speech, but it has limitations, such as not expressing hate speech or infringing on others' rights. The rights approach contradicts the utilitarian approach, which aims to maximize good over harm. Key rights include the right to life, human dignity, freedom, free speech, assembly, freedom of religion, and property ownership. However, the utilitarian approach may support the approach of killing one workman to achieve good over harm, as seen in the hypothetical trolley situation[11].

Communal Conflicts and Emerging Technologies

Social media significantly influences African election dynamics, with countries like Nigeria, Kenya, Madagascar, and Uganda experiencing disinformation operations by operations instigated by states such as Russia (for example, the campaign led by Russia's Private Military Company (PMC), the Wagner

---

[11]See R Arneson, *Deontology's Travails Moral Puzzles and Legal Perspectives* (Cambridge University Press 2019), 355

Group), [12]or by non-state and illusive actors.[13] These operations have caused turmoil, increased anxiety and fear among civilians, and decreased trust between the population and authorities. For instance, in the 2017 Kenyan elections, Cambridge Analytica launched a microtargeting campaign, resulting in people being victims of these operations. A company targeted Kenyans using their private data, exposing them to horrific messages about past violence and fear of the opposition's future annihilation of certain tribes. This has significant psychological effects on the population, who are deeply entrenched in fear and suspicion.

Disinformation or misinformation plays a significant role in situations involving violence and community conflict. In cases where it is difficult to trace individuals or groups involved, the distribution of content, such as images, memes, videos, and voice messages, can lead to high levels of violence among communities. For example, in Nigeria, images of mass graves were used to fuel animosity between Fulani Muslims and Berom Christians, resulting in violence and killing. In Ethiopia, misinformation cases involving the Tigray conflict, where fabricated content was shared, could also fuel violence among conflicting parties.

Africa's social media users have grown significantly, with AI playing a significant role. However, there has been a rise in de-

---

[12]The Wagner Group, a Russian PMC supported by Putin, has been conducting disinformation operations in Africa targeting elections using tactics such as fake Facebook profiles, news pages, think tanks, and local newspapers.
[13]Tessa Knight, 'Social Media Disinformation Campaign Targets Ugandan Presidential Election', (*Daily Maverick*, 12 January, 2021) <https://www.dailymaverick.co.za/article/2021-01-12-social-media-disinformation-campaign-targets-ugandan-presidential-election> Accessed 17 June 2023.

structive AI technologies, such as deep-fake technologies and Generative Adversarial Networks, which manipulate images, videos, and sounds to alter source files. Deep learning has also been used in the autoregressive language model of GPT-3, which generates texts independently. This has led to surprising results, as many of these texts appear to be written by humans, but are actually not.

Selective editing and shallow or cheap fakes are becoming increasingly prevalent in the digital world. "Deepfakes" are videos altered through machine learning to generate human bodies and faces, while cheap fakes are audiovisual manipulations created with cheaper software. Malevolent actors in Africa are using these fakes to target innocent civilians, unaware of the potential impacts of their actions.[14] They share these fakes with friends, colleagues, and loved ones without checking their veracity and origin. Many people believe these fakes are true because they received information from trusted individuals, leading to automatic re-sharing. Some people are unaware that this content was created to achieve specific aims, such as instigating collective violence. In 2018, a deepfake video of President Ali Bongo was cited as the trigger for an unsuccessful coup by the Gabonese military.[15]

Algorithms play a significant role in social media platforms, creating addictive behaviors, echo chambers, and trust dynamics among users. Platforms like YouTube suggest videos to watch, Facebook groups to join, and recommend popular articles with fake news, amplifying extremist rhetoric, violence,

---

[14]Britt Paris and Joan Donovan, 'Deepfakes and Cheap Fakes', (2019) Data & Society. <https://datasociety.net/library/deep-fakes-and-cheap-fakes> Accessed 19 July 2023

[15]Mika Westerlund, 'The Emergence of Deepfake Technology: A Review' (2019) (9) (11) Technology Innovation Management Review

hatred, and discrimination. As people view, share, and watch repetitively, ideas and news become deeply anchored in their minds, affecting both online and offline interactions.

Symbolic Violence and Biometric Technologies

Biometric technologies are being used in border control, predictive policing, banking, health, and identification. China has become a dominant player in this field, spreading biometric technologies globally. Some argue that China is creating global AI norms based on its own values. Africa has recently been the beta-testing ground for emerging technologies, with civilians unaware of their involvement. China has partnered with African countries through the Belt and Road initiative to roll out facial recognition technologies in elections, schools, and other situations. Civilians are unaware that their private data, including images and videos of their faces, has been collected for AI-enhanced technologies.

Biometric technologies often create situations where civilians are subjected to symbolic violence, such as surveillance capitalism and data colonialism. This violence is rooted in asymmetrical power dynamics, where powerful actors control the collection, gathering, selling, and storage of biometric data. Vulnerable populations, minorities, and those living in under-regulated areas face symbolic violence due to the lack of control over the type of data collected, its purpose (policing minorities), storage duration, and access to it. This violence is not direct or physical but stems from asymmetrical power dynamics.

Authoritarian and 'thug' states are increasingly deploying facial recognition technologies for mass surveillance, with countries like Ghana, Kenya, South Africa, Uganda, and Zimbabwe being targeted. Huawei, a Chinese company, has been accused of spying on the African Union. Huawei's projects in Africa are part of initiatives like safe city programs. In 2018, Chinese firm Cloudwalk Technology partnered with Zimbabwe to launch a large-scale facial recognition program as part of the Belt and Road Initiative.[16]

Smaller companies like Transsion are using cheap technologies like smartphones and facial recognition to collect data from African people without oversight. This lucrative business allows marketing companies to microtarget the local population, posing a threat to privacy and liberty. In authoritarian and police states, such as Uganda, facial recognition is used to identify and track opposition politicians during protest movements, posing a significant threat to democratic processes and peace in post-conflict zones.[17]

---

[16]Lynsey Chutel, 'Zimbabwe Introducing a Mass Facial Recognition Project with Chinese AI Company CloudWalk' (*Quartz Africa* 2018) <https://qz.com/africa/1287675/china-is-exporting-facial-recognition-to-africa-ensuring-ai-dominance-through-diversity> Accessed 22 January 2023
[17]Amy Hawkins, 'Beijing's Big Brother Tech Needs African Faces', (Foreign Policy 2018). <https://foreignpolicy.com/2018/07/24/beijings-big-brother-tech-needs-african-faces> Accessed 27 June 2023; Wilson Tom and Murgia Madhumita, 'Uganda Confirms use of Huawei Facial Recognition Cameras', (*The Financial Times*, 20 August 2019) <https://www.ft.com/content/e20580de-c35f-11e9-a8e9-296ca66511c9> 25 September 2023

Colonial Governance Practices and Lethal Autonomous Weapons Systems (LAWS)

The Foucauldian boomerang effect refers to the shift in technology production and deployment, originating from colonial practices in the global South or conflict zones. These technologies, initially used for pacification, militarization, and control, are now being deployed in America, Europe, and East Asia. For instance, North American police are now using Israeli drones for civilian policing, originally used to protect Palestinians[18].

Despite the global shift towards technology, many technologies used in wars and conflicts are still developed in the global North without strict regulations, perpetuating colonial practices. In the postcolonial era, these practices are transferred, copied, and diffused in the deployment of emerging technologies like AI, as seen in the LAWS case.

The Future of Life Institute defines lethal autonomous weapons as systems that can identify, select, and engage targets without human control.[19] The US and Israel have acknowledged AI's role in operations against Hamas in the Gaza Strip. However, there have been no major incidents where AI has targeted innocent civilians in conflict zones in Africa. The use of AI in the Israeli-Palestinian conflict signifies the future of warfare, where laws of war will be used, causing harm to civilians.[20]

---

[18]Stephen Graham, 'Cities as Battlespace: The New Military Urbanism' (2009) (13) (4) City, 383–402

[19]Future of Life Institute 'Lethal Autonomous Weapons Systems' (Future of Life Institute) <https://futureoflife.org/lethal-autonomous-weapons-systems> Accessed 11 March 2021

[20]Zoe Kleinman, 'Mohsen Fakhrizadeh: "Machine-gun with AI" Used to Kill Iran Scientist' (BBC News, 2021) <https://www.bbc.com/news/world-middle-east-55214359> Accessed 16 May 2023

The US and its allies have been dominating the governance of AI in the military and defense sector, inviting only technological powerhouses from the global South, such as India, to participate. This transatlantic governance platform aims to develop standards, norms, and regulations with "western" and "democratic" values. However, these violent and colonial technologies will be adopted and used in wars in the global South, including Africa. African governments, supposed to protect African people, are excluded from the spaces where the military governs AI. The only platform many African governments are part of is the Group of Governmental Experts on Lethal Autonomous Weapons Systems in Geneva.[21]

Invisible Threats and 5G Technology

Emerging technologies pose invisible threats to civilian peace, including disinformation, misinformation, and fake news. The diversity of digital threats, including the COVID-19 pandemic, has led to distrust and fear, leading to actions like protests, riots, and conflicts. These threats are diverse and can be spread through the cybersphere and offline methods like rumour.

Civilians in Africa are playing a crucial role in securitizing the fifth-generation mobile network (5G), which is believed to provide high-speed, optimal performance, and improved connectivity. However, some Africans have joined an anti-5G conspiracy, viewing 5G as a threat due to its role in diffusing coronavirus. This global movement has led to arson attacks and threats to engineers. An example of this securitisation is the

---

[21]Sydney Freedberg, 'Military AI Coalition of 13 Countries Meets on Ethics', (*Breaking Defense*, 16 September 2020) <https://breakingdefense.com/2020/09/13-nations-meet-on-ethics-for-military-ai> Accessed 8 November 2023

recent influence of a global conspiracy theory online in South Africa, where Vodacom and MTN towers were burned due to conspiracy theories linking COVID-19 to 5G. Civilians' actions, such as destruction of public goods, signify dissatisfaction and fear, highlighting the vulnerability of the population if drastic measures are not taken to manage and regulate the deployment of emerging technologies.

Potential of Emerging Technologies in African Peace and Conflict Processes

Cyber peace and security initiatives are being implemented by scholars, practitioners, and actors from public and private sectors. These initiatives focus on defining responsible state behaviors, controlling the internet based on democratic principles, cyber peacekeeping, arms control, and using AI in peacebuilding, conflict resolution, and mediation. They also aim to combat cyberwarfare, cyber conflict, mass surveillance, espionage, disinformation operations, and misinformation. The list of initiatives is long due to the rapid evolution of digital technologies and slow regulation.[22]

AI is being used by malevolent actors in certain countries to create conflict and war. In the Middle East, particularly in Syria, AI has been used by Russians and the Assad regime to organize and amplify disinformation campaigns, using anti-imperialist messages and pretending to denounce human rights violations.[23]

Emerging technologies, despite their decentralised and empowering aspects, are often exploited by malevolent actors to create conflict and insecurity. These technologies often target

---

[22]Reto Inversini,'Cyber Peace: And How It Can Be Achieved' (2020) Markus Christen, Bert Gordijn and Michele Loi (eds), *The Ethics of Cybersecurity* (Springer Link 2020) 259–276
[23]Ibid

vulnerabilities within people, such as feelings, identities, historical past, attachment to loved ones, and anger. Africa is embracing these technologies, but people are already paying a high price with community violence, trust erosion during elections and the pandemic, online organized crime, and disinformation operations targeting vulnerable populations. Extremist groups like ISIS have found a new home in Africa, using digital tools for recruitment.[24]

Emerging technologies pose significant threats to societies and individuals in Africa, and their role in peace and security is under-researched. Organizations like the UN Department of Peace Operations use AI to support decision-making and analyze data for conflict forecasting. Sentiment analysis, using Natural Language Processing, helps identify and classify opinions and emotions in data from platforms like Facebook, Twitter, and YouTube. This technique can help predict the occurrence of crises or conflicts. However, the extent to which these technologies support peace processes and help resolve conflicts remains unclear. Further research is needed to understand how these technologies interact with civilians during peace and conflict periods.

Conclusion and Recommendations

In conclusion, emerging technologies pose threats to peace and security, often with local governments' complicity. For instance, facial recognition is deployed in Africa, where technology is under-regulated, creating loopholes for colonial actors. Africa's colonial past has led to the deployment of technologies like AI, which have been used to manipulate issues such as colonialism and imperialism. Africa's youth and technology

---

[24]Ibid

talents have been employed in misinformation operations, involving physical violence and manipulation of issues. The cyber domain has been central to these tactics, as seen in Russia's disinformation operations against France in the Central African Republic (CAR). These campaigns targeted France's presence and led to violent street protests.

Based on the challenges posed to the peace and security of Africa as discussed above, the following recommendations have been suggested as a way forward: Africa needs to be prioritized in international governance platforms dealing with emerging technologies in peace and security. Local regulations are needed to protect civilians against such threats, and Africa must be brought to the forefront of these discussions. There should be investigation into the implications of these technologies on peace and security on the continent is necessary to address these issues and ensure a more just and equitable future for Africa.

The Politics and Challenges of State Creation in Nigeria

Joel Adelusi Adeyeye, PhD[1]

Introduction

In Nigeria, the process of creating a state entails the establishment of independent governing bodies that function as secondary units.[2] The national government is the first, while municipal governments are the third. Nigeria has created state policies in 1967, 1976, 1987, 1991, and 1996 for various reasons. Political, economic, and cultural justifications are the most common ones for founding governments. These justifications for state formation are put forth in an effort to improve nation-building (socio-cultural), effective governance (political), and economic advancement.[3]

---

[1]Acting Head of Department of Private and Property Law, Faculty of Law, Ede, Osun State, Nigeria
[2]K Ezeji-Okoye, Political, Economic and Cultural Rationale for State Creation in Nigeria. (Unpublished Dissertation Submitted to the Faculty of Clark Atlanta University, in Partial Fulfillment of the Requirement for the degree of Doctor of Philosophy, 2009)<<https://radar.auctr.edu/islandora/object/cau.td%3A2009_ezeji_okoye_kentu/datastream/OBJ/download> accessed 25 November 2023.
[3]Ibid.

In an attempt to colonize the region, the British ordered a survey of the Bight of Benin from 1822 to 1826. In 1830, the British Navy, displaying its power and presence, apprehended a Spanish ship in Bonny Port on suspicion of engaging in the trafficking of human beings.[4] In retaliation, the chief of Bonny Kingdom detained the British officers for meddling in his internal affairs. In retaliation, the British overthrew the coastal chieftaincy and methodically ended the Bonny Kingdom's sovereignty in an attempt to obtain inland access and purchase palm oil directly from the source. Chiefs from other coastal regions were also overthrown or put in jail. In 1861, the British took control of the region after they overthrew King Kosoko of Lagos. The pivotal event occurred in 1884–1885 when, at the Berlin Conference, agreements were made to divide up African countries, and the British asserted Nigeria as their territory or colony.[5]

The north and south remained separate protectorates after 1885. To balance the budget deficits of the northern Nigeria, the British merged the palm oil and cocoa rich south with the northern protectorate in 1914.[6] What still plagues Nigeria today began with just one act. The issue that united was how to govern more than 374 ethnic groups as a one country. There were

---

[4]JIM Okeke, DO Nnamani & EL Akajife 'Federal Character Principle and Nation Building in Nigeria: focus on Federal civil Service Commission<https://acjol.org/index.php/njrcs/article/download/2125/2101>accessed 25 November 2023.
[5]Ezeji-Okoye (n 1).
[6]H Alapiki, 'State Creation and its Endemic Problem in Nigeria' in D Iwarimie-Jaja (ed.) The Nigeria Enviroment and Socio-Economic Development, (SIJ Publishers)<https://www.cambridge.org/core/journals/african-studies-review/article/state-creation-in-nigeria-failed-approaches-to-national-integration-and-local-autonomy/FC8C452DA461AC0F4082E8E4312E898B>accessed 25 November 2023.

independent ethnic and sub-ethnic groupings in Nigeria prior to the union of the southern and northern protectorates. The British understood after merger how difficult it would be to govern various ethnic groupings as a single nation.[7] The British established Native Authorities (NA) with two distinct missions: (1) to ensure greater autonomy of groups and subgroups in the south, and (2) to reinforce domination of various groups in the north under the Muslim overlords in Muslim and non-Muslim areas (except for areas designated as NA which enjoyed some measure of autonomy) in order to allay some of the concerns of once autonomous groups arbitrarily merged together under one umbrella called Nigeria.[8]

After the British created regions in the East, West and North in the late 1940s, the 374 ethnic groups that were mostly autonomous now fell under the new "majority" and "minority" classifications. The elite of the new majority (consisting of the Ibo, Hausa/Fulani, and Yoruba) sought to unite their various subgroups (which were already autonomous under the NA system) in an effort to push the minorities to the periphery and cash in on the opportunities of their new positions.[9] Ibo State Union and *Egbe Omo Oduduwa* are political and cultural movements that were founded by the East and the West, respectively. The only goal of these ethnic organizations was to further the hegemonic politics of the majority groups by securing their dominance and keeping the minority groups out of positions of power, both locally and centrally. Minorities were pushed to the periphery as a result of the Hausa-Fulani's dominance over the North, the Ibos' over the East, and the Yorubas

---

[7]Ibid.
[8]Ibid.
[9]Ezeji-Okoye (n 1).

over the West. In the 1950s, the minorities used protest and separatist actions to seek justice.[10]

Nigeria has struggled to manage its numerous minority issues from the colonial era till the present. Nigeria has attempted to address its numerous minority challenges by pursuing varying degrees of federalism, the Bill of Rights, and secularity. Nigeria has prioritized the establishment of states and local administrations as a means of addressing issues pertaining to minorities. According to Osaghae, he defined minority problem as 'discrimination of various groups due to their inferior numbers, diffusion, and historical evolution within the modern Nigeria state, have been subjected to subordinate political, social and economic positions in the federation and its constituent units'.[11] The elites and movements of minority groups have focused their efforts on finding solutions to end discrimination in the nation's resource distribution and power dynamics. Sadly, minority issues have not been remedied by the foundation of states.[12]

---

[10]Ibid.

[11]S Bayero, 'Geopolitical Structure and Development in Nigeria' in IES Amdi & W Hinjira, (eds) *Party System, Democracy and Political Stability in Nigeria* (NPSA, 1990)<https://books.-google.com/books/about/Party_Systems_Democracy_and_Political_St.html?id=QIIwAAAAYAAJ>accessed 25 November 2023..

[12]Ibid.

Implications of Federalism

In contrast to a unitary government, a federal government has two or three tiers of authority.[13] Each level is independent of, but co-ordinate with, the other in the exercise of its powers and functions.[14] Usually, there is a central or federal government constituting the first level of government and the governments of the constituent units (variously called allied regions, states, provinces, cantons) making up the second level of government. Citizens of a federal government owe direct allegiance to both the federal or central and unit governments and expect some services from them directly.[15] The 1979[16] and 1999[17] constitutions of Nigeria made Local Governments a third level of government.

The federal or central government is typically in charge of communications, defense and security of the nation, international affairs, and other crucial and delicate issues of national importance, while the unit governments are in charge of more local and routine issues, especially those that have an im-

---

[13]KC Wheare, *Federal Government* (Oxford University Press, 1963) <https://www.scirp.org/(S(lz5mqp453edsnp55rrgjct55))/reference/ReferencesPapers.aspx?ReferenceID=2105757 accessed 13 October,2023

[14]Ibid.

[15]Ibid.

[16]The Constitution of the Federal Government of Nigeria, 1979 <https://constitutionnet.org/vl/item/constitution-federal-republic-nigeria-1979#:~:text=This%20document%20is%20the%20Constitution,Territory%20and%20general%20supplementary%20provisions>accessed 13 October,2023.

[17]The Constitution of theFederal Government of Nigeria, 1999<https://ilo.org/dyn/natlex/docs/ELECTRONIC/54097/99986/F774356846/NGA54097%202.pdf>accessed 13 October,2023.

pact on specific units.[18] A clear and precise division of authorities and functions between the two levels of government in a federation is exceedingly challenging, despite these broad boundaries, due to the complexity of modern administration. These days, local and community concerns, as well as state and regional affairs, are heavily involved in the federal or central government. At the same time, the unit governments are getting more and more involve in national programmes in co-operation with the federal or central government.[19]

The federal form of government is, therefore, a product of the desire of a people to maintain a modicum of national identity and unity in spite of these differences.[20] Federalism then is an attempt to cultivate and nurture unity in diversity.[21] In order to maximize certain goals deemed advantageous to all of them, people who are different from each other in terms of culture, ethnicity, geography, economy, history, politics, and religion may want political unity, yet they may also be unwilling to set aside their differences.[22] Such a people must opt for federalism as a form of government so as to achieve political unity in the face of heterogeneity.[23]

---

[18]O Nnoli, *Ethnic Politics in Nigeria* (Fourth Dimension Publishers, 1983) <https://www.scirp.org/(S(lz5mqp453edsnp55r-rgjct55))/reference/referencespapers.aspx?referenceid=2105749> accessed 13 October,2023.
[19]Ibid.
[20]C Ake, *Democracy and Development in Africa,* (Spectrum Books Limited, 2001) <https://www.amazon.com/Democracy-Development-Africa-Claude-Ake/dp/0815702191> accessed 18 November 2023.
[21]Ibid.
[22]EF Okoli & FC Okoli, *Foundations of Government and Politics,* (African-Fep Publishers Limited, 1990)
[23]Ibid.

The implication of this situation is that the governments of the constituent units pre-date that of the federal or central government.[24] But once in existence, the federal or central government is not always subordinate to the unit government.[25] The majority of federal states give residual powers to the units, whereas some states give them to the center. Strong federal administrations are found in nations where the center retains residual authority, such as Nigeria. Weak federal governments are seen in nations where the constituent parts retain residual authority, such as the United States of America.[26]

A written constitution is one of the fundamental elements of a federal government.[27] All federal governments have written constitutions.[28] It would be challenging to determine which governmental levels have what authority without a written con-

---

[24]EO Awa, F*ederal Government in Nigeria* (Berkeley Press, 1946) <https://www.scirp.org/(S(czeh2tfqyw2orz553k1w0r45))/reference/ReferencesPapers.aspx?ReferenceID=764823 accessed 14 November 2023.

[25]Ibid; J Hicks, *Federalism and Economic Growth in Underdeveloped Countries*, (George Allen & Unwin Ltd, 1961)https://discovered.ed.ac.uk/discovery/fulldisplay? vid=44UOE_INST%3A44UOE_VU2&search_scope=UoE&tab= Everything&docid=alma99508033502466&lang=en&context=L &adaptor=Local%20Search%20Engine&query=sub%2Cexact% 2C%20International%20business%20enterprises%20--%20Europe>accessed 14 November 2023..

[26]AO Akinyemi, PD Cole & W Ofonagoro, *Readings in Federalism* (Nigerian Institute of International Affairs, 1980) <http://www.worldcat.org/title/6633941>accessed 14 November 2023.

[27]EO Ojo,'Federalism and the Search for National Integration in Nigeria'*,African Journal of Political Science* (2009) 3 (9)<https://academicjournals.org/journal/AJPSIR/article-full-text-pdf/AB630EE40478>accessed 14 November 2023.

[28]Ibid.

stitution.[29] Most federal constitutions spell out clearly the functions of each level of government.[30] Others, however, spell out the powers and functions of only one level and provide that all powers and functions not included belong to the other level.[31] The majority of federal constitutions are inflexible, meaning that only one level of government, one organization, or a coalition of groups may attempt to amend them for their own benefit.[32]

A federation collapses when one unit, or a combination of units, in a federal setup is strong enough to jeopardize the independence and autonomy of the other units.[33] Therefore, the second tenet of federalism is that no single unit or group of units will be strong enough to rule the federation.[34] The Northern Region, which ascended to this dominant status due to its geographic size and population, was held responsible for the collapse of Nigeria's first republic. Northern Region was able to force its will on the other federations during the last years of the first republic.[35]

---

[29]Ibid.

[30]O Awolowo, *The Peoples Republic* (Oxford University Press, 1968) <https://books.google.com/books/about/The_People_s_Republic.html?id=2Q-PAAAAIAAJ>accessed 14 November 2023.

[31]Ibid.

[32]Ibid.

[33]BO Nwabueze, *Federalism in Nigeria* (Sweet & Maxwell, 1983) <https://www.scirp.org/(S(lz5mqp453edsnp55rrgjct55))/reference/referencespapers.aspx?referenceid=2105751>accessed 14 November 2023.

[34]Ibid.

[35]A Abebe & AZ Huq, 'Foreign Affairs Federalism: A Revisionist Approach', (2013) 66 *Vanderbilt Law Rev.* 7230-796<https://scholarship.law.vanderbilt.edu/vlr/vol66/iss3/1/>accessed 14 November 2023.

A federal form of government requires not only that no one unit should be large enough to threaten or control the others, but also that each constituent unit should be large enough to be economically and politically viable.[36] In terms of population and economic resources, each constituent unit should be able to carry out an effective government.[37] According to Awa, 'the 552 princely states of India were consolidated into larger units between 1947 and 1950' to give effect to this requirement.[38] In Nigeria, the former regions of the federation were broken down, first into twelve states under Gowon in 1967 and later into nineteen states under Mohammed in 1976 to give effect to the principle of viability.[39] It would be recalled that during the first republic of Nigeria, the minority ethnic groups inhabiting the four regions complained bitterly of economic and political neglect.[40] Although the Willink Commission appointed by the British government in 1957 to look into the fears of the minorities recommended against the splitting of the regions, it recognised the need for even development throughout the federation and to allow the minorities some degree of self-

---

[36]EO Anthony, 'Federalism and National Integration in Nigeria' in EO Obi & others, *Federalism and National Integration in Nigeria* (Book Point Limited, 2004) <https://www.scirp.org/(S(lz5mqp453edsnp55rrgjct55))/reference/referencespapers.aspx?referenceid=2105735>
[37]EO Ewa, *Issues in Federalism* (Ethiope Publishing Corporation,1973) <https://books.google.com/books/about/Issues_in_Federalism.html?id=xCovAAAAYAAJ>accessed 14 November 2023.
[38]DD Basu, *Commentary on the Constitution of India,* (Sarka & Sons, 1950) <https://www.amazon.com/BASU-COMMENTARY-CONSTITUTION-INDIA/dp/9350359464>accessed 14 November 2023.
[39]Ewa (n 25).
[40]Ibid.

determination.[41] That Nigeria grew from three regions in 1960 to four in 1963, to twelve states in 1967 and to nineteen states in 1967 is a testimony to this recognition. Viability of the constituent unit is, therefore, the third bedrock of a federal form of government.[42]

The Supreme Court explained in great details, in the case of *Attorney General of Abia vs. Attorney General of the Federation*,[43] the meaning and rationale of federalism. His lordship, Tobi, J.S.C., who delivered the lead judgment of the apex Court, explained the concept of federalism and stated as follows:

Federalism, as a legal and political concept, generally connotes an association of states; formed for certain common purposes, but the states retain a large measure of their original independence or autonomy. It is the coordinate relationship and distribution of power(s) between the individual states and the national government, which is at the centre. Federalism, as a viable concept of organizing a pluralistic society such as Nigeria, for governance, does not encourage so much concentration of power in the centre, which is the Federal Government. In federalism, the component states do not play the role of errand boys. The other extreme is also true, and it is that they do not

---

[41]RT Akinyele, 'State Creation in Nigeria: The Willink Report in Retrospect', *African Studies Review* (1996) 39 (2)<https://www.cambridge.org/core/journals/african-studies-review/article/states-creation-in-nigeria-the-willink-report-in-retrospect/6DF2D4-FA9C868BC9E1C3089AE824A335> accessed 15 November 2023; R Hyam, *Britain's Declining Empire: The Road to Decolonisation*, (Cambridge University Press, 2007) 274 275 <https://www.academia.edu/8939322/Hyam_Ronald_Britain_s_Declining_Empire._The_Road_to_Decolonization> accessed 15 November 2023. .
[42]Anthony (n 35).
[43](2006) All FWLR (PT. 338) 604.

exercise sovereignty, which only belongs to the nation as a sovereign entity. States in a federation rather exercise the middle role, if I may say so, for lack of a better expression, of exercising legislative and fiscal autonomy as provided for in the constitution.[44]

In summary, His Lordship concluded that the goals of federalism are twofold: first, to "greatly reduce the power of the majority at the center and thus minimize the danger of its domination of the other groups"; second, to "allow each group to develop at its own speed and along its own characteristic lines within the unity of the whole" by localizing some of the central government's powers in the component states.

In a nutshell, the doctrine of mutual non-interference, also known as implied prohibition, as it relates to a federation, states that in a nation governed by a federal Constitution, there exists an unsigned agreement between the Federal Government and State Governments on the one hand, and the federating units on the other, prohibiting any of them from interfering with the affairs of the other, particularly through legislative action. The Court of Appeal, in *Kwara State, INEC. vs. P.D.P.*,[45] expounded deeply on the notions of federalism and mutual non-interference, as follows:

In a federation, the federating units or in our case, States, agree to surrender some of their sovereignty to a central of federal authority, which is established to cater for their joint and common interest. In every other respect, however, each unit or state is autonomous and independent of the others and of the federal authority, subject, of course, to the agreed level of cooperation necessary to make the federation work. Generally, therefore, one unit or State cannot establish organs of government for another or for the federal authority and vice versa.

---

[44]Ibid at 647.
[45](2004) All FWLR (PT. 227) 980.

Nor can it, without the consent of another unit or State or of the federal authority, impose a duty on an organ of government established for that other unit or State or federal authority, either by that other authority itself or by the federation charter, the constitution. Just as the units or States cannot impose on the federal authority, so, by the law of reciprocity, the federal authority cannot impose on the units or States.[46]

Furthermore, the Supreme Court defined 'federalism' and held in *Hon. Minister for Justice & Attorney General of the Federation vs. Attorney-General of Lagos State*, that[47] the different levels of government within a federation such as Nigeria enjoy "independence" and the ability "to make laws that benefit their development," concluding that these powers "cannot be taken away from them, as long as they do not breach any constitutional requirement." His lordship, I.T. Muhammad, held that the concepts of "covering the field" and "mutual non-interference" were equivalent. In actuality, however, the theories of "implied prohibition" and "mutual noninterference" have no place when standard construction rules are used to ascertain the declared or unavoidably implied meanings of the instrument's real terms.

The situation is not different in Nigeria. Indeed, *Amalgamated Society of Engineers v Adelaide Steamship Company Ltd*,[48] was cited with approval by the Supreme Court, in *Attorney General of Ondo State vs. Attorney General of the Federation*.[49] In this case, the plaintiff had, by originating summons, at the Supreme Court, called for a determination of the question whether or not the Corrupt Practices and other Re-

---

[46]At 1001-1002.
[47](2013) All FWLR (PT 704) 1.
[48](1920) 28 CLR 129.
[49](2002) 9 NWLR (PT. 772) 222

lated Offences Act[50] was valid as a law enacted by the National Assembly and was validly in force in every State of the Federation, particularly Ondo State. The plaintiff then sought for a declaration that the Act was not in force in Ondo State, and also sought for a perpetual injunction restraining the Attorney General of the Federation from enforcing the provisions of the Act or prosecuting offenders thereof in Ondo State. It was the contention, *inter alia*, of the plaintiff and of some of the *amici curiae,* that the promulgation of this Act, which was an act of the National Assembly to cover all the States of the Federation, was a violation of the doctrine of mutual non-interference or implied prohibition. In rejecting this submission, the Supreme Court held that the provisions of the 1999 Constitution, which allocate powers to the three tiers of government, should be the guiding point, as opposed to a nebulous consideration of such constitutional law doctrines as the doctrine of mutual non-interference. That those provisions, and not those doctrines, actually define the extent to which each tier of that government can perform its duties, although it is legitimate to have those doctrines in one's mind while interpreting those constitutional provisions. Uwaifo, J.S.C., held as follows:

Without meaning to discount these doctrines which, indeed, may be useful reminders when the application of an Act may appear to be a blatant invasion of or interference with the affairs of a State, I have to say, however, that it has been held that what decides ultimately is the effect of the distribution of powers under the Constitution.[51]

This effectively means that, although these doctrines might be helpful in assessing whether a Federal Act has violated a state's right to semi-autonomy under the Constitution, they must undoubtedly make way for explicit constitutional provi-

---

[50]No. 4 of 2000, Laws of Federation of Nigeria, 2004.
[51]At 339.

sions regarding the division of powers between the Federal Government and the federating units, or States. This makes sense because the specific provisions of a given Constitution cannot be superseded by constitutional ideas or concepts.

The doctrine of mutual non-interference, however, still remains a good constitutional theory that can be applied in any relevant situation. Thus, in *Attorney General of Lagos State vs. Attorney General of the Federation*,[52] the Supreme Court held that section 2(2) of the Constitution has re-enacted the doctrine of federalism. The supreme Court claims that this clause guarantees the independence of the federal and state governments and that no government is in charge of the other. According to the Supreme Court, this indicates that, in terms of the relationship between the States and the Federal Government, each is an independent entity in the sense that it is free to express its own will in conducting its business within the bounds of the Constitution without interference from another governmental body. Several decisions of superior courts of law have explained further the implications of the federal structure of Nigeria. In *Attorney General of the Federation vs. Attorney General of Abia State*, one[53] of the major contentions was what the boundary of a littoral State was. In other words, whether it was correct, as contended by the eight littoral States, that their southern boundaries, extended to the high seas, or the continental shelf of Nigeria. For the States had argued that by sections 2(2) and (3) and (2) of the CFRN 1999, including the first schedule thereto, Nigeria consists of the aggregate of the territories of all the 36 States ofNigeria and the Federal Capital territory; and that constitutionally therefore, Nigeria cannot have any other territory outside this aggregation. Moreover, for the sake of argument, Nigeria will collapse if the 36 states vanish. Conse-

---

[52](2003) FWLR (PT. 168) 909.
[53](2002) 4 SCNJ 1.

quently, the plaintiff's claim that the federal government owns the continental shelf without regard to the states will result in a breach of the constitutionally established boundaries. Lastly, the eight littoral States—which are, by the Nigerian Federation's Constitution, constituent parts—own the continental shelf or exclusive economic zone, which extends deep into the Atlantic Ocean. This argument was denied by the Supreme Court's entire court. It was held that as the sea forms Nigeria's southern border as a sovereign nation, the sea cannot logically be a part of the eight littoral states' territory. Ogundare, J.S.C., who read the lead judgment, held:

As I have found earlier in this judgment, the southern boundaries of the littoral States of Nigeria are the sea. This makes them riparian owners. And as riparian owners the seaward extent of their land territory, at common law, is the low-water mark or seaward limit of their internal waters.[54]

The Supreme Court further declared that "Nigeria exercises jurisdiction beyond that limit in accordance with its sovereignty and by custom of the international community," even if "the seaward limit of Nigeria is [the] low water mark." The Court further held that, in contrast to the sovereignty such states have over their land territories, the 1958 Geneva Conventions on the Territorial Sea and the Contiguous Zone, 1958 Geneva Convention on the Continental Shelf, and 1958 Geneva Convention on the High Seas all granted coastal States only limited sovereignty over their territories. Since Nigeria's land territory is limited to what is specified in sections 2 and 3 of the constitution, the Supreme Court held that the plaintiff, or the Federal Government, does not have the right to assert sovereignty over the country's exclusive economic zone and territorial sea.

---

[54]At 33.

The Court of Appeal, in *F.R.S.C. vs. Omono-Obla*,[55] incisively explained the import of the Federal structure of Nigeria as provided for in section 2(2) of the constitution. It held that in a federal structure like Nigeria, there are two levels of government – the central government on the one hand and the state, provincial or territorial governments on the other. Mika'ilu, J.C.A., who delivered the lead judgment of the Court of Appeal, concluded thus:

Thus, countries with federal political system(s) have both a central government and governments based in smaller units, usually called states, provinces or territories. These smaller political units surrender some of their political powers to the central government, relying on it to act for (the) common good.[56]

After going into further detail on what federalism entails, His Lordship came to the conclusion that while the goal of federalism is to 'allow each group or federating unit to be free from interference or control of others,' it also ensures that "these differing interests and circumstance[s] are accommodated...for the peace, security, and stability of the country. Additionally, it was decided that because each of the Nigerian federating states has its own set of delineated borders, they are all "autonomous from the others."

Similarly, all States of the federation, existing or newly created, are equal in the eyes of the Constitution. Thus, in *Attorney General of Ondo vs. Attorney General of Ekiti State*,[57] even though the dispute in this case bordered on the sharing of assets of the old Ondo State upon on the creation of Ekiti State, the Supreme Court once again made findings on the geopolitical structure of States of the Federation. It held that all States of

---

[55](2010) 15 NWLR (PT 1217) 617
[56]At 632.
[57](2001) 10 SCNJ 117

the Federation, whether created or existing, are equal before the law. Ayoola, J.S.C., held:

A State is first and foremost a community of persons in political association exercising jurisdiction and authority within defined borders. In a federation, the community as described above is recognised as a federating unit sharing with the central government powers within a larger state. When the composition of the community comprising a state changes as fundamentally as in this case, by a redefinition of the areas comprising the state, it will be legalism carried to rather absurd limits to hold that the old order remains. What is real is that the old state is dissolved, and new entities are created, none of them representing, and exclusively succeeding to, the assets and liabilities of the dissolved state.[58]

Politics of State Creation

Generally, the need to bring government closer to the people and satisfy long-standing anxieties among some ethnic groups about the oppressive influence of their more populous neighboring communities were the main drivers for the founding of states in Nigeria.[59] As previously mentioned, ethnic minorities in the former eastern region began advocating for their own State or region as early as the 1950s. In addition, proponents of state creation contended that these actions would guarantee equality in political participation and the distribution of federal government resources, promote development, and curb region-

---

[58]At 179.
[59]JA Oni, Federalism in Nigeria-Principle and Practice, *Sage Journal*<https://journals.sagepub.com/doi/ 10.1177/001132559002200201>15 November 2023.

al economic disparities.[60] However, opponents of State creation, such as former President Shehu Shagari, saw such an exercise as unnecessary.[61] This was due to the enduring repercussions. For example, it was contended that the establishment of new states would not only hinder development by depleting the federal government's meager resources, but also promote state indolence and extravagant spending by large contractors.[62] Also, given Nigerian's heterogeneous nature, it has been contended that the idea of State creation would constitute an unnecessary distraction from the task of government because of the unending competition for the resources of the Nigeria state which, more or less, has as its basis ethnically-defined constituencies.[63] Put differently, the argument put up by those opposed to the establishment of states is that, far from promoting nation-building and national integration, this endeavor will only serve to perpetuate centrifugal forces rather than foster patriotism and national unity. The movement for the establishment of a state has been specifically attributed to Nigeria's federal system. This results from the distributive approach in federal-state relations and the federal monopoly of national resources. In other words, people who feel that they are not receiving enough have been constantly calling for more states to be included in the federal financial aid program. This has confirmed Suberu's assertion that 'the pervasive influence of the

---

[60]Ibid.
[61]S Shagari, 'The Time for Muddling Through is Over' *Speech Delivered at the Usman Dan Fodio University, Sokoto*, 13 January, 1996.
[62]Ibid.
[63]R Suberu, 'State Creation and the Political Economy of Nigeria Federalism' in K Amuwo & others, (*eds*), *Federalism and Political Restructuring in Nigeria* (Spectrum Books, 1998) <https://searchworks.stanford.edu/view/3975454> accessed 25 November 2023.

norm of inter-unit equality is also reflected in the practice of providing equal federal financial aid to new States.'[64] As a result, the federal government will certainly face more financial strain and pay less attention to matters pertaining to national growth the more States it creates.[65]

There are also arguments that the creation of States in Nigeria over the years had been informed more by political considerations than any other factor.[66] This school of thought holds that military officers from the former northern region, which is primarily Hausa-Fulani and Muslim, have dominated the federal government since 1967. The north has benefited more than the south because military regimes have created all states to date (formed up of previous eastern and western regions). For example, in the 1967 exercise, the former western area consisted mainly of the Western and Lagos States with a part in Kwara State, while the former northern region was divided into five states (Benue-Plateau, Kano, North-Central, North-Eastern, and North-Western States).[67] The former eastern region had three States, namely, East Central, Rivers and South-Eastern States.[68] As a matter of fact, it has been argued that the Creation of Rivers and South-Eastern States by Gowon was intended specifically to break the Igbo by turning them into a minority in the former eastern region vis-à-vis the ethnic minorities who had two States as against one for the more popu-

---

[64]Ibid.
[65]ibid
[66]HGA Ofoeze, *The Nigeria State and the Human Rights of the Igbo* (Data Globe Nigeria, 2009)<https://www.arjonline.org/papers/arjhss/v6-i1/5.pdf>accessed 25 November 2023.
[67]Ibid.
[68]Ibid.

lous Igbo.[69] Similarly, Murtala Mohammed gave seven States to the former Northern Region in 1976, three more to the former western region, and only two to the former eastern region.[70] The trend of favouring the North was sustained in the 1987, 1991 and 1996 States creation exercises by the predominantly Hausa-Fulani Muslim north has fourteen States, while ethnic minorities in the north have five; the Yoruba have six States, with stakes in two, while the Igbo have five States, just one State more than the ethnic minorities in the former eastern region.[71]

Nigeria's federal system is such that the centre has an overwhelming control over the financial resources of the country.[72] The number of States and local governments determines how these resources are allocated as well. More States and local government districts are found in the former northern region than in the combined former eastern and western regions. Since crude oil production in the former eastern zone provides the majority of Nigeria's financial resources, the ethnic groups residing in that region have called for the establishment of true federalism and have expressed feelings of marginalization.[73] Over time, the politicization of state creation has exacerbated tensions between different ethnic and regional groups, particu-

---

[69]MIO Ikejiani-Clark 'The Igbo in Contemporary Nigeria' in GEK Ofomata (ed), *A Survey of the Igbo Nation* (Africana –Fep Publishers Ltd, 2002) <https://searchworks.stanford.edu/view/5747458> accessed 25 November 2023.

[70]Ibid.

[71]Ibid.

[72]S Oguedo, 'Stepping into the Minefield Struggle for National Resources Polarises Nigerian into the North against South' *This Week* No 161, 12 February,1990<https://www.arjonline.org/papers/arjhss/v6-i1/5.pdf> accessed 25 November 2023.

[73]Ibid.

larly between those who feel they have been shortchanged and those who think everything is fair.[74]

The introduction and validation of criteria like the federal character principle and the quota system, along with the utilization of land mass and the quantity of local government areas in the distribution of national resources, have significantly intensified calls for the creation of additional States and local government units, particularly in the southern region of the nation.[75] The argument appears to be, as earlier stated that the former northern region has been unduly favoured in all the State creation exercises. Thus, there have been cries of internal colonisation from the domination of Nigerians by the northern Nigerian oligarchy, a situation which has favoured the flowering of new dimensions of interethnic and interreligious conflicts in the country.[76] Because they have been in control of the Federal government for most of Nigeria's independence, the northern Nigerian oligarchy has been accused of using its advantage to alienate and subdue other Nigerians.[77] For example, following the end of the Nigeria-Biafra conflict in 1970, the Federal Government has continued to favor the North in social amenities and infrastructural development as well as political

---

[74]Ibid.

[75]EN Ota, CS Ecoma and CG Wambu, 'Creation of States in Nigeria, 19670-1996: Deconstucting the History and Politics' *American Journal of Humanities*<https://scholar.google.com/citations?user=arOdWyYAAAAJ&hl=en>http accessed 25 November 2023.

[76]Ibid.

[77]JAA Ayoade, 'The Federal Character Principle and the Search for National Intergration' in K Amuwo *et al, Federalism and Political Restructuring in Nigeria* (Spectrum Books,1998) <https://www.scirp.org/(S(czeh2tfqyw2orz553k1w0r45))/reference/ReferencesPapers.aspx?ReferenceID=1446093> accessed 25 November 2023.

appointments.[78] Similarly, the Federal Character Principle has resulted in the discarding of merit in recruitments into and promotions in the federal civil service and federal parastatals.[79] The story is basically the same in the admission of students into federal government-owned secondary and tertiary institutions, where merit is often sacrificed on the altar of federal character in order to enable some so-called educationally-disadvantaged groups catch up with those considered better off.[80] Over time, this has led to ongoing competition and conflict between the various ethnic groups over more States and, consequently, improved access to the nation's financial resources. This is the case because, as was already mentioned, the number of States and local government units determines how resources are distributed by the "almighty" federal government.[81]

Most importantly, as has been correctly noted, the attempt to address the north-south regional imbalance directly led to the creation of the States, but this has resulted in the north's domination of the south, making the north literally determine the political destiny of every Nigerian.[82] Among other aspects, the legitimacy of the federal character idea has not led to the fair and equitable treatment of all Nigerians in any observable or acceptable way. Instead, because appointments to federal government-owned businesses, organizations, and institutions continue to prioritize State of origin and ethnolinguistic affinities,

---

[78]Ibid.
[79]Ibid.
[80]EJ Ellah, *Nigeria and State Creation Based on 'the Unfinished Nation'* (Ellah & Sons Company Ltd, 1983) <https://www.re-searchgate.net/publication/342142383_CREATION_OF_S-TATES_IN_NIGERIA_1967-1996_DECONSTRUCT-ING_THE_HISTORY_AND_POLITICS> accessed 25 November 2023.
[81]Ibid.
[82]Ibid.

it has jeopardized efforts at national integration. "The operationalization of the Federal Character Principle has tended more to differentiate than to integrate," according to Ayoade.[83] This is due to the obvious fact that the people of the former eastern region especially those of the Niger Delta, whose crude oil-bearing lands have experienced environmental degradation over time, feel marginalized, deprived, and dominant as a result of the nation's unfair distribution of financial resources and infrastructure development.

The Ethnic Configuration of Nigeria.

In all multi-ethnic countries, the ethnic-minority relationship is a universal problem. The problem in Nigeria arose in 1914 when Sir Lord Frederick Lugard combined the colony, or the protectorates in the south and north. The marginalization of minorities by majorities, particularly with regard to prospects for economic and political advancement, has historically been the source of outcry.[84] But over time, historic political developments like the division of the nation into states and local government districts from its three regional structures—which had previously solidified the unequal power dynamics between the two groups—and intensified their fierce rivalry for scarce economic resources helped to allay some of these fears. Even after the Nigerian state was restructured and power was devolved, the issues facing minorities have not yet been sufficiently addressed.[85]

Nonetheless, the researchers made several suggestions to address the issues, and it is believed that these would help Nigeria

---

[83]Ayoade (n 77).
[84]Ibid.
[85]Ibid.

become a more prosperous and peaceful country in the future. There will inevitably be certain individuals who benefit in a multicultural country like Nigeria because of their population, early exposure to colonialists, or level of education. These invariably spark rivalry and the fight for equity and justice in the allocation of resources, positions, and offices open to the society they are a part of.[86]

Since gaining independence in 1960, Nigeria has been in precisely this circumstance. Minority ethnic groups have been fighting for justice, equality, and complete inclusion in the preparation and distribution of the "national cake." Igbo, Yoruba, and Hausa-Fulani make up the main tribes. People from various ethnic groups who live in Nigeria's northern and southern regions make up the minority.[87]

At the vortex of the ethnic minority question is the disenchantment with the structure of the Nigerian federation perceived by the ethnic minorities to be skewed in favour of the three dominant ethnic groups by the three ethno-regional blocs: Hausa in the North, Yoruba in the West and the Igbo in the East. For the ethnic minorities, the federation is not inclusive and this results in political, economic and cultural marginalisation. According to Anugwom, marginalization exists when an ethnic group or any kind of group feels disenchanted with the political system.[88]

---

[86]GA Danaan, *Brothers against Brothers: The Press, Identity Politics and Conflict Management in Northern Nigeria.* (Selidan Publishers 2010) 13 < https://theartsjournal.org/index.php/site/ article/view/953> Accessed 25 November 2023
[87]Ibid
[88]EE Anugwom, 'Ethnic Conflict and Democracy in Nigeria: The Marginalisation Question'(2000) 15 (1) Journal of Social Development in Africa 15, 61-78<https://www.ajol.info/index.php/ jsda/article/view/23854>Accessed 25 November 2023

The three regions, North, West and East have within them minority populations and each of these has its own peculiar problems. In the South West, the minorities asserted that the government at Ibadan was dominated by the Yoruba and that it would be difficult for a non-Yoruba ethnic group to become the Premier of the Western region.[89] This led to the demand for a mid-Western Region. In the South East, the minorities expressed fear that the Igbos would over-run them commercially and politically.[90] They therefore urged the establishment of a distinct area to reconcile the states of Calabar, Ogoja, and Rivers. The Ilorin and Kabba Division in northern Nigeria protested that the system had been authoritarian and that there had not yet been a transition to democratic practices. They insisted on being sent to the West. The application of Muslim rule, or Sharia law, was strongly opposed in the non-Muslim portion of the Emirate.[91] There was a strong agitation by minorities in the North central Nigeria for the creation of Middle Belt region to cater for their interest and self-autonomy.

Miller emphasizes that 'democracies ought to be willing to include certain basic rights in the constitution, precisely, to protect minorities against the unfriendly nature of the majorities at any moment' in his reflection on the issue of minorities in general. It is crucial to note, though, that the absence of constitutional protection for minorities' fundamental rights is not the root of the country's minority problems. Instead, their issue

---

[89]JO Ojiako, *Nigeria: Yesterday, Today And....*(Africana Educational Publishers, Nig. Ltd) <https://discovered.ed.ac.uk/discovery/fulldisplay?docid=alma993938283502466&context=L&vid=44UOE_INST:44UOE_VU2&lang=en&adaptor=Local%20Search%20Engine&tab=Everything&query=sub%2Cexact%2CNkrumah%2C%20Kwame%2C%201909-1972> accessed 26 November 2023.
[90]Ibid
[91]Ibid

stems from a few existential circumstances that make the provision unworkable. Toyo stated that:

how constitutional provisions are translated into practice depends on who is in power and this applies to federal, state and local government levels and the party in power are of crucial importance. A political party of tribalists, power sharers, sycophants, greedy opportunists and get-rich-quick gangsters can never translate intentions of the constitutions into practice.[92]

The main source of ethnic unrest and bloodshed worldwide is minority groups. A United Nations source defines minorities as groups that are numerically inferior to the rest of the population in a state in a non-dominant position, whose members possess ethnic, religious, or linguistic characteristics different from the rest of the population, and who have, if only implicitly, a sense of solidarity directed towards preserving their culture, tradition, religion, or languages. This definition adequately captures the critical properties of the concept.[93] Consequently, minorities are viewed as comparatively cohesive, culturally different groups that hold a position of numerical inferiority and real or potential socio-political subordination in relation to other cultural sections within a political community. According to Ukpo (1977:99), an ethnic group is 'a group of people having a common language and cultural values.' Regular contacts

---

[92]E Toyo, 'Youth, Women, Workers and Minority Interests in Nigeria Constitutions: Personal Reflections' in Okon E Uya, *Issues in the 1995 Nigerian Draft Constitution* (CATS Publishers 1999) <https://www.africabib.org/rec.php?RID=W00097374> accessed 26 November 2023.
[93]Ibid.

among members of the group, community, or region define these shared factors.[94]

In Nigeria, assimilation, intermarriage, and/or intermingling occasionally result in the fusion of ethnic groups. The groups that make up these fusions retain some degree of individual identity. In the context of competitive politics, Jega defines identity politics as the reciprocally reinforcing interaction between identities and the pursuit of pecuniary gains.[95] This means that identities are used mostly in political competition by groups within a society for the distribution of scarce resources and procurement of positions, appointments, winning of elections.[96]

Ethnic minority movements in the 1950s and 1960s believed that state establishment was the answer. However, actual existential circumstances seem to run counter to this optimism. In actuality, the dominance of regions has been overthrown, and in the micro-spaces known as States, the majority inside minorities has taken its place. Larry claims that the concerns and complaints of ethnic minorities were centered on getting an equitable share of the benefits and resources of a growing state and economy, including jobs, loans, scholarships, processing

---

[94]U Ukpo, *Ethnic Minority Problems in Nigerian Politics,* (LiberTryck AB, 1977) <https://books.google.com/books/about/Ethnic_Minority_Problems_in_Nigerian_Pol.html?id=CtNPAQAAIAAJ> accessed 26 November 2023
[95]A Jega, *Identity Transformation and Identity Politics under Structural Adjustment in Nigeria,* (Afrikainstitute/Apsalla/CRD-Jimida.S.I 2012) <https://www.diva-portal.org/smash/get/diva2:248993/FULLTEXT01.pdfSimilarIdentity&usg=ALkJrhhDsCZFsdGz-PyA2Cm6sUymNvOj4w> accessed 26 November 2023.
[96]Ibid.

facilities, water supply, street lights, schools, and hydroelectric projects.[97]

Challenges of State Creation

Statehood has, in fact, been an important factor in the allocation of a wider range of social opportunities in the Nigerian federation.[98] For instance, the principle of 'federal character', which has been a key constitutional issue since 1979, enjoins the representation of every state in crucial federal institutions and positions, and also prescribes an important role for the states in the election of the president and the formation of political parties. Socio-economically, the federal character principle has been widely interpreted as prescribing equality between the states of the federation in the distribution and utilization of federal development projects, including the location of, and admission of candidates into, federal educational institutions.[99]

The more overtly political justification that supported the state construction process prior to 1970 can be contrasted with the distributive imperatives that emerged to define state agitation and reorganization after this time. In fact, the official tenets used to establish new states in Nigeria indicate a preference for political goals over economic ones.[100] The more important of these principles include the need to prevent the domination of the federal government by a single state, enhance administrative convenience and political security, give adequate recognition to the facts of history and the wishes of the

---

[97]L Diamond, 'Class, Ethnicity and Democratic State: Nigeria, 1950-1966' (1983) 25(3) Comparative Studies in Society and History

[98]Nnoli (n17)

[99]Ellah (n80)

[100]Ibid.

people, bring government nearer to the people, ensure even development, preserve the federal structure of government, maintain peace and harmony within the federation and minimize minority problems.[101] While their actual application in specific reorganizations has been mediated by a 'strong dose of expediency or pragmatism', these principles have provided the basic parameters for territorial reforms in Nigeria.[102]

Thus, the creation of states in 1967 derived from the need to satisfy the longstanding demand by ethnic minority groups for independent constituent units, a demand that was only very partially satisfied by the creation of the Midwest in 1963.[103] Resolving the ingrained fears of dominance caused by the Northern region's disproportionate size was another factor taken into account during the 1967 exercise. In order to maintain some symmetry between the two regions, the region was split into six states and the number of constituent units in the South was increased from three to six.[104]

Practically speaking, the establishment of an autonomous unit for minority groups in 1967 was essential to the federation's survival because it quickly reduced support for secession in the Eastern area.[105] Similarly, the creation of the Lagos State out of the Western region was designed to weaken autonomist pressures in that region by denying it independent access to the sea.[106]

---

[101]K Ezera, 'Nigeria's constitutional Road to Independence' (1959) 30 (2) The Political Quarterly
[102]Ibid.
[103]EE Osaghae, 'Ethnic Minorities and Federalism in Nigeria' (1991) 90 (359) African Affairs: The Journal of the Royal African Society
[104]Ibid.
[105]Okpu (95)
[106]Ibid.

While ethnic minority groups' agitation for new states and opposition to the regional system in the 1950s and 1960s included allegations of sectional discrimination in the distribution of developmental opportunities, the creation of states was only closely linked to the fight for a larger share of national resources after the revenue allocation decree of 1970 was enacted and subsequent changes to the revenue sharing system increased the states' overall financial dependence on the federal government.[107] Therefore, General Murtala Mohammed stated that 'the basic motivation in the exercise is to bring government nearer to the people while at the same time ensuring even development within a federal structure of government' when he announced the Federal Military Government's decision on the 19-state structure in February 1976. The process of "bringing government nearer to the people" effectively entails making resource distribution less contentious and access to resources more direct. It also means "more" because of how revenue is distributed among the states, as has been correctly noted.[108]

One significant effect of this focus on the redistributive goals of reorganization was the total devaluation of the ethnolinguistic premise, which was long espoused as the most objective foundation for state formation in Nigeria, among others, including Chief Obafemi Awolowo. The sheer number of ethnic groups in Nigeria made it nearly impossible to apply this principle strictly, and the homogeneous majority ethnic formations of Hausa-Fulani, Yoruba, and Igbo were now undergoing new subdivisions in response to internal sub-ethnic pressures for a larger share of the country's resources.[109]

---

[107]Akinyele, (n 40)
[108]Ibid
[109]DC Bach, 'Managing a Plural Society: The Boomerang Effects of Nigerian Federalism' (1989) 27 (2) The Journal of Commonwealth and Comparative Politics

Constitutionally, to create a state in Nigeria is a big challenge. The Constitution of the Federal Republic of Nigeria 1999 (as amended) provides as follow:

An Act of the National Assembly for the purpose of creating a new State shall only be passed if –

a request, supported by at least two-thirds majority of members (representing the area demanding the creation of the new State) in each of the following, namely –

the Senate and the House of Representatives;

the House of Assembly in respect of the area;

the local government councils in respect of the area,

is received by the National Assembly;

a proposal for the creation of the State is thereafter approved in a referendum by at least two-thirds majority of the people of the area where the demand for creation of the State originated;

the result of the referendum is then approved by a simple majority of all the States of the Federation, supported by a simple majority of members of the Houses of Assembly; and

the proposal is approved by a resolution passed by two-thirds majority of members of each House of the National Assembly.[110] By this provision, to create a state in Nigeria is a herculean task, since the constitution is rigid. The moment there is move for creation of a state by any part of the country; other parts will also agitate for it, thereby frustrating the process. It has always been difficult to the concurrence of two-thirds of the states of the federation to approve the creation of the new states. Even in creating Local Government, Council has not been successful because of this rigidity, to the extent that no local government can also be created without the concurrence of the National Assembly. In *AG of Lagos State v AG of the Federation*[111]the dispute in this case was whether or not

---

[110]S 8 (1) of the 1999 Constitution of Nigeria (as amended).
[111](2004) ALL NLR 90.

a Local Government Council created by the Appellant herein to replace the ones recognized under the constitution can automatically come into being and enjoy benefits accruing to Local Governments under the constitution without the input of the National Assembly as provided for by s 8 (5) and s 3 (6) of the 1999 Constitution (as amended)? The Supreme Court held that the law made by the Lagos State Government was not sufficient to give life to the new local governments areas until the National Assembly passes a consequential Act amending the Section 3 (6) and Part 1 of the First Schedule to the constitution and that for a new local government to be created the provisions of s 8 (3) of the 1999 Constitution (as amended) must be complied with by the House of Assembly of the State where the local government or Council is to be created. See also *AG Federation of Nigeria v AG Abia State and 35 others*[112]

Conclusion

The politics and many obstacles associated with the establishment of new states have been covered in this work. There has been emphasis on federalism, which demands the establishment of states and the ethnic structure. It is clear from this research that the fear of the majority wishing to rule the minority is the main driver behind the demand for new states. Up till the present, this fear of dominance has persisted, even before the Willink Commission. Some believe that the 1914 amalgamation of Nigeria is the root cause of this issue. After more than a century, it is now necessary for the populace to tolerate one another in order to minimize tension and conflict. The aforementioned accounts and conversations indicate that Nigeria's ethnic makeup will likely lead to ongoing calls for the establishment

---

[112](2002) 6 NWLR (PT 764) 524

of a state. Despite all of this, the suggestions listed below are suggested. From now on, Nigeria should not create any new states over the next fifty years; instead, the current states should be strengthened to better serve the requirements of the nation's population. Secondly, it is necessary to uphold fiscal federalism. More than ever, the people should hold the government responsible for its financial operations. Three, the federal government's authority must be transferred to the states and local government councils. Since the other levels of government are closer to the people, they should be given more authority to carry out functions that directly affect citizens' lives; hence the Exclusive Legislative List should be reviewed. State police should be permitted to operate in the same manner as other federating nations, such as the US and Australia. State and municipal governments should be in charge of road infrastructure and related issues. Four, the revenue allocation system should be changed to provide state and local governments more money so they can carry out citizen-oriented activities. However, this should be closely watched to avoid office misuse.

Reducing Legal Constraints in Obtaining Judicial Dissolution of a Statutory Marriage in Nigeria

Nathal Kehinde Adegbite[1]

Introduction

The family[2] is the basic unit of the society, and central to family is marriage. Marriage is a social contract between two or more persons, which may be formal or informal. When two people of the opposite sex cohabit without a formal ceremony declaring them as husband and wife, they may nonetheless be loosely regarded as a couple if they both perform activities

---

[1]Lecturer and Ph.D candidate, Faculty of Law, Obafemi Awolowo University, Ile-Ife, Nigeria, +2348038556525, nkadegbite@oauife.edu.ng, https://orcid.org/ 0000-0002-1819-8225.
[2]A family is taken to consist of a man, a woman and their children. Black's Law Dictionary defines family as "A group consisting of parents and their children." See Bryan A. Garner, *Black's Law Dictionary* (9th Edition, WEST 2004) 679

such as sexual relations and procreation.[3] On the other hand, a marriage is seen as formal when the State (including traditional institutions, especially in most African societies) has roles to play in a marital contract between two or more persons.

The State in most nations of the world, if not all, extends its roles in marital contracts to determining which relationships would be regarded as marriage and which ones would not. For instance, at a time in England, only unions between a man and a woman were accorded legal recognition as marriage. Thus, in the old English case of *Hyde V. Hyde*,[4] marriage was defined as a '...voluntary union for life of one man and one woman, to the exclusion of all others.'[5] While the definition paints the picture

---

[3] In many common law jurisdictions, this type of relationship is referred to as common law marriage, although with varied legal recognition in such jurisdictions. In Nigeria, it is doubtful if cohabitation, no matter how long, can transform into a legally recognised marriage. If it will be regarded as marriage at all in Nigeria, it may be either customary or Islamic law marriage. This may be inferred from the provision of the Evidence Act 2011, s 166 which states:

When, in any proceeding whether civil or criminal, there is a question as to whether a man or woman is the husband or wife under Islamic or Customary law, of a party to the proceeding the court shall, unless the contrary is proved, presume the existence of a valid and subsisting marriage between the two persons where evidence is given to the satisfaction of the court, of cohabitation as husband and wife by such man and woman.

[4] (1866) L.R.1 P. & D 130

[5] ibid, the definition was offered by Lord Penzance.

of a monogamous marriage,[6] the idea of 'voluntary union' connotes that any party to it could as well exercise the liberty to exit it when they want. The idea of 'for life' simply presupposes that parties to the marriage intend their union, at the time of its celebration, to endure until death do them part. Although the case[7] was decided in England, the definition aligned with the old prevailing conception of marriage in many other countries.[8] However, both England and many other jurisdictions have in recent past expanded the definition of relationships now regarded as marriage. For example, in England, America, Canada

---

[6]Like a statutory marriage, a monogamous marriage is a union of two persons, usually a man and a woman. By law, a statutory marriage must be monogamous. For example, the Criminal Code, Cap. 38, Vol. II, Laws of Oyo State of Nigeria 2000, s 1 defines "monogamous marriage" as "…a marriage which is recognized by the law of the place where it is contracted as the voluntary union for life of one man and one woman to the exclusion of all others during the continuance of the marriage…" Identical definition can be found in the laws of many other States in Nigeria especially Southern States. It is in this sense that statutory marriage is used interchangeably with monogamous marriage.
[7]N 3, *Hyde v. Hyde*
[8]For instance, under the Australian Marriage Act 1961, s 5 marriage was defined as "…union of a man and a woman to the exclusion of all others, voluntarily married for life." However, from 2017, the section was amended to read, "…union of 2 persons to the exclusion of all others, voluntarily married for life." See Australian Marriage Act 1961, s 5 <https://www.refworld.org/pdfid/4dd1432a2.pdf> accessed 15 October 2023 and compare with the amended version,< http://www5.austlii.edu.au/au/legis/cth/consol_act/ma196185/s5.html#marriage> accessed 15 October 2023

and a good number of European countries,[9] persons of the same sex can now lawfully marry one another, though this is not so in many African countries, including Nigeria.[10] In Nigeria, what relationship is regarded as marriage or how marriage is defined is determined by three factors – inherited colonial

---

[9]In these countries, marriage between persons of the same sex is not only legal but couples in such relationships also enjoy the same set of rights that couples of heterosexual relationships enjoy.

[10]Homosexual relationships are viewed from both cultural and religious angles in most African countries and to that extent, the relationships are not legalised except South-Africa where marriage between persons of the same sex is legal.

legal system,[11] religion[12] and culture.[13] Being a former British colony,[14] Nigeria adopts the definition offered in *Hyde v.*

---

[11]Babafemi Odunsi elucidates on this thus, "…the colonial relationship between Nigeria and England engendered the introduction of supervening English law and legal system into Nigeria." See Babafemi Odunsi, "Customary Law as a Source of Nigerian Law" in S. B. Odunsi, O. S. Oyelade and M. O. Adeleke (ed.) *Nigerian Legal System* (A Book in Honour of Paul Usoro, SAN, FCIArb) (UP PLC 2019) 95

[12]The religion in this context is Islam being the dominant religion in the Northern part of Nigeria and again, prior to the inception of colonial rule in Nigeria, Islamic law had taken roots in the North and the colonial overlords decided to allow it exist side by side with the imported English legal system. This explains the applicability of native law and customs to Nigerians as personal law in certain areas of their lives such as inheritance, marriage, real property, and succession, although, unlike the general law, native law and customs has to be proved as fact, until it has gained such notoriety to be judicially noticed. Its application must also pass the validity tests set by the English law in which case any rules of native law and customs to be applied must not be repugnant to natural justice, equity and good conscience. It must not also be incompatible with any written law in force nor be contrary to public policy. See generally, Akintunde Olusegun Obilade, *The Nigerian Legal System* (Spectrum Books Ltd 2005) 83-100

[13]In the case of the Southern part of Nigeria, customs and traditions functioned as binding rules over the people in that part of the country and the arrival of the British colonialists and the importation of their laws did not totally overthrow the pre-existing traditional legal order.

[14]Nigeria was ruled by the Great Britain from 1861 to 1960 when the country gained its political independence but relics of the erstwhile colonial master remain visible in the former colony's legal, economic and political systems.

Hyde[15] in addition to the legal recognition she accords a marital relationship between a man and many women.[16] In essence, the imported English law,[17] Islamic religion[18] and diverse indigenous cultures[19] in Nigeria respectively define marriage. Polygamy is as legally recognised in Nigeria as monogamy. However, same-sex marriage is both prohibited and crimi-

---

[15]ibid, n 3. In *Amobi v. Nzegwu & Ors.*, (2013) LPELR-21863 (SC) 61, the Nigerian Supreme Court adopted the definition of marriage in *Hyde v. Hyde*

[16]Polygamy as an alternative legal marriage in Nigeria exists under both Islamic and customary laws. Willing Muslims can marry according to the dictates of their religion which implies that a man can have more than one wife and any Nigerian, irrespective of their religion, can also choose to marry under their respective native laws which allow men to marry as many wives as they wish, although some men married under these two systems of law choose to be monogamous, not marrying more than a wife at a time.

[17]This coinage is used to refer to received English law, and other pieces of legislative enactments made by Nigerians or elected Nigerian legislators such as Nigerian legislation, and the Constitution in that they are all laws influenced by the English law principles and concepts as opposed to Islamic and customary laws which can be regarded as different systems of law.

[18]Islam as a religion commands a huge followership in Nigeria especially in the Northern part of the country and its legal system is also entrenched in the country.

[19]Prior to the introduction of colonialism and the English legal system to Nigeria, the local communities constituting the present-day Nigeria ruled themselves through their customs and traditions which they regarded as binding on them.

nalised.[20] The rationale behind the criminalisation of same-sex marriage in Nigeria may be traced to the strong influence of religion and culture in the formulation of legal rules, public policies and official matters despite that the country is regarded

---

[20]In Nigeria, Same-Sex Marriage (Prohibition) Act was passed by Nigeria's National Assembly in 2013 and till date, the law is in force under which it is a crime for persons of the same sex to have amorous relationship or enter into marriage. Specifically, the Same-Sex (Prohibition) Act 2013, s 3 provides "Only a marriage contracted between a man and a woman shall be recognised as valid in Nigeria." In section 5 (1) of the same Act, it criminalises same sex marriage or relationship thus, "A person who enters into a same sex marriage contract or civil union commits an offence and is liable on conviction to a term of 14 years imprisonment."

as a secular nation,[21] though the secular status of Nigeria is of-

---

[21] The idea of secularity of Nigeria is typically associated with the provision of section 10 of the Constitution of the Federal Republic of Nigeria 1999 (CFRN 1999) which provides, "The Government of the Federation or of a State shall not adopt any religion as State Religion." However, this constitutional provision has not received the benefit of judicial interpretation till date as such judicial intervention would have helped to determine whether the section confers a secular status on Nigeria and if it does, the Judiciary should further clarify the meaning of secularity in relation to the involvement of the Government in matters of religion.

ten enmeshed in controversy.[22]

Although polygamy exists as an offshoot of religion and culture, it is not on the same footing with monogamy on a number

---

[22]While pro-secular advocates anchor their position on CFRN 1999, s 10, those who counter the secular status of Nigeria contend that the drafters of the Constitution would have specifically tagged the country a secular nation, if they had intended the section to make the country a secular nation. To such persons, Nigeria is a multi-religious society, not secular. See Osita Nnamani Ogbu, 'Is Nigeria a Secular State? Law, Human Rights and Religion in Context' (2014) 1 The Transnational Human Rights Review. However, from the available evidence, the arguments against the secularity of Nigeria appear more convincing when the Constitution itself is properly scrutinised as the Sharia law and courts feature prominently in it. A secular Constitution would not have accorded a religious law such degree of recognition and validation. In addition, the involvement of governments in religious activities at all levels fail to portray Nigeria as a secular nation. State resources are often used to sponsor government officials and private persons on pilgrimage to both Mecca and Jerusalem. These are religious obligations of individual believers for which state resources ought not to be applied except in moderate measures of providing pilgrims security and other minimal logistic support. Again, the failure of the Federal Government of Nigeria to file a suit at the Supreme Court against the actions of some Northern States in the early 2000s introducing penal Sharia laws in their States in spite of the provisions of CRFN 1999, ss 10 and 36 (12) which run contrary to such religious laws appears to support the argument that Nigeria is not a secular nation. Between 1999 and 2004, a number of Northern States such as Zamfara, Kano, Katsina, and Kebbi had introduced penal aspects of Sharia law in their respective States. See also Hon. Justice Kayode Eso, CON, "Law, Religion and A Secular State" in Hon. Justice Kayode Eso, CON, *Thoughts on Law and Jurisprudence* (MIJ Professional Publishers Limited 1990) 291-305

of grounds. Monogamy[23] appears to enjoy greater recognition and protection under the law. One obvious instance of legal protection for monogamous marriage, also known as statutory marriage, is in the area of its dissolution. Polygamous marriage may either be dissolved extra-judicially[24] or by judicial means.[25] In contrast, dissolution of a monogamous marriage can only occur by judicial means.[26] Unlike a polygamous marriage which may be dissolved for any reason or no reason at

---

[23]In appropriate contexts in this paper, monogamy or monogamous marriage is used interchangeably with statutory marriage.
[24]Both Islamic and customary marriages can be dissolved without a court order. In the case of Islamic marriage, a spouse may pronounce on the other spouse "I divorce you" three times consecutively and the marriage will stand dissolved. This practice is known as *talaq*. As regards customary marriage, it may be dissolved without the judicial process when a man hands over his wife to her parents or family members and a woman may also dissolve it by returning the bride price paid over her by her husband back to him. Despite that both Islamic and customary marriages may be dissolved extra-judicially, persons married under them do have reasons to file for judicial dissolution especially where claims for child custody and maintenance are involved.
[25]Petitions for the dissolution of Islamic and customary marriages are entertained by Sharia and customary courts respectively and not by a High Court which is regarded as an "English" court.
[26]High Courts excluding Federal High Court are the only courts empowered to dissolve statutory marriage in Nigeria. They are courts established by the Constitution which also defines qualifications of persons who may preside over such courts, their jurisdiction and powers, among others. See generally CFRN 1999, s 270

all, though subject to the type of such polygamous marriage,[27] a monogamous marriage must be shown to have broken down irretrievably. While the protection offered monogamous marriages is good in that it offers some degree of stability in homes, it is argued that facts constituting circumstances for its dissolution be expanded to permit couples who have other reasons for asking for divorce outside those stipulated in section 15 (2) Matrimonial Causes Act (MCA)[28] to do so through judicial process. Adding new but less stringent conditions to the existing requirements for dissolution of marriage does not mean that the Nigerian State can no longer keep the sanctity of marriage as the dissolution of marriage must still pass through the judicial process and on the other hand, the new conditions will give couples greater control in deciding when to remain in marriage or when to opt out with minimal legal impediments.

---

[27]Mutual agreement to dissolve a marriage is allowed in both Islamic and customary marriages and both marriages can be dissolved for any reason or no reason at all, though where reasons are given for divorce, different reasons avail in the two marriages, that is, Islamic and customary marriages. In Islamic divorce, mutual consent of a couple to dissolve their marriage is known as *Khula*.

[28]Matrimonial Causes Act, Cap. M7, Laws of the Federation of Nigeria 2004

Types of marriage

Nigeria is a federation[29] comprising thirty-six states and Abuja as the Federal Capital Territory. In many ways, Nigeria is a pluralistic society,[30] especially as it relates to her religious and ethnic composition, and legal systems. S. Ayooluwa St. Emmanuel writes, 'Nigeria's legal system is composed of three sources.'[31] By 'three sources,'[32] the author means the received English law, customary law, and Islamic law.[33] The classifica-

---

[29]Nigeria is a federation because she embraced a federal system of government in 1954 which is in practice till date, though in the 1960s, unitary system was briefly introduced by the Government of General Johnson Aguiyi-Ironsi. See Emmanuel Ibiam Amah, 'Federalism, Nigerian Federal Constitution and the Practice of Federalism: An Appraisal' (2017) 8 (3) Beijing Law Review

[30]Nigeria is home to three dominant religions of Islam, Christianity, and African traditional religion in addition to diverse ethnic groups with different languages and dialects. The country is said to consist of more than 250 ethnic nationalities. See The People <https://foreignaffairs.gov.ng/nigeria/the-people/> accessed 3 October 2023

[31]S. Ayooluwa St. Emmanuel, 'Legal Pluralism: An Examination of Conflicting Standards in Statutory, Customary and Islamic Law Marriage in Nigeria' (2021) 4 (1) Ajayi Crowther University Law Journal 3

[32]ibid, 2-3

[33]A. A. Oba appears to agree with the approaches which classifies the Nigerian law into three different systems. Oba wrote, 'Perhaps the most important expression of legal pluralism in the country is that not only the type of legal regime is applicable in the country. Rather, English style law (common law), Islamic law, and customary law apply variously.' See AA Oba, 'Islamic Law as a Customary Law: The Changing Perspective in Nigeria' (2002) 51 (4) International and Comparative Law Quarterly. Even though Oba expressed his views in 2002, his position is valid till date as regards the current state of the Nigerian law.

tion of the Nigerian law into three sources, each of which is a distinct system of law, forms the basis why some writers[34] claim Nigeria has three types of marriage, while some argue they are two.[35]

Types of marriage in Nigeria may be grouped into two or three, depending on how they are viewed. When viewed in terms of their nature, they are polygamous and monogamous marriages. If considered, on the other hand, in relation to the law governing their celebration and validity, they are statutory marriage, Islamic marriage, and customary marriage. While both Islamic and customary marriages are potentially polygamous[36] in nature, statutory marriage is necessarily monogamous. Olokooba S. M., in his paper,[37] classified types of mar-

---

[34]See ON Ogbu, *Modern Nigerian Legal System* (CIDJAP Press 2007) 91-92

[35]See EI Nwogugu, *Family Law in Nigeria* (3rd Edition, HEBN Publishers Plc 2014) 4-5

[36]See n 14

[37]SM Olokooba, 'Analysis of Legal Issues Involved in the Termination of "Double-Decker"' Marriage under Nigeria Law" (2007-2010) 7 Nigeria Current Law Report 3

riage in Nigeria into two,[38] monogamous and polygamous. For

---

[38]It appears those who classify types of marriage into two do so on account of their position on the sources of the Nigerian law in which case they classify Islamic law as part of customary law, while those who classify marriages into three seem to separate Islamic law from customary law. Nwogugu is one of the writers who subscribe to the idea of two types of marriage in Nigeria. See EI Nwogugu, *Family Law in Nigeria* (3rd Edition, HEBN Publishers Plc 2014) 4-5. See also Ikechukwu D Uzo, *Guide to Matrimonial Proceedings: With Matrimonial Causes Act and Rules* (2nd Edition, Law Digest Publishing Co 2012) 2-3. However, Nasiru Tijani in his book, Matrimonial Causes in Nigeria: Law and Practice, does not appear to take a clear position regarding the types of marriage in Nigeria. At page 2 of the book, he writes, "In Nigeria two systems of marriage are recognised." Again, at page 4 of the same book, he writes, "It is therefore clear from this Constitutional provision that three forms of marriage are recognised in Nigeria..." The author made this assertion on account of Item 61 in the Exclusive Legislative List. See Nasiru Tijani, *Matrimonial Causes in Nigeria: Law and Practice* (2nd Edition, Renaissance Law Publishers Limited 2017) 2-4. On the other hand, it is interesting to note the provision of the Evidence Act 2011, s 258 which defines wife and husband to mean "...respectively the wife and husband of a marriage validly contracted under the Marriage Act, or under Islamic law or a Customary law applicable in Nigeria..." the Same-Sex Marriage (Prohibition) Act 2013, s 7 defines marriage as "...a legal union entered into between persons of opposite sex in accordance with the Marriage Act, Islamic law or Customary Law..." It seems that on the basis of the Constitution and other statutes, it is more correct to claim that Nigeria has three types of marriage rather than two.

those who classify types of marriage into three,[39] the Constitution[40] constitutes one of their sources of legal support. In the Constitution, it is stated thus, 'The formation, annulment and dissolution of marriages other than marriages under Islamic law and Customary law including matrimonial causes relating thereto.'[41] Apart from the constitutional recognition given to the three marriages, only statutory marriage is placed under the legislative competence of the National Assembly.[42]

Statutory marriage originates from the inherited English law; Islamic marriage is from Islamic/Sharia law which applies mainly in the Northern part of Nigeria, while customary marriage emanates from customary law, being the native law and customs mainly in force in Southern Nigeria. These marriages co-exist in Nigeria and citizens are at liberty to contract any of them, though it is unlawful to combine a statutory marriage with any other type,[43] being a monogamous marriage. Statutory marriage is a marriage celebrated in compliance with the re-

---

[39]See the Same-Sex Marriage (Prohibition) Act 2013, s 7. See also Andreas Rahmatian, 'Termination of Marriage in Nigerian Family Laws: The Need for Reform and the Relevance of the Tanzanian Experience' (1996) 10 International Journal of Law, Policy and the Family

[40]CFRN 1999

[41]Item 61, Second Schedule, Part 1, CFRN 1999. Legislative lists in the Constitution are two, that is, the Exclusive Legislative List and Concurrent Legislative List. While the former contains matters over which only the National Assembly can legislate, the latter is a list of matters within the legislative competence of both the National Assembly and States' Houses of Assembly.

[42]ibid

[43]By virtue of the Marriage Act, ss 39, 46, and 47 and the Criminal Code, s 370, anyone who does so may be charged with bigamy.

quirements of a valid marriage[44] as spelt out in the Marriage Act[45] and for the dissolution of this type of marriage, it is the MCA[46] which is the applicable law.

Current State of Law on Dissolution of Marriage

Prior to the passage of the Matrimonial Causes Act which came into force in 1970,[47] Nigerian courts would always resort to any divorce legislation in force in England, which changed

---

[44]Some of the requirements of a valid marriage are single status of a person entering into it, the marriage ceremony to be witnessed by at least two witnesses and mutual consent of each party to it.

[45]Marriage Act, Cap. M6, Laws of the Federation of Nigeria 2004

[46]Both the Marriage Act and MCA are federal statutes. They are subjects under the Exclusive Legislative List over which only the National Assembly can legislate as distinct from Islamic and customary marriages where state legislative houses are competent to legislate. See Item 61, Second Schedule, Part I, CFRN 1999. Given that both statutory marriage and its dissolution are federal matters, any person who wishes to petition for its dissolution can present the petition in any state of the federation irrespective of where couples involved or any of them resides, although occasions may arise where an application can be made for transfer of a petition filed in one state to another state which is considered more convenient for parties to the case. Courts seized of such matters are usually disposed to order their transfer.

[47]The Matrimonial Causes Act 1970 was the first legislation locally promulgated by the Nigerian legislators to govern matrimonial matters such as dissolution of marriage, nullity of marriage, judicial separation, etc., since the English system of monogamous marriage was introduced to Nigeria through the Marriage Act, although the matrimonial legislation essentially copied the provisions of the English Divorce Reform Act of 1969.

from time to time. Before 1970, the English divorce law was based on the matrimonial offence theory,[48] which required a petition for dissolution of marriage to be brought upon the commission of such matrimonial offences by one of the spouses as cruelty, adultery, and desertion. As Nigeria changed her direction in the early 70s with the passage of MCA, likewise England enacted her own Matrimonial Causes Act in 1973. Both the Nigerian and English MCAs made "irretrievable breakdown" as an omnibus ground for dissolution of marriage. While section 15 (2) of Nigeria's MCA has eight conditions[49] for dissolution of marriage, section 1 (2) of the English MCA had five conditions.[50] However, England recently jettisoned the provision of section 1 (2) MCA by substituting it with section 1 (1) of the Divorce, Dissolution and Separation Act (DDSA) 2020,[51] a new legislation, which came into force on 6 April 2022. With DDSA, England has become another jurisdiction of

---

[48]Michael Attah and Linda Osagie, 'Reforming the Irretrievable Breakdown Rule – Historical Perspectives from Common Law Jurisdictions and Lessons from Nigeria' (2020) 11 (1) Nnamdi Azikiwe University Journal of International Law and Jurisprudence 3

[49]The eight conditions are discussed in details below.

[50]The five conditions are adultery, unreasonable behaviour, two years of desertion, living apart for two years, and living apart for five years. See MCA 1973, s 1 (2) (a) – (e).

[51]See Katie O'Kelly, 'Five key changes introduced by the Divorce, Dissolution and Separation Act 2020' (Russell Cooke, 8 April 2022) <https://www.russell-cooke.co.uk/news-and-insights/news/five-key-changes-introduced-by-the-divorce-dissolution-and-separation-act-2020-no-fault-divorce> accessed 21 November 2023

'no-fault' divorce law system[52] where couples seeking dissolution of their marriages do not have to provide reasons for wanting a divorce. It is enough they state that their marriage has broken down irretrievably and the marriage will be pronounced dissolved by a court.

Unlike the current English DDSA, "irretrievable breakdown" as the sole ground for dissolution of marriage under Nigeria's MCA continues to apply whereby a party seeking dissolution of a marriage has to convince a court of one or more conditions contained in section 15 (2) (a) to (h) MCA. One of the obvious consequences of this system is that the Nigerian law makes divorce more difficult to obtain in Nigeria than it is now the case in England.[53] Again, the demands of the law to obtain a divorce often turn estranged couples to more bitter enemies. In view of certain key provisions of the MCA, Nigeria cannot claim to have substantially moved away from the old concept of matrimonial offence theory, although the phrase "matrimonial offence" is not used in the country's MCA. To paint a clear picture of the legal requirements to obtain a dissolution of a statutory marriage in Nigeria, it is necessary to reproduce *verbatim* the provisions of sections 15 (1) and (2), and 30 (1) MCA for a more detailed discussion and analysis. Section 30 (1) being a condition precedent before a petition can be entertained at all, it is logical to quote it first while section 15 (1) and (2) follows:

Section 30 (1):

---

[52]No-fault divorce system enables couples who apply for divorce in court to obtain a divorce order without providing evidence to establish the wrongdoings of any of them as a condition for the grant of divorce No-fault divorce system is common with all the States of America.

[53]It is interesting to note that England which exported her monogamous marriage system to Nigeria has relaxed her divorce law but the latter is still keeping her own rigid divorce law.

Subject to this section, proceedings for a decree of dissolution of marriage shall not be instituted within two years after the date of the marriage, except by leave of the court.

15 (1):

A petition under this Act by a party to a marriage for a decree of dissolution of the marriage may be presented to the court by either party to the marriage upon the ground that the marriage has broken down irretrievably.

15 (2):

The court hearing a petition for a decree of dissolution of a marriage shall hold the marriage to have broken down irretrievably if, but only if, the petitioner satisfies the court of one or more of the following facts:

that the respondent has wilfully and persistently refused to consummate the marriage;

that since the marriage the respondent has committed adultery and the petitioner finds it intolerable to live with the respondent;

that since the marriage the respondent has behaved in such a way that the petitioner cannot reasonably be expected to live with the respondent;

that the respondent has deserted the petitioner for a continuous period of at least one year immediately preceding the presentation of the petition;

that the parties to the marriage have lived apart for a continuous period of at least two years immediately preceding the presentation of the petition and the respondent does not object to a decree being granted;

that the parties to the marriage have lived apart for a continuous period of at least three years immediately preceding the presentation of the petition;

that the other party to the marriage has, for a period of not less than one year, failed to comply with a decree or restitution of conjugal rights made under this Act;

that the other party to the marriage has been absent from the petitioner for such time and in such circumstances as to provide reasonable grounds for presuming that he or she is dead.

Application of Two-Year Rule

Section 30 (1) is otherwise known as the "two-year rule" meaning that persons who desire to terminate their marriage within two years of being married are barred from presenting a petition to court without first applying for leave of court and obtaining an order of court granting them the leave. However, under section 30 (2) there are six circumstances in which the need for leave will not be necessary before filing for divorce when a person has not been in marriage for two years. Section 30 (2) provides, 'Nothing in this section shall apply to the institution of proceedings based on any of the matters specified in section 15 (2) (a) or (b) or 16 (1) (a) of this Act, or to the institution of proceedings for a decree of dissolution of marriage by way of cross-proceedings.'

By virtue of the quoted section 30 (2), the wordings clearly show that where lack of consummation of marriage,[54] adultery,[55] rape,[56] sodomy,[57] bestiality[58] is involved or where a cross-proceeding/cross-petition[59] is filed in response to a petition, the two-year rule in section 30 (1) will not be activated. In other words, the two-year rule is only applicable when the basis of a divorce petition rests on any of the conditions or a combination of conditions in section 15 (2) (c), (d) and (g). As regards section 15 (2) (e), (f) and (h), the two-year rule does not also apply at all because a marriage would not have been less than two years in such situations, although these circumstances are not specifically exempted by section 30 (2). However, notwithstanding situations not covered by the two-year rule, the rule still constitutes a serious constraint where only reasons for desiring a divorce relate to unreasonable behaviour

---

[54]MCA, s 30 (2). However, the Act does not specify the length of time within which a spouse may present a petition based on lack of consummation of marriage. Does it mean that a petition for lack of consummation may be brought if a request or two are made for sexual intercourse and the other spouse refuses to allow it within a month of being married? It is reasoned that a petition for lack of consummation within a month of marriage may be entertained by court as the Act seems to confer the liberty on individuals to determine how long or short, they can endure or not endure a marriage without sexual intercourse since its inception.

[55]Under s 30 (2), like lack of consummation of marriage, the two-year rule does not apply where a spouse commits adultery. It follows that an aggrieved spouse can present a petition for dissolution of marriage upon the occurrence of one incident of adultery which happens few days after a marriage celebration as long as there is evidence to prove it in court.

[56]MCA, s 30 (2) and 16 (1) (a)

[57]ibid

[58]ibid

[59]MCA, s 30 (2)

of a spouse,[60] desertion of a spouse for less than two years[61] or where a spouse fails to comply with an order of restitution of conjugal rights.[62]

The provision in section 30 (1) imposes two options on persons who want to terminate their marriage before two years of entering into it and whose situation falls outside any of the exceptional circumstances under section 30 (2) or 15 (2) (e), (f) and (h) in which they can present their petition for dissolution of marriage without first applying for leave. The two options require they either endure a failed marriage for two years after contracting it before presenting a petition for its dissolution or to apply for leave, whose success in court is not guaranteed because so much depends on a judge's discretion.[63] For those who cannot endure the trauma of their failed marriage for two "long" years before terminating it, then they have to apply for leave.[64] Applying for leave implies that such persons have to

---

[60]MCA, s 15 (2) (c)

[61]ibid, s 15 (2) (e)

[62]ibid, s 15 (2) (g)

[63]MCA, s 30 (3) provides – "The court shall not grant leave under this section to institute proceedings except on the ground that to refuse to grant the leave would impose exceptional hardship on the applicant or that the case is one involving exceptional depravity on the part of the other party to the marriage." The Act fails to define what is meant by "exceptional hardship" or "exceptional depravity" which means an individual Judge has the discretion to determine what amounts to any of these in each case. Although Judges may be guided by decisions of higher courts on similar matters, the place of their discretion is not eliminated.

[64]MCA, s 30 (1)

embark on two litigations[65] – one to obtain leave and the other to file for the real dissolution of their marriage, provided the application for leave succeeds[66] in the first place. Two litigations entail incurring more expenses than would have been incurred if only a petition for dissolution was undertaken. Many financially weak persons will be unable to undertake two litigations. Again, given the notorious slow-pace of administration of justice in Nigeria,[67] anyone who applies for leave may end up spending two years in court before obtaining the leave itself, which means the system indirectly forces people to endure failed marriages for two years before applying for their dissolution.

An Overview of the Ground and Facts for Dissolution of Marriage

Section 15 (1) introduces the concept of irretrievable breakdown, although it is nowhere defined in the Act. It is in reading of section 15 (1) along with 15 (2) that the full import of the former provision becomes clearer. In other words, a petitioner does not have to prove that a marriage has broken down irre-

---

[65]By virtue of MCA, s 30 (3) and the Matrimonial Causes Rules (MCR) 1983, Order IV Rules 1 and 2 two separate suits have to take place. Leave must first be obtained by an *ex parte* application and divorce petition will be filed pursuant to MCR 1983, Order V Rules 1.

[66]A community reading of section 30 (1) and other sub-sections of the section shows that an application for leave to file a divorce petition before a marriage exists for two years may either fail or succeed.

[67]Mojeed Olujinmi A Alabi, "'Justice Denied': Problems and Prospects of Decongesting the Supreme Court of Nigeria" (2005) 3 (2) Nigerian Bar Journal 3

trievably but rather to prove a fact or more as contained in section 15 (2) (a) to (h) and upon such proof, the court shall hold that the marriage has broken down irretrievably. Thus, the idea of irretrievable breakdown appears unnecessary, as it cannot stand on its own. Submitting on the meaninglessness of the concept, Itse Sagay argues, 'It is clear that the irretrievable breakdown provision in Section 15 (1) is just an empty form of words, a ritual phrase that is tagged on to every real ground – those contained in Section 15 (2) and 16 (1).'[68] In section 15 (2) (a) to (h) are eight situations, each of which, if proved, can form the basis for a court to order the dissolution of a marriage. These situations make the Nigerian divorce law to qualify for being labelled "fault-based"[69] divorce. Of the eight, only two circumstances can be classified as 'no-fault'[70] divorce, and they are living apart for three years[71] and presumption of death.[72] This means that for each of the other six situations, a petitioner has to produce evidence to prove wrongdoings of the other spouse to be able to secure a divorce. It is reasoned that the State's interests in protecting the marriage institution is be-

---

[68]Itse Sagay, *Nigerian Family Law: Principles, Cases, Statutes and Commentaries* (Malthouse Press Ltd 1999) 137

[69]Fault-based divorce requires persons who present petitions for marriage dissolution to provide the wrongdoings of the other party as the basis of their divorce petitions.

[70]No-fault divorce law was first introduced in the State of California in 1969 and subsequently, all the remaining States in the United States of America followed suit. No-fault divorce legislation allows couples to present petitions for the dissolution of their marriages without proving wrongdoings of their spouses or giving any reason at all for wanting a divorce. See Denese Ashbaugh Vlosky and Pamela A. Monroe, 'The Effective Dates of No-Fault Divorce Laws in the 50 States' (2002) 51 (4) Family Relations 3

[71]MCA, s 15 (2) (f)

[72]ibid, s 15 (2) (h)

ing taken too far when persons who voluntarily enter into it cannot freely exit it without 'washing… their dirty linen in the open'[73] at the end of which their relationship is damaged beyond repairs. As regards living apart for two years,[74] a petition based on it can only succeed without proving the other spouse's wrongdoings, if the other spouse is not opposing the petition.

Experience shows that the majority of persons who want to opt out of their marriage in court do not wish to disclose details of their reasons for wanting a divorce, provided they can achieve what they want without doing so. However, by reason of the provisions of section 15 (1) and (2), couples who want a divorce must present a petition in court and give oral or documentary evidence to show that their marriage has broken down irretrievably especially on such accounts as lack of consummation,[75] adultery,[76] unreasonable behaviour,[77] desertion of at least one year,[78] living apart for two years,[79] or disobedience of restitution order.[80] Each time a petition is premised on any of these situations, sordid accounts of unwholesome conduct of spouses are often rendered in open court, where strangers can listen and hear what should be treated as secrets between husbands and wives. However, many persons have had to reluctantly render details in court of how their spouses fail to consummate their marriage due to physical or biological inability which was concealed before marriage and in some other cases,

---

[73]See the case of *Oguntoyinbo v. Oguntoyinbo* (2017) LPELR-42174 (CA)
[74]MCA, s 15 (2) (e)
[75]MCA, s 15 (2) (a)
[76]ibid, s 15 (2) b)
[77]ibid, s 15 (2) (c)
[78]ibid, s 15 (2) (d)
[79]ibid, s 15 (2) (e)
[80]ibid, s 15 (2) (g)

details of adulterous acts of spouses have been provided, while it is a series of unreasonable behaviour in others.

For those who want divorce in any of the six situations and do not wish to provide details of their spouses' wrongdoings in court in the attempt to convince the court that their marriage has truly broken down irretrievably, they may choose to stay out of marriage without having any relationship with the other spouse for good three years. This appears a difficult path, as many consider three years of living apart and living single not to be convenient. In reality, however, many who desire a divorce and cannot stay without entering into another marriage (or for any other reasons) for three solid years have devised some ingenuous means, though usually unlawful and unethical, to obtain their divorce as quick as possible.

Some persons choose to predicate their petition for dissolution of marriage on a series of falsehood[81] which may include claims of desertion by the other spouse for three years or filing a divorce petition based on unreasonable behaviour of the other spouse, for instance, though without serving the other spouse with their petition. One of the improper ways this is done is by using a wrong address for the other spouse, in which case evidence of service will be produced in court to satisfy the requirement of putting the other party on notice, though the other party will not be in court for genuinely not being aware of the pending case. Some other persons will enter into an agreement with another person different from the real spouse so as to impersonate the actual spouse. Where this is done, the impersonator will come to court and choose not to oppose the petition. All these are probably done to avert disclosing details of the

---

[81]Also, in some cases, unlawful means by which people obtain divorce include paying for divorce certificates. Some persons who want to dissolve their marriage because they have entered into another relationship which is more promising may go to the extent of patronising corrupt court officials to obtain fake court documents dissolving their marriages. They need to dissolve the existing marriage in order to formalise another one with a different person when they know that the existing conditions for divorce in Nigeria do not apply to their circumstances. This is common with married people who want to marry other persons outside Nigeria especially in places such as the United Kingdom, Canada or United States of America for obvious reasons and to obtain divorce, they deploy unlawful means or concoct series of lies. However, some persons who toe this path only divorce their spouses on paper as they continue to maintain conjugal relationships with their spouses, either virtually or physically. Some 'divorced' spouses in this situation are aware of and privy to what the other spouse has done for survival purpose, while some other spouses do not know, totally unaware of any illegally obtained divorce judgments or certificates against their marriage.

degeneration in their marriage in open court to the hearing of others, or to achieve a divorce without acrimony. In some others, it may be because they want a divorce, despite the fact that their reasons for divorce do not fall into any of the six or eight circumstances recognised for presenting a divorce petition in Nigeria.

In *Kizito Adetokunbo Taiwo v. Felicitas Adedayo Taiwo*,[82] the Appellate Court of Maryland found that a divorce petition initiated in Nigeria by Mr. Taiwo against his wife was served at a Nigerian address which the wife had not visited in twenty years. The Court refused to regard the service as proper and also did not allow the husband to use the excuse of the earlier divorce petition initiated in Nigeria against the one started by the wife against him in the United States. Experience has shown that many times when parties initiating divorce petitions serve their petitions at "the last known address or place of abode" of opposing parties, it is often because they do not want parties purportedly served to become aware of the pending matter and not because the current address is unknown to them or that they honestly believe parties served will become aware of such cases through the last known address.

An Analysis of Section 15 (2) (a) to (h)

A more careful review of each factual situation in section 15 (2) will help to provide a clearer picture of their meanings based on judicial attitude and approach in adjudicating matrimonial proceedings as deduced from decided cases. In applying for divorce, it is enough if a petitioner predicates his or her

---

[82]Circuit Court for Baltimore County (2022) <https://www.md-courts.gov/sites/default/files/unreported-opinions/0069s22.pdf> accessed 12 October 2023

petition on any or a combination of situations contained in section 15 (2) (a) to (h), though in practice petitions are commonly brought on the basis of more than one factual situation; so, if one situation fails, the other may succeed. However, in some cases, none may succeed. Each situation in section 15 (2) is now serially discussed below:

Lack of consummation (s. 15 (2) (a))

In section 15 (2) (a), a petition may be presented in court on the basis "that the respondent has willfully and persistently refused to consummate the marriage;" but the Act fails to define what is meant by "consummation" or "to consummate the marriage". In interpreting this provision, courts have defined consummation[83] to mean the first sexual intercourse that a couple have since they are married. In other words, in determining whether consummation of a marriage has taken place, courts will consider if a couple have had a sexual relationship from the time they are married and when a divorce petition premised on lack of consummation is presented in court. It is immaterial if sexual intercourse happens only once, despite the long period of time that a couple are married. Where sexual intercourse takes place between two people before they marry each other and none has taken place since they are married, it will be taken that no consummation has taken place since they are married.

---

[83]*Adetunji v. Adetunji,* suit no. FCT/HC/PET/101/2011 (Unreported) High Court of the Federal Capital Territory, Apo Abuja Judicial Division, M. A. Nasir J., 8 July 2013, the Court defines consummation thus, "To consummate a marriage means to bring to completion, especially to make a marriage complete by sexual intercourse." In *Black's Law Dictionary,* 359, consummation of marriage is defined as 'The first post-marital act of sexual intercourse between a husband and wife.'

From reported cases,[84] it appears, in some instances, that lack of consummation is confused with cessation of cohabitation. Although cessation of cohabitation can be linked to desertion or living apart, it is not related to lack of consummation. It is not enough that a petitioner pleads that there is no consummation since marriage, it is required that such a petitioner further pleads and provides evidence showing that a respondent refuses consummation in spite of requests for it. In *Owobiyi v. Owobiyi*,[85] the Court refused to dissolve the marriage between the petitioner and the respondent on the basis of lack of consummation of marriage as it was held that there was no evidence that the petitioner made requests for consummation to the respondent. However, in *Imianvan v. Imianvan*,[86] the Court believed the unchallenged evidence of the petitioner that there was no sexual intercourse between her and the respondent who refused to consummate their marriage despite that the petitioner reported him to his family members.

---

[84]ibid. In the case, the Court refused the divorce petition in that the petitioner failed to convince the Court that her marriage was not consummated. The Court premised its decision on a finding that both the petitioner and the respondent have a five-year-old child since they were married. In this case, it seems the petitioner confused cessation of cohabitation for lack of consummation. However, the Court went ahead to dissolve the marriage on the basis that the couple have lived apart for not less than three years despite that the petition was not presented on that ground. The order of the Court seems to run contrary to a settled principle of law to the effect that courts do not grant prayers that parties fail to seek.

[85](1965) 2 All NLR 200. It is noted that this case was decided prior to 1970 when the MCA came into force, although the principle followed in it remains valid till date.

[86]FCT/HC/PET/170/2012 (Unreported) High Court of the Federal Capital Territory, Abuja Judicial Division, M. A. Nasir J., 20 November 2013

Adultery (s. 15 (2) (b))

As regards predicating a divorce petition on the allegation of adultery, section 15 (2) (b) states 'that since the marriage the respondent has committed adultery and the petitioner finds it intolerable to live with the respondent...' Nigerian courts have ascribed to adultery its ordinary meaning, which is a voluntary sexual intercourse between a married person and another person not married to that person. Nwogugu in his book[87] argues that sexual intercourse must be one between two persons of the opposite sex and not between two homosexuals. While this argument appears strong, it may only be so in Nigeria and other places where same-sex relationship is outlawed. As the definition of marriage has expanded in some places, it is logical that adultery as a basis for divorce will be applicable to homosexual marriages as it is to heterosexual marriages in jurisdictions where same-sex marriage is legal. It is, however, reasoned that where sexual intercourse occurs in Nigeria between two persons of the same sex in which one of them is married to a different person, allegation of adultery as a basis for divorce in such instance may fail, although the same conduct may successfully be cited as an act of unreasonable behaviour under section 15 (2) (c). Again, where sexual intercourse takes place against the will of a spouse as in the case of rape, the allegation of adultery cannot stand.

To ground a divorce petition on the allegation of adultery, it is required to also plead that a petitioner finds it intolerable to live with the adulterous spouse, the respondent, as the failure to state that is fatal to the success of the petition. Adultery must have taken place during the period of marriage and not prior to it. In many cases, petitioners who allege adultery against their spouses are unable to prove the allegation for one reason or

[87]E. I. Nwogugu, (n 36) 178

another. In some cases, the failure of proof is due to lack of evidence, as direct evidence of adultery is often difficult to have. In some others, a petition premised on adultery may fail as a result of one technical error or another. For instance, it is required by section 32 (1) MCA[88] that whenever a petition is founded on adultery, a party with whom adultery is allegedly committed by the other spouse must be joined in the petition. Even if a party confesses to adultery, the allegation will be considered unproved where a co-adulterer is not joined in a petition as a party.

In *Aguolu v. Aguolu*,[89] the Court refused to grant the husband's divorce petition of the petitioner on account of adultery allegedly committed by his wife because the petitioner only alleged marital unfaithfulness instead of specifically pleading adultery,[90] joining the co-adulterer and pleading further that he found it intolerable to continue to live with his wife. However, the divorce was granted on the ground of unreasonable behaviour of the wife, who aborted her pregnancy without the petitioner's consent. Contrastingly, in *Erhahon v. Erhahon*,[91] the Court held that the petitioner committed adultery as alleged by his wife in her cross-petition in that she joined three women with whom the petitioner committed adultery coupled with the evidence of four children that they had for him which he did not deny. The allegation of adultery was established in this case by reason of proof that the petitioner was the father of four children from the three women joined in the cross-petition as

---

[88]The only exception to this requirement is when the joinder is waived by the rules of court. See also *Ebe v. Ebe* (2004) 3 NWLR Pt. 860, 215
[89]FCT/HC/PET/47/2011 (unreported) High Court of the Federal Capital Territory, Apo Abuja Judicial Division, M. A. Nasir J., 16 January 2013
[90]ibid. See also *Obajimi v. Obajimi* (2011) LPELR-4665
[91](1997) 6 NWLR Pt. 510, 667

co-adulterers. Even though he was not found having sexual relations with any of the women, it is naturally deducible that sexual intercourse must have preceded childbirth. The marriage was therefore dissolved on the strength of the wife's cross-petition and not the husband's petition.

Unreasonable behaviour (s. 15 (2) (c))

While section 15 (2) (c) simply provides thus, "that since the marriage the respondent has behaved in such a way that the petitioner cannot reasonably be expected to live with the respondent...", section 16 (1) supplies a long list of conduct which may amount to unreasonable behaviour of a respondent that a petitioner may find intolerable to endure. Although conduct of unreasonable behaviour stipulated in section 16 (1) is not exhaustive, examples of behaviour contained in the section include bestiality, rape, habitual drunkenness, criminal acts, imprisonment, insanity, and violence. Other forms of behaviour which may qualify as unreasonable, though not specifically provided in section 16 (1), are: destruction of a spouse's educational credentials, emotional abuse, a spouse fond of fighting with neighbours, abortion of pregnancy without the consent of the other spouse, among others.

Once an alleged unreasonable behaviour is proved to the satisfaction of the court, a marriage may likely be dissolved. The test for determining the unreasonableness of a spouse's behaviour is usually objective, as the court will consider whether a right-thinking person can be expected to tolerate a respondent's conduct complained of.[92] For a conduct deemed unreasonable by a spouse to ground a divorce petition, such conduct must have taken place from the time of marriage, not one before the marriage. This factual situation as a basis for divorce is

---

[92]See *Nanna v. Nanna* (2006) 3 NWLR Pt. 966, 1

one of the commonest reasons in the divorce judgments examined in this study, and the success rate is relatively high in relation to marriages held by courts to have broken down irretrievably for the reason of this fact.[93]

In *Olugbebi v. Olugbebi*,[94] the Court granted the petitioner's prayer for dissolution of his marriage with the respondent on account of his evidence that his wife was fond of drinking alcohol, coming home late-, and frequenting-night clubs. The behaviour of the wife was considered unreasonable, for which the husband could not be expected to continue to tolerate. Also, in *Aguolu v. Aguolu*,[95] the Court held that the action of the wife terminating a 5-month-old pregnancy without the consent of the petitioner was considered unreasonable behaviour and the marriage was dissolved on that account. However, unlike the cases of Olugbebi and Aguolu, the Court in *Amaizemen v.*

---

[93]In the course of this research, 50 divorce judgments consisting of decisions of High Courts of the Federal Capital Territory, Abuja and High Court of Benin, Edo State were reviewed on their websites and ten percent of these decisions were based on unreasonable behaviour of a spouse alone. See Court Judgments, <https://www.fcthighcourt.gov.ng/the-family-court/current-cases-submissions/> accessed 16 October 2023 and Archive: Matrimonial Cases, <https://edojudiciary.gov.ng/category/judgements/matrimonial-cases/> accessed 16 October 2023. This author searched the Internet for judgments from other Nigerian States but only the Edo State High Court and the High Court of the Federal Capital Territory, Abuja have their divorce judgments uploaded online.

[94]FCT/HC/PET/188/2012, High Court of the Federal Capital Territory, Apo Abuja Judicial Division, M. A. Nasir J., 4 June 2013

[95](n 80)

Amaizemen,[96] failed to rule in favour of the husband's allegation of unreasonable behaviour against his wife, the respondent. Instances cited for the unreasonable behaviour of his wife were her refusal of sex, reporting him to the Police for bigamy, and writing a petition to the American Embassy in opposition to his application for an American visa. Giving evidence in her defence, the respondent narrated how her husband abandoned her and the children for Dubai, where he entered into another marriage with an American woman, one Diane Uwadiale. The wife said she became aware of the marriage when her husband posted pictures of his new marriage on Facebook, as well as pictures of twins he and the American woman had together. She thereafter printed out the pictures and formally lodged a complaint of bigamy against the petitioner to the Police. She also narrated writing to the American Embassy to prevent the petitioner from eloping to America to join his 'wife.' Although the Court dissolved their marriage on finding that the petitioner and the respondent had been living apart for more than three years, the Court refused to be persuaded by the petitioner's allegation of unreasonable behaviour against the respondent. On the contrary, given the wife's evidence, the Court reasoned that the wife's behaviour was not unreasonable but rather that it was the behaviour of the husband which was unreasonable.

---

[96]HCU/7D/2016, High Court of Edo State, Uromi Judicial Division, A A Akhihiero J, 12 March 2019. Similarly, in the English case of *Owens v. Owens* [2018] UKSC 41, the Court refused to grant the divorce petition on the basis that the wife was not able to prove unreasonable behaviour of Mr. Owens to the Court's satisfaction. It is widely believed within the United Kingdom's legal circles that the circumstance of this case was one of the factors which precipitated the passage of DDSA 2020. See Sarah Trotter, "The State of Divorce Law" <https://eprints.lse.ac.uk/100740/3/Trotter_1601_FIN_FOR_LRO.pdf> accessed 23 November 2023

Desertion (s. 15 (2) (d))

Section 15 (2) (d) deals with desertion, and it states, 'that the respondent has deserted the petitioner for a continuous period of at least one year immediately preceding the presentation of the petition ...' A petitioner whose suit for divorce is premised on this factual situation has to prove that a respondent deserts the matrimonial home without the other spouse's consent and that the desertion has lasted for at least one year prior to the presentation of the divorce petition in court. In addition, it has to be proved that the one who deserts has the intention of bringing marriage and cohabitation to an end. Desertion may be actual or constructive.[97] It is actual when a person who deserts the other is also the guilty party, while constructive if the party deserted is the guilty spouse. For example, where a spouse deserts the matrimonial home due to the violence or any offensive conduct of the deserted party, it will be taken that the one who deserts is the innocent party. Only an innocent party can bring an action for divorce on account of desertion. In other words, a spouse who deserts the matrimonial home cannot bring a petition for divorce, unless it is a case of constructive desertion. However, in case an innocent party chooses not to file for divorce, the other spouse cannot file for it and has to

---

[97]Desertion is actual when a spouse leaves the other spouse and begins to live apart from the other spouse due to no fault of the latter. In the case of constructive desertion, section 18 MCA is applicable which provides thus:
A married person whose conduct constitutes just cause or excuse for the other party to the marriage to live separately or apart, and occasions that other party to live separately or apart, shall be deemed to have willfully deserted that other party without just cause or excuse, notwithstanding that that person may not in fact have intended the conduct to occasion that other party to live separately or apart.

wait for two or three years of living apart before bringing a petition for divorce under section 15 (2) (e) or 15 (2) (f).

In *Ajayi v. Ajayi*,[98] the husband brought an action for divorce on the ground of desertion of his wife. He gave evidence as to how his wife, the respondent, left the matrimonial home as if she were going to work and has since refused to return. Prior to her desertion, the woman was involved in a case of financial misappropriation in her office and the husband had to refund the amount involved because her employer decided to place a disclaimer against her in a newspaper. The husband felt embarrassed by what his wife did and the publicity it generated. Subsequently, their relationship degenerated. Without informing her husband, the woman left the matrimonial home and did not return even when the husband contacted her on phone. Finding that it was a clear case of desertion, the court dissolved their marriage.

Two years of living apart (s. 15 (2) (e))

Closely related to desertion is the provision of section 15 (2) (e) which states, "that the parties to the marriage have lived apart for a continuous period of at least two years immediately preceding the presentation of the petition and the respondent does not object to a decree being granted..." In this case, husband and wife must have stopped living together for at least two years. This condition is also similar to the provision of section 15 (2) (f) but a court can only dissolve a marriage under this ground if the other spouse is not opposed to dissolution. It is generally considered risky to predicate a divorce petition only on living apart for two years because, in addition to proving the number of years of living apart, the other spouse must

---

[98]FCT/HC/PET/174/2011, High Court of the Federal Capital Territory, Abuja Judicial Division, M. A. Nasr J., 15 May 2013

not be opposed to divorce. In other words, where the other spouse objects to the dissolution of marriage, a court cannot grant an order for divorce, unless it is found that the period of living apart is three years or more. In that case, the order of dissolution will be made pursuant to section 15 (2) (f) and not section 15 (2) (e).

In *Akinwande v. Akinwande*,[99] the wife petitioned for dissolution of marriage on the basis of living apart from her husband for two years. The court gave an order dissolving the marriage in view of the husband's agreement to dissolution of their marriage.

Three years of living apart (s. 15 (2) (f))

Like two years of living apart, section 15 (2) (f) provides for three years of living apart in these words, 'that the parties to the marriage have lived apart for a continuous period of at least three years immediately preceding the presentation of the petition…' However, unlike section 15 (2) (e), this provision is fully qualified as "no-fault" ground under the Nigerian divorce law as parties citing this as a basis for seeking dissolution of their marriage have no burden to prove the wrongdoings of the other spouse, although in practice evidence of wrongdoings is often provided. All that has to be proved is the commencement of desertion from one of the spouses or cessation of communication as husband and wife for a period not less than three years prior to the presentation of the divorce petition in court. If husband and wife live separately on account of the demands of their jobs, such will not qualify as living apart irrespective of the number of years, unless they provide evidence showing a collapse of their relationship during the period. When husband

---

[99]FCT/HC/PET/65/2010, High Court of the Federal Capital Territory, Abuja Judicial Division, M. A. Nasir J., 3 April 2013

and wife live in the same apartment, it is usually uncommon for a court to hold that they are living apart. When a couple have lived apart for three years, a court is bound to dissolve such a marriage even if one of them does not want a divorce.

In *Ahukannah v. Ahukannah*,[100] the husband filed a divorce petition against his wife. The petition was filed on 24th April 2009, while living apart started in July 2004. The husband gave evidence of circumstances leading to their living apart. He narrated how he agreed with his wife prior to their marriage that they would both be worshipping in Catholic denomination given that he was a Catholic and the wife was an Anglican but upon getting married, the wife reneged on their agreement. She started attending a different church. It was their inability to resolve their differences which culminated into the wife's decision to desert her husband. Under section 15 (2) (f), irrespective of which of the spouses is guilty of events leading to living apart, any of them can initiate divorce proceedings as soon as it is three years of living apart, and they desire a divorce or one of them desires it. Although living apart for three years without entering into another relationship may be difficult for many persons, filing a divorce suit on this basis is the surest means to successfully obtain a divorce order in Nigeria.

Non-compliance with an order of restitution of conjugal rights (s. 15 (2) (g))

By section 15 (2) (g), a divorce petition may be brought when '...the other party to the marriage has, for a period of not less than one year, failed to comply with a decree or restitution of conjugal rights made under this Act...' Out of the eight factual

---

[100]FCT/HC/PET/100/2009, High Court of the Federal Capital Territory, Abuja Judicial Division, I. M. Bukar J., 7 December 2011

situations for which a divorce petition may be predicated, this is one of the few rarely invoked situations to sue for divorce. The wordings of the section suggest the existence of a prior conflict in a marriage leading to the institution of a litigation in which the other spouse is ordered to resume conjugal relationship. It is interesting to note that failure to comply with a court order in this instance will only empower the innocent spouse to file for divorce instead of citing the spouse in disobedience of court order for contempt of court. It seems the law reckons with the fact that it takes two people to make a marriage work and when one of them is no longer interested in the union, no force of law can make such a marriage work.

Presumption of death (s. 15 (2) (h))

A divorce petition may be presented pursuant to section 15 (2) (h) which states thus, 'that the other party to the marriage has been absent from the petitioner for such time and in such circumstances as to provide reasonable grounds for presuming that he or she is dead.' To have a full understanding of this section, then section 16 (2) (a) and (b) MCA has to be read together with it. Thus, section 16 (2) (a) and (b) provides –

Where a petition is based on the fact mentioned in section 15 (2) (h) of this Act:

> *Proof that, for a period of seven years immediately preceding the date of the petition, the other party to the marriage was continually absent from the petitioner and that the petitioner has no reason to believe that the other party was alive at any time, within that period is sufficient to establish the fact in question, unless it is shown that the other party to the marriage was alive at a time within that period; and*

*A decree made pursuant to the petition shall be in
the form of a decree of dissolution of marriage by reason of presumption of death.*

Like section 15 (2) (g), a careful search through reported judicial authorities and available literature reveals that there is no
single reported judgment by Nigerian courts bordering on a
divorce petition predicated on this condition. It appears the
need for bringing a divorce petition on this basis may arise
where a spouse is missing without any conflict with the other
spouse. It is, however, difficult to imagine how any person
whose spouse is missing will wait for seven years before approaching a court for dissolution. Waiting for such length of
time may be easier for a person who is old and may no longer
think of remarrying. In that instance, it may be needless to apply for divorce. However, in the case of a young person, it may
not be unthinkable that people in such a situation will prefer to
file for divorce on account of living apart for three years, for
instance, without disclosing that the other spouse is missing
rather than to wait for seven years.

Apart from the rarity of people waiting for such a length of
time, it may be considered 'unAfrican' in this part of the world
that spouses in this situation will be disposed to ask courts to
presume their husbands or wives dead in their attempt to terminate marriages with their missing spouses. The fact that cases
are not found in this section may also speak to the "unAfrican-
ness" of the idea it promotes. No matter how long a person is
not seen, relatives of that person will prefer to believe that he
or she is alive somewhere and not dead. Rather than retaining
the redundant provision in the Act, it is better to replace it with
a condition which will enable a spouse to ask for divorce after
three years of not seeing the other spouse. The petition for divorce in this instance will be premised on the fact that the person not seen is missing, instead of presuming the person dead.

Arguments for the Reform of the Current State of Law on Dissolution of Marriage

Apart from strict requirements for dissolution of marriage which require people to gather evidence of wrongdoings of their spouses before they can obtain a judicial dissolution of their marriage, the list of situations for which a divorce petition may be brought is too limited. There are many other situations which wreck marriages and which inform some people's decisions for wanting to end their marriages, but unfortunately, such situations are not among the eight legally recognised circumstances in Nigeria. From a general studying of courts' judgments in Nigeria[101] and professional experience of this author as a practising lawyer of twenty years' standing coupled with information gathered from other professional colleagues, some other problems which beset people's marriages and for which they desire to terminate their marriages include cessation of love, incompatibility, childlessness, lack of sexual satisfaction, religious differences, lack of trust, laziness of a spouse, external influences, among others. Adding these to the existing conditions under section 15 (2), though some of the proposed conditions also entail recounting the wrongdoings of a spouse, will enable more people to be freed of unhappy, loveless and abusive marriages.

Given the limited reasons for which a petition for dissolution of marriage may be initiated, there are occasions when divorce cases have failed in courts even when both parties in such marriages want divorce but unable to prove their cases to the satis-

---

[101]The same MCA governs dissolution of statutory marriages in Nigeria nationwide; so, irrespective of States covered in relation to judgments discussed, the law is uniform.

faction of courts.[102] An example is the case of *Orebe v. Orebe,*[103] in which the trial court held that the petitioner (the husband) failed to prove adultery against his wife. The decision of the trial court was also confirmed by the Court of Appeal. One wonders the rationale behind a situation when law forces two people to continue to live together as husband and wife despite that they are tired to remain so. Many problems, if not all, that the current Nigerian law on divorce impose on persons in troubled marriages will be removed when new conditions for divorce are added to the existing ones. For example, when cessation of love is added to the existing situations, many couples who desire divorce, for whatever reason, will be able to rely on

---

[102]In *Oguntoyinbo v. Oguntoyinbo* (n 71), the Court made this pronouncement –
…it will be in the interest of society, that divorce is not granted unless the Court is fully satisfied upon unassailable facts that its grant is the only remedy to the marriage. In other words, the jurisdiction of the Court to dissolve a marriage is one which one which should not be readily applied, because such jurisdiction involves the status of the parties. Accordingly, public interest demands that the marriage bond should not be set aside without strict proof of the grounds alleged or without painstaking and strict judicial enquiry.
The above pronouncement is symptomatic of the mindset of the Nigerian Judges which is a direct influence of the current state of the Nigerian divorce law that deprives Judges of powers to dissolve a marriage with palpable evidence of collapse, although parties are unable to establish their case as required by law. Also in *Adetunji v. Adetunji* (n 82) the presiding Judge held, "Dissolution of marriage is a serious thing which cannot be granted at the whims and caprices of the parties."
[103](2017) LPELR-42160 (CA). In this case, the Appellate Court held thus, "For a petition for the dissolution of marriage to succeed, the petitioner must prove one of the ingredients contained in 15 (2) … failing which the petition will not succeed…" See also *Akinbuwa v. Akinbuwa* (2002) SMC 1, 10-11

it to exit their marriage even if their reasons for wanting divorce are more serious than cessation of love.

Adding new factual situations for divorce will enable people to have options in which those who want to tell stories of their marriage in court can do so and those who want to keep details of their marital problems can find a mild condition to provide instead of revealing the real problems in their marriage. Ultimately, new conditions for divorce will enable couples who desire a divorce, though not because they are no longer in good terms, to exit their marriages while they still remain as friends, especially where children are involved to do so. For those whose relationships have seriously deteriorated, new conditions will give them opportunity to exit their marriages with less toxicity and bitterness.

Arguments against the Reform of the Current State of Law on Dissolution of Marriage

Some people argue in favour of the extant Nigerian matrimonial law, as it makes obtaining divorce difficult.[104] When divorce is not easily available, more marriages survive, and this in turn helps to minimise the number of broken homes. They argue that difficult divorce law enables people to have time for possibility of settling their differences and keeping their marriages. It is further argued that, apart from the fact that difficult divorce reduces divorce rates, it sustains the sanctity of marriage

---

[104]See Jonathan Gruber, 'Is Making Divorce Easier Bad for Children? The Long-Run Implications of Unilateral Divorce' (2004) 22 (4) Journal of Labor Economics 3

institution and instils the values of appreciating marital vows in the married and yet to be married.

While arguments in favour of the current Nigerian divorce law are reasonable, it is submitted that the dangers of the current state of the Nigerian divorce law outweigh its benefits. Difficult divorce law may force people to stay in abusive and violent relationships, which endanger their health and lives. When persons in violent and abusive marriages stay put because of the difficulty in obtaining a divorce as evidence has to be presented, and gory stories recounted in court in order to successfully obtain a divorce, they may end up losing their lives and even the lives of children raised in such homes may be negatively affected. Some cases of mariticide and uxoricide[105] have been linked to prolonged domestic abuse. Human lives are sacred, and losing lives in the name of keeping marriages is unjustifiable. It holds more wisdom when people can easily exit their marriages if necessary, rather than being forced down in an unhappy and broken marriage due to difficulty in obtaining a divorce.

Reducing legal constraints in obtaining dissolution of marriage in Nigeria may not translate into losing the sanctity of marriage institution. Persons who want to keep their marriages can continue to do so. As already pointed out in this study, three types of marriage exist in Nigeria and marriage under the Act (statutory marriage) is the most difficult[106] to dissolve as the law governing its dissolution does not provide for extra-judicial or mutual dissolution. The conditions for its dissolution

---

[105]TA Yusuf, 'Judicial Approach to Uxoricide Cases in Nigeria' (2020) International Journal of Science and Research
[106]It is further reasoned that if England which introduced statutory marriage to Nigeria can remove the rigid rules governing divorce under her erstwhile MCA, then Nigeria has no justifications to continue to keep hers.

through the judicial means are nonetheless limited and difficult to meet. However, in spite of the relative ease in obtaining divorce in both Islamic and customary marriages, many people still remain married under these other types of marriage. While there is no official record to show which of the three marriages commands the highest number in Nigeria, it may be suggested that both Islamic and customary marriages are far more popular and command greater number than statutory marriage given that there is a seeming widespread impression that statutory marriage is mainly for the educated and elites. It cannot also be said that there is available official record regarding rates of divorce in the three marriages, but experience shows that a higher and overwhelming population of married people in Nigeria keep their marriages due to strong influences of religion and culture.

Conclusion

The Nigerian society, like most African communities, presents a peculiar circumstance in contradistinction to Western societies in the area of marriage. Generally, only monogamous marriage is recognised in the Western world, though it could be heterosexual or homosexual. In Nigeria, people have the options of entering into any of the three types of marriage: Islamic marriage, customary marriage and statutory marriage. Considering that a vast majority of Nigerians who are married according to the Islamic system or their local customs continue to keep their marriages despite the liberality of marriage dissolution under the systems in which they are married, it is reasonable to modify the more rigid rules of divorce as currently applicable to statutory marriage. Expanding the situations by which people can present divorce petitions in court is incapable of completely removing the moderating influence of the Nigerian State on the institution of marriage, especially as it relates to statutory marriage. It is believed that none of the three marriages legally recognised in Nigeria is superior or inferior to the other and to that extent, the arguments presented in this study deserve serious consideration in that statutory marriage cannot be turned into a *"cul-de-sac"* for parties who enter into it in the name of protecting marriage institution or keeping the sanctity of marriage, while the rules of exit in respect of the other types of marriage remain relaxed and less cumbersome. On the principles of equality and non-discrimination, reducing legal constraints of obtaining judicial dissolution of statutory marriage is a direction requiring both scholarly and legislative attention.

Examining the Environmental Protection Responsibilities in Nigeria: A Human Rights-Based Approach for Effective Implementation

Ayobami O. Aluko[1]

Introduction

Like most developing countries, Nigeria faces difficulties with environmental protection responsibilities. Responsibilities simply mean ensuring the effective implementation and enforcement of domestic laws and policies, as well as internationally ratified instruments. Therefore, access to justice through the implementation of environmental laws has been elusive because of factors such as loose laws, complexities facing the ju-

---

[1]Dept. Jurisprudence and Private Law, Faculty of Law, Obafemi Awolowo University, Ph.D. Candidate, Tilburg Law School, Tilburg University.

diciary and a lack of political will.[2] In Nigeria, loose laws include those that are not capable of handling present environmental realities and experiences of duplicity and multiplicity of laws. Judicial complexities resulting from environmental litigation involve 'challenges and questions regarding the role of judges in allowing matters to be litigated. For instance, issues of standing, private rights of action, political questions, admitting and evaluating scientific evidence, establishing the appropriate standard of review, applying the precautionary principles and other environmental principles and designing redress.'[3] The lack of political will makes the state complicit many times on environmental degradation issues. In essence, access to environmental justice may involve the formulation of proper laws, policy implementation and the adjudication of these laws along with obligatory environmental governance. Meagre efforts to protect the environment may restrict citizens' ability to exercise and enjoy their human rights. The absence of regulations, inadequate regulations, or insufficient oversight of their implementation can harm the environment and result in human rights violations.[4] In terms of economic concerns related to the

---

[2]a.o.aluko@tilburguniversity.edu
Godwin Uyi Ojo and Nosa Tokunbor, 'Access to Environmental Justice in Nigeria: The case for a Global Environmental Court of Justice' (2016). Available online: https://www.foei.org/wp-content/uploads/2016/10/Environmental-Justice-Nigeria-Shell-English.pdf> accessed 14 Oct. 22

[3]Dinah Shelton, 'Complexities and Uncertainties in Matters of Human Rights and the Environment: Identifying the Judicial Role' in John H Knox and Ramin Pejan (eds), *The Human Right to a Healthy Environment* (Cambridge University Press 2018)., at 98.

[4]ibid., quoted from Inter-American Commission on Human Rights (IACHR), *Report on the Human Rights Situation in Ecuador*, OEA/Ser.L/V/II.96, Doc. 10 rev., (April 24,1997), chapters 8-9.

environment, the state should consider international and national health and safety standards and ensure that environmental standards do not decline and are properly enforced.[5]

The chapter aims to understand the influence of current legal frameworks and judicial activism on the application of the rights-based approach to environmental protection. In the quest to explore the human rights-based approach to environmental protection in Nigeria, it is trite to appreciate the existing legal frameworks that support this approach as well as the attitude of the judiciary. First, using an expository approach, the formalities prescribed by the environmental legislation were examined. The examination will be carried out, particularly regarding key environmental legislation that enhances the rights-based approach. Second, this chapter explores discourse on environmental justice through the agency of environmental litigation in Nigeria. Focusing on case law, this study brings to the fore the progress and shortcomings within the ambit of environmental law cases. Accordingly, this can be achieved by reviewing environmental cases using the human rights-based approach, as examined in the previous chapter. Comparatively, the jurisprudence of the ECtHR serves as the normative framework for this study. Finally, an examination of environmental protection responsibilities that encourage effective implementation of environmental laws and policies through the jurisprudence of the ECtHR, with focus on human rights for environmental protection. The conclusions of the chapter then follow.

---

[5]John H Knox and Ramin Pejan, 'Introduction' in John H Knox and Ramin Pejan (eds), *The Human Right to a Healthy Environment* (Cambridge University Press 2018)., at 4

The idea of environmental protection in Nigeria: Law on the books

Section 20 of the 1999 Constitution of the Federal Republic of Nigeria as amended provides a foundation for environmental protection. It provides that: '' The State shall protect and improve the environment and safeguard the water, air and land, forest and wildlife of Nigeria.'' We find the fundamental provision which caters for the protection of the environment generally in the above section. It provides that the state shall protect and improve the environment and safeguard the water, air and land, forest, and wildlife of Nigeria. It can be deduced that the main aim of this provision is simply to protect and ensure a healthy environment.[6] Prior to this Section 20, the preamble to the Constitution states that the constitution is provided for the purpose of promoting good government and the welfare of all persons in our country on the principles of freedom, equality, and justice. Section 17 (1) of the constitution further gave assurances to the preamble and provides thus: ''The State social order is founded on the ideals of freedom, equality, and justice.''

The above provisions confirm the foundation for the right based approach in the constitution. In furtherance of this foundation, Section 17 (2) provides that every citizen shall have equal rights and opportunities before the law, governmental action shall remain humane, exploitation of both human and natural resources in any form shall only be for the good of the community and human sanctity and dignity shall be recognised, maintained, and enhanced; the independence, impartiality and integrity of the judiciary is guaranteed and ease of ac-

---

[6]Gozie Ogbodo, 'Environmental Protection in Nigeria: Two Decades After Koko Incidence' (2010) 15 Annual Survey of International and Comparative law 1, 18

cessibility thereto shall be secured and maintained.[7] These provisions are well articulated to provide assurance of both human and environmental rights in Nigeria. However, the reverse is true as there is unregulated environmental degradation leading to various human rights violations.

One major setback to these provisions is enforceability and justiciability in the court. According to Chapter 2 of the constitution titled *"Fundamental objectives and Directive principle of state policy"* under which they are all categorised, and in conjunction with the provision of section 6 (6) (c) which provides the following: 'The judicial powers vested in accordance with the foregoing provisions of this section shall not except as otherwise provided by this Constitution, extend to any issue or question as to whether any act of omission by any authority or person or as to whether any law or any judicial decision is in conformity with the Fundamental Objectives and Directive Principles of State Policy set out in Chapter II of this Constitution.'

The effect of this section 6 (6) (c) simply does not make the provision of section 20 justiciable in a court of law in Nigeria. The provision of section 20 has been taken only as a guide to the decision-making responsibilities of the government. This is the crux of the legal issue as it pertains to the protection of the environment in the constitution, which must be addressed if we are to create a sustainable environment. It is argued that this provision only places a mandatory duty on the state and without any corresponding legal rights for citizens to enforce

---

[7]See s 17(2)(a) to (e) of the 1999 constitution.

against the state in the event of non-compliance.[8] In *Attorney-General, Ondo State v Attorney-General, Federal Republic of Nigeria*,[9] the Court held that 'as to the non-justiciability of the Fundamental Objectives and Directive Principles of State Policy, s 6 (6) (c)... says so. While they remain mere declarations, they cannot be enforced by legal process but would be seen as a failure of duty and responsibility of State organs if they acted in clear disregard of them ... the Directive Principles can be made justiciable by legislation'.[10] This chapter will not argue whether or how can section 20 be made justiciable. Rather, it argues for the prospects of reinterpreting the core rights outlined in the Constitution, particularly those pertaining to life, human dignity, fair trial, freedom of expression, private and family life, and property, in accordance with the provisions of Section 20, with the aim of safeguarding the constitutional right of every Nigerian to exist in a setting that promotes their physical and mental health and well-being.

However, the effect of section 6 (6) (c) as stated above does not affect the provision of section 33 (1) which is found in Chapter 4 and specifically provides for fundamental rights such as the right to life, right to property, right to private and family life and so on. These rights unlike the provision of section 20 are justiciable and enforceable in a court of law in Nigeria. Chapter IV provides substantial fundamental rights that can be classified as substantive and procedural rights for the purpose

---

[8]Emeka Polycarp Amechi, 'Litigating Right to Healthy Environment in Nigeria: An Examination of the Impacts of the Fundamental Rights (Enforcement Procedure) Rules 2009, In Ensuring Access to Justice for Victims of Environmental Degradation', (2010) 6 Law, Environment and Development Journal 3, p. 320, at 325.

[9](2002) 9 Sup. Ct. Monthly 1.

[10]Ibid. See also, *Okogie (Trustees of Roman Catholic Schools) and others v Attorney-General, Lagos State*, [1981] 2 NCLR 337.

of environmental governance. It is paramount to state that the right to the environment is absent, and the rights herein have no environmental underpinning until some of the provisions are given a form of wide interpretation. Let's look at section 33 (1) which provides thus: 'Every person has a right to life, and no one shall be deprived intentionally of his life, save in execution of the sentence of a court in respect of a criminal offence of which he has been found guilty in Nigeria.'

The above section does not directly affect the environment; however, it is established that allowing anyone to live in an environment that is harmful to life and sustenance may threaten and endanger life. It is also cardinal to state the provisions of Section 34 (1) (a) which states: 'Every individual is entitled to respect for the dignity of his person, and accordingly- no person shall be subject to torture or to inhuman or degrading treatment...' Emphasis has to be placed on the essence of dignity for human life and existence. There is no dignity in which human activities have destroyed the essence of living and have left environments that thrive in deplorable living conditions. The environment has been a source of livelihood for some years, and they have seen the environment destroyed and no more of use to them because of various activities for national economic gains. These activities run against the principle of sustainable development, which simply gives a generation the opportunity to meet their needs without sabotaging the ability of future generations to meet their needs.

In *Jonah Gbemre v Shell Petroleum Development Company of Nigeria and 2 Ors*,[11] the Federal High Court determined that the conduct of the 1st and 2nd respondents, in persistently flaring gas during their oil exploration and production operations

---

[11]Unreported Suit No. FHC/B/CS/53/05, Delivered on 14 November 2005.

in the applicant's community, constituted a flagrant breach of their constitutionally protected rights to life (including a healthy environment) and the dignity of the human person.[12]

Section 12 (1) of the Constitution makes it possible for treaties to have the force of all in Nigeria only if it is enacted into law by the National Assembly. It states that: "No treaty between the Federation and any other country shall have the force of law except to the extent to which any such treaty has been enacted into law by the National Assembly." Accordingly, such treaties must pass a test of non-availability on the Exclusive Legislative List[13]. It must be in respect of matters not included in the Exclusive Legislative List and shall not be enacted unless it is ratified by the majority of the House of Assembly in the Federation.[14] Treaties on the environment that have been enacted accordingly include the Convention on International Trade in Endangered Species of Fauna and Flora, the Convention on the Prevention of Pollution by the Sea by Oil, and the African Charter on Human and Peoples Rights. The African Charter has since been ratified, which brought into existence the African Charter on Human and Peoples' Rights (Ratification and Enforcement) Act.[15] Therefore, the Act makes the provisions of the African Charter a part of Nigerian law. The decision made by the Court in the Gbemri case embodies this notion, as it concluded that a legislative measure enabling the 1st and 2nd Respondents to continue gas flaring is at odds with several provisions, such as articles 4, 16, and 24 of the

---

[12]Ibid, paras. 3-4.
[13]This is provided for under the Second Schedule: Legislative Powers and in Part I. It has 68 items with no mention of environmental issues.
[14]See section 12 (2) and (3) of the 1999 Constitution.
[15]African Charter on Human and Peoples' Rights (Ratification and Enforcement) Act, Cap A9, Vol. 1, LFN 2004.

Act.[16] Accordingly, any individual who perceives that any of the rights conferred by the Act, particularly the right to a healthy environment, has been or is likely to be violated or jeopardized by actions of the state or private individuals may initiate legal proceedings in any of the Nigerian high courts, depending on the specifics of the case, to seek appropriate remedial measures.[17] The requirement for reevaluating and implementing existing human rights for environmental protection, as indicated by this research, could potentially become obsolete. According to Amechi, this is plagued by procedural constraints that frequently hinder the efficient preservation of the environment through the utilization of current human rights.[18]

However, pursuant to the provisions of the Nigerian Constitution and any subsequent law that may repeal or modify it, Article 24 and other relevant sections of the Act are subject to such modifications or amendments as may be necessary.[19] The implication of this is that in the event of any discrepancy between the provisions of the Act and those of the Nigerian Constitution, particularly with regard to fundamental human rights;

---

[16]Art. 4 states that human beings are inviolable. Every human being shall be entitled to respect for his life and the integrity of his person. No one may be arbitrarily deprived of this right.; Art. 16(1) states that every individual shall have the right to enjoy the best attainable state of physical and mental health. (2) provides that States Parties to the present Charter shall take the necessary measures to protect the health of their people and to ensure that they receive medical attention when they are sick; Art. 24 states that all peoples shall have the right to a general satisfactory environment favorable to their development.

[17]Emeka Polycarp Amechi, n 7, at 327. See also, *Ogugu v the State* [1994] 9 NWLR (Part 366) 1.

[18]Ibid.

[19]*Abacha v Fawehinmi* [2000] FWLR 585G-P; 586A-C; & 653G.

the latter will take precedence.[20] Furthermore, in this section, some of the operational environmetal laws in Nigeria, particularly for the petroleum sector, are considered because the sector is responsible for major environmental degradation. This evaluation will be carried out in no specific order, rather the relevance of these laws to the idea of a human rights-based approach will serve as a guiding factor.

National Environmental Standards and Regulations Enforcement Agency (Establishment) Act 2007[21]

Ensuing from the provision of Section 20 of the 1999 Constitution as amended, the agency remains the major federal government agency saddled with the responsibility of protecting the Nigerian environment. The Agency functions under the supervision of the Federal Ministry of Environment, Housing and Urban Development. The National Environmental Standards and Regulations Enforcement Agency (NESREA) is responsible for enforcing compliance with laws, guidelines, policies and standards regarding environmental matters. It goes further to ensure compliance with international instruments on the environment and to coordinate cooperation with stakeholders within and outside Nigeria regarding environmental standards and regulations.[22] Nigeria has ratified a number of international instruments on the environment but has refused to domesticate

---

[20]The 1999 Constitution FRN, s 1(3). See also *Ransome-Kuti v Attorney-General, Federation* [2001] FWLR 1677F and *Akulega v B.S.C.S.C* [2002] FWLR 288E-F.
[21]Act No. 25 of 2007
[22]See section 7(a) to (m) for the functions of the Agency.

them.[23] As stated by Ladan, the idea of enforcing compliance with the provisions of international agreements, protocols, conventions and treaties on the environment can be interpreted in two ways. First, it could mean giving NESREA the authority to enforce such environmental treaties in Nigeria, whether or not they have been domesticated in the country. Second, it could mean limiting the powers of NESREA to international agreements and treaties on the environment that have been domesticated in Nigeria by an Act of the National Assembly.[24]

According to the NESREA (Establishment) (Amendment) Act of 2018, the oil and gas sector was completely removed from the purview of NESREA. Section 7(c) initially empowered the Agency to enforce compliance with the provisions of international treaties on the environment, including the oil and gas sector, among other environmental matters. Section 7(g) empowers the agency to enforce compliance with regulations on the import, export, production, distribution, storage, sale, use, handling and disposal of hazardous chemicals and waste other than in the oil and gas sector. The exclusion of the oil and gas sector from the enforcement powers of the Agency is repeated in Section 7(h, j, k, and l). Therefore, it is clear that the intention of the legislature is to remove the authority of NESREA from the oil and gas sector. Section 8, which provides the power given to the Agency, also excludes the oil and gas sectors. For instance, in subsection (g), it empowers the Agency to

---

[23]In matters such as climate change, biodiversity, desertification, forestry, oil and gas, hazardous waste etc. See Muhammed Tawfiq Ladan, 'Review of NESREA Act 2007 and Regulations 2009-2011: A New Dawn in Environmental Compliance and Enforcement in Nigeria - Country Legislation' (2012) 8 Law, Environment and Development Journal 116., at 122

[24]For a comprehensive insight on these views, see ibid., at 122-123

conduct investigations on pollution and the degradation of natural resources, except for investigations on oil spillage. Accordingly, Section 29 states that the Agency shall co-operate with other government agencies for the removal of any pollutant, excluding oil and gas related ones discharged into the Nigerian environment, and shall enforce the application of the best clean-up technology currently available and the implementation of the best management practices as appropriate.

Environmental Impact Assessment Act[25]

'Environmental Impact Assessment (EIA) is a process of evaluating the likely environmental impacts of a proposed project or development, taking into account inter-related socio-economic, cultural and human-health impacts, both beneficial and adverse'.[26] The EIA Act came into force on December 10, 1992, with the aim of providing general principles, procedures, and methods to enable the prior consideration of environmental impact assessment with respect to public and private projects.[27] Furthermore, the objectives of environmental impact assessment are to promote the implementation of appropriate policies and to encourage the development of procedures for information exchange and consultation when proposed activities are likely to have significant environmental effects.[28]

---

[25]CAP E12, Laws of the Federation of Nigeria (LFN) 2004
[26]Hakeem Ijaiya, 'PUBLIC PARTICIPATION IN ENVIRONMENTAL IMPACT ASSESSMENT IN NIGERIA: PROSPECTS AND PROBLEMS' (2015) 13 Nigerian Judicial Review 83.
[27]Junaidu Bello Marshall and Fauziyah Bashir, Human Rights Approach to Environmental Protection in Nigeria: An Appraisal' (2020) 8 International Journal of Business and Law Research 4, p. 135-147 at 144
[28]See s 1(a)-(c) of the Environmental Impact Assessment Act

Both the public and private sectors of the economy shall take into account the environmental impact assessment at an early stage. Also, whenever it is established that the proposed project or activity is likely to significantly affect the environment, its environmental impact assessment shall be undertaken in accordance with the provisions of the Act. The Act provides the criteria and procedure to determine whether an activity is likely to significantly affect the environment.

Environmental Impact Assessment is required in any project to be carried out by the federal, state, or local government council.[29] Projects excluded from the assessment are such that in the opinion of the agency that the environmental impact is minimal, such a project should be carried out as a result of a national emergency or in the interest of public health or safety.[30]

National Oil Spill Detection and Response Agency Act[31]

The Act is the principal law on environmental protection in Nigeria's oil and gas sectors. As an oil and gas sector-specific law, this may provide a better understanding of why legislators excluded the sector from the scope of the NESREA Act but did not justify it. The Act is intended to regulate the detection of oil spills during oil production and exploration.[32] It established the National Oil Spill Detection and Response Agency, which is responsible for preparedness, detection and response to all oil spillages in Nigeria. It is an Agency body corporate and may

---

[29]Section 13, ibid.
[30]Section 14(1) (a)-(c), ibid.
[31]Cap N157, Laws of the Federation (LFN) 2006.
[32]Section 19 (2), ibid.

sue and be sued.[33] Similarly, the Act established the National Control Response Centre (NCRC), which was charged with response coordination for oil spills, evaluation of oil spills and compliance monitoring of all existing environmental legislation.[34]

The objective of the agency was to coordinate and implement the National Oil Spill Contingency Plan. To achieve this main objective, the agency shall ensure a safe, timely, effective and appropriate response to major or disastrous oil pollution. Establish the mechanism to monitor and assist or where expedient directs the response, including the capability to mobilize the necessary resources to save lives, protect the threatened environment, and clean up to the best practical extent of the impacted site. Ensuring funding and appropriate and sufficient pre-positioned pollution combating equipment and materials, as well as functional communication network systems, are required for effective response to major oil pollution.[35]

The Act states that the Agency is responsible for surveillance, ensuring compliance with all existing environmental laws, and the detection of oil spills in the petroleum sector. The Agency shall receive reports of oil spills and coordinate oil spill response activities throughout the country. In addition, the Agency shall coordinate the implementation of the plan as may be formulated from time to time and for the removal of hazardous substances as may be issued by the federal government. Finally, it shall perform other functions as required to achieve the aims and objectives under the Act or any plan formulated by the federal government pursuant to the Act.[36] The National

---

[33]Section 1, NOSDRA Act.
[34]Section 18 (1) (a)-(c), ibid.
[35]Section 5 (a-n), ibid. See also the National Oil Spill Contingency Plan, Second Schedule to the NOSDRA Act.
[36]Section 6 (a)-(e).

Oil Spill Contingency Plan is an effort by the federal government to tackle oil spill incidents and associated environmental problems in Nigeria. The implementation of the plan complies with national objectives and the international convention on Oil Pollution Preparedness, response, and cooperation (OPRC 90, which Nigeria ratified).[37]

Land Use Act[38]

The Land Use Act is not strictly aimed at protecting the environment. However, environmental protection is one of the considerations that a holder of a certificate of occupancy that a private owner has to observe, although it is not explicitly provided for in any of the provisions of the Act. If the Act is read without such importation, the result is bound to be absurd and environmentally unsound,[39] simply because issues of health, well-being and life are raised when the environment is polluted. The objectives of the Act have been narrowed down to include the following: to effect structural change in the system of land tenure; to achieve fast economic and social transformation; to negate economic inequality caused by the appropriation of rising land values by land speculators and landholders; and

---

[37]See Foreword to the National Oil Spill Contingency Plan (NOSCP) 2010 for Nigeria, at *vi*
[38]CAP 202, Laws of the Federation (LFN) 2004.
[39]Sylvanus Abila, Stephen Timi Kalama, Prosper Ayawei, 'Environmental Law and Land Use in Nigeria' a paper for the second colloquium on Environmental Law and Land Use organized by the IUCN academy of Environmental Law, Bonn, Germany and in collaboration with the University of Nairobi, Kenya. 4-8 October 2014.

to make land available easily and cheaply to both the government and private individual developers.[40]

Petroleum Industry Act (PIA), 2021[41]

The Act aims to provide legal, governance, regulatory, and fiscal frameworks for the Nigerian petroleum industry and the development of host communities. As a newly enacted law, it brings to an end the effort to reform Nigeria's oil and gas sector through the creation of an environment more conducive to the growth of the sector and addressing legitimate grievances of communities most affected by extractive industries.[42] The president of Nigeria appoints NNPC Ltd.'s president as well as the heads and members of the regulatory agencies. Separately, the Minister of Petroleum will head the industry with a wide range of powers to formulate, monitor, and administer government policies under the Act. Under its general administration, NNPC Ltd. aims to ensure that petroleum operations are conducted in a manner that protects the health and safety of persons, property and the environment.[43] In addition, the administration and management of petroleum resources and their derivatives shall be conducted in accordance with the Act and the principles of

---

[40]Omotoso Olatunji John, 'Authoritarianism and the Question of Environmental Justice in Africa: The example of Land Use Act of 1978 in Nigeria' (2017) VIII Afro Asian Journal of Social Sciences No. 1 Quarter 1., at 13.

[41]Act No. 6 of 2021.

[42]Kasirim Nwuke, 'Nigeria's Petroleum Industry Act: Addressing old problems, creating new ones' (Brookings, 24 November 2021) <https://www.brookings.edu/blog/africa-in-focus/2021/11/24/nigerias-petroleum-industry-act-addressing-old-problems-creating-new-ones/> accessed 11 January 2023

[43]Section 68 (1) (m), ibid.

good governance, transparency, and sustainable development in Nigeria.[44]

A fundamental provision is the discretionary power of the minister to revoke a petroleum prospecting license or petroleum mining lease, where the licensee or lessee fails to conduct petroleum operations in accordance with good international petroleum industry practices, the provisions of the Act, and any other relevant legislation.[45] The Commission ensures that it meets health, safety and environmental standards, including an environmental management plan for the elimination of routine natural gas flaring.[46] The Environmental Guidelines and Standards for the Petroleum Industry (EGASPIN)[47] in Nigeria outlines environmental guidelines and safety standards for petroleum production operations. For projects that require environmental impact assessment, a licensee or lessee shall submit an environmental management plan. The environmental plan shall be approved only where it complies with relevant environmental acts, the applicant has the capacity or has provided for the capacity to rehabilitate and manage negative impacts on the environment.[48] The Act also prohibits the flaring or venting of natural gas except in the case of an emergency, as an acceptable safety practice under established regulations such as the Flare Gas (Prevention of Waste and Pollution) Regulations. The regulations also prescribe a penalty for the purpose of environmental remediation and relief of the settlors' host communities on which the penalties are levied.[49]

---

[44]Section 67, PIA 2021
[45]Section 96 (1) (a), ibid. For a complete list of the grounds for revocation, see subsection (1) (b) to (n).
[46]Section 79 (2) (a), (d), (h) and (j).
[47]EGASPIN was issued in 1991 and subsequently revised and updated in 2002, 2016 and 2018.
[48]Section 102, ibid.
[49]Sections 104 and 105, ibid.

Considering the nagging issues that have beset the Nigerian petroleum industry, Nwuke opines that the PIA possesses the potential to address these issues only 'if implemented properly and vigorously. The PIA can represent the gold standard of natural resource management, with clear and separate roles for the subsectors of the industry; the existence of a commercially oriented and profit-driven national petroleum company; the codification of transparency, good governance, and accountability in the administration of the petroleum resources of Nigeria; the economic and social development of host communities; environmental remediation; and a business environment conducive for oil and gas operations to thrive in the country.'[50]

The Nigerian justice system and access to Environmental Justice: Law in practice

As an intrinsic part of access rights, access to justice in environmental matters is key to public engagement in environmental decision-making. Access to justice is the right to have decisions, acts, and omissions by the state and its agents, and by private actors reviewed legally.[51] Access to environmental justice through the Courts in Nigeria has not seen so much of a green light since the inception of environmental litigation in Nigeria. The lack of access to justice through the Courts in Nigeria in cases of environmental degradation has been ascribed to judicial bars such as *locus standi* (right to sue), high cost of litigation, burden of proof and jurisdiction. Generally,

---

[50]Kasirim Nwuke, n 41.
[51]Jonas Ebbesson, 'Public Participation' in Lavanya Rajamani and Jacqueline Peel (eds), *The Oxford Handbook of International Environmental Law* (Second Edition, Oxford University Press 2021).

litigation is a common response to governance failure. 'In the context of human rights and the environment, cases may aim to prevent a project or activity from receiving approval, to challenge approval that has been given and thus enjoin initiation or continuation of a project, or to obtain redress when harm has occurred or is imminent.'[52] Some cases may be instituted to challenge a particular law or regulation as opposed to human rights, rather than challenging the lack of proper application or enforcement of such laws.[53] In the words of Ebbesson, access to justice relates to the following situation: 'first, where an applicant's request for environmental information has been ignored, refused, or not dealt with in accordance with the law, and second, where any member of the public having a sufficient interest challenges the substantive and procedural legality of any decision, act, or omission concerning specific activities that may affect the environment'.[54]

As one of the procedural aspects of the rights-based approach, access to justice is key to achieving a healthy and sustainable environment. It has also been referred to as one of the pillars of environmental democracy.[55] According to the Rio Declaration on the subject of access to justice, 'effective access to judicial and administrative proceedings, including redress and remedies, shall be provided'.[56] Within the discourse on en-

---

[52]Shelton (n 2)., at 98
[53]ibid.
[54]Jonas Ebbesson, 'Information, Participation and Access to Justice: The Model of the Aarhus Convention', Joint UNEP-OHCHR Expert Seminar on Human Rights and the Environment, Background Paper No 5. Geneva, 14–16 January 2002.
[55]Linda Hajjar Leib, *Human Rights and the Environment: Philosophical, Theoretical and Legal Perspectives* (Brill Nijhoff 2010)., at 81
[56]See Principle 10, Rio Declaration on Environment and Development 1992.

vironmental governance, access to justice is key, placing trust and reliance on the judiciary to play a significant role in ensuring good environmental governance. Citizens may wish to approach the court seeking access to relevant environmental information, challenge procedurally or substantively unfair environmental decisions, prevent environmentally deleterious actions, or seek compensation for any damage caused.[57] As the last resort within the ambit of procedural rights, the idea is that environmental issues should not be left to government discretion.[58]

Locus Standi

Locus standi simply refers to the right to sue in matter before a competent court. This is the right to bring about an action before and subsequently be heard by the court. Apart from the notion that it disallows judicial time-wasting, the court is unable to assume jurisdiction of a matter before it without legal standing. Therefore, in Nigeria, this implies that a plaintiff must show sufficient interest in the matter to sue successfully. Nigerian courts have applied this principle in a narrow and strict manner, allowing only persons who demonstrate a personal interest in a matter or persons who have been directly impacted by violations of the law to sue.[59] This restrictive approach requires that there is an interest that is individualistic to

---

[57]Muhammed Ladan, 'Nigeria' in in Louis J. Kotzé and Alexander R. Paterson (eds.), *The Role of the Judiciary in Environmental Governance: Comparative Perspectives* (Kluwer Law International BV 2009) at 537

[58]Leib, n 55 at 86

[59]Dejo Olowu, *An Integrative Right-Based Approach to Human Development in Africa* (Pretoria University Law Press 2009) at 175. *Nworika v Ononeze-Madu and Others* (2019) SC 307/2008.

the plaintiff and not representative, which is shared in common with the general members of the public.[60] The case of *Abraham Adesanya v the President of the Federal Republic of Nigeria*[61] a classical authority stated in a ruling by Justice Mohammed Bello:

'It seems to me that upon the construction of the subsection, it is only when the civil rights and obligations of the person who invokes the jurisdiction of the court, are in issue for determination that the judicial powers of the court may be invoked. In other words, standing will only be accorded to a plaintiff who shows that his civil rights and obligations have been or are in danger of being violated or adversely affected by the act complained of.'[62] In this above case, it is interesting to note that the judges were not in accord. In the ruling given by Justice Uwais, he stated that the issue of locus standi will depend on the specific situation of each case and that no hard and fast rule should be established. According to Fatayi Williams CJN[63] (he was then):

'To deny any member of such society who is aware or believes, or is led to believe, that there has been an infraction of any of the provisions of our Constitution... access to the court of law to air his grievance on the flimsy excuse (of lack of sufficient interest) is to provide a ready recipe for organized disenchantment with the judicial process.'[64]

In environmental matters, the restrictive approach to the right to sue may have led to injustice. According to Oputa JSC[65],

---

[60]Godwin Uyi Ojo and Nosa Tokunbor, n 1 at 4
[61][1981] 1 All NLR 1
[62]Ibid, para. 82
[63]Chief Justice of Nigeria.
[64]Ibid, para. 9
[65]Justice of the Supreme Court.

'...there is perhaps no question more fundamental in the whole process of adjudication than that of access to justice, access to the courts. He who cannot even reach the court cannot talk of justice from the court. It is in this context and for the fundamental reason that many legal systems are now relaxing the erstwhile severity of their rules governing locus standi. '.[66]

Access to remedies for environmental harm is based on the ability to access the judiciary in the absence of dispensable barriers. The connection between human rights and the environment often lies in the right to a healthy environment, which places an obligation on the state to ensure access to justice. Interestingly, access to justice is indispensable in the discourse of human rights norms and is an acceptable and recognised procedural aspect of environmental rights. The restrictive approach has limited the activities of non-governmental organizations and human rights advocates saddled with litigating environmental matters impacting the poor and their communities. Those willing to assist the socially concerned through their resources and expertise to litigate environmental issues have denied them legal standing before the courts, leading to injustices.[67] In *Oronto Douglas v Shell Petroleum Development Company Limited and Others*,[68] the plaintiff, an environmental activist, sought the compliance of the respondents with the provisions of the Environmental Impact Assessment (EIA) Act in relation to the Liquified Natural Gas (LNG) project at Bonny being executed by defendants. The court held that the plaintiff had no standing to institute the action since he had shown no

---

[66]*A.G. of Kaduna State v Hassan* [1985] 2 NWLR (pt. 8) 522
[67]Alex Cyril Ekeke, 'Liberalization of the Rule on Locus Standi before Nigerian Courts: Lessons from India' (2022) 66 Journal of African Law 339.
[68][1998] LPELR-CA/L/143/97

evidence prima facie that his right was affected, or that any direct injury caused to him or that he suffered any injury more
than the generality of the people. This decision inspired the
practice of environmental NGOs sponsoring victims of environmental degradation to obtain redress against those responsible.[69]

In *Jonah Gbemri v Shell Petroleum Development Company
Nigeria Ltd and Ors*,[70] the court granted leave to institute these
proceedings in a representative capacity for himself and for
each member of the Iweherekan Community in Delta State of
Nigeria. It was held that these constitutionally guaranteed
rights[71] inevitably included the right to a clean, poison-free,
pollution-free, and healthy environment.[72] It was declared that
continuing to flare gas in the course of their oil exploration and
production activities in the Applicant's Community was a violation of their fundamental rights to life (including a healthy
environment) and the dignity of the human person guaranteed
by the Constitution of the Federal Republic of Nigeria (1999)
and reinforced by the African Charter on Human Rights Procedure Rules (Ratification and Enforcement) Act.[73] In the court's
ruling, the failure of the respondents to carry out an environmental impact assessment in the Applicant's Community concerning the effects of their gas flaring activities was a violation
of the Environment Impact Assessment Act and contributed to
the violation of the applicant's fundamental rights to life and
the dignity of the human person. The court ordered respondents
to take immediate steps to stop further gas flaring in the appli-

---

[69]Emeka Polycarp Amechi, n 7 at 330.
[70][2005] Suit No. FHC/B/CS/53/05.
[71]Fundamental rights to life and dignity of the human persons as
guaranteed by the Constitution in sections 33(1) and 34(1), respectively.
[72]Ibid, para. 15
[73]Ibid, para. 17-18

cant's Community. The Court did not award any damages, costs, or compensation whatsoever.

However, the principle of *locus standi* has recently been relaxed by the Supreme Court in environmental litigation. In terms of environmental rights and possibly all socio-economic rights, the Court has established a unique foundation for safeguarding these rights, enabling non-governmental organizations to enforce environmental rights.[74] In *Centre for Oil Pollution Watch v Nigerian National Petroleum Corporation (NNPC)*,[75] the appellant sought the reliefs against NNPC, a state-owned oil company over the oil spillage in the Acha Community of Isukwuato Local Government Area of Abia State. As part of the relief, there was reinstatement, restoration and remediation of the impaired and/contaminated environment that was contaminated by oil spills. The NNPC denied liability for the oil spillage and filed an objection challenging the centre's locus standi. The Federal High Court agreed with the NNPC's objection and struck out the centre's action. The Centre appealed the decision, but the Court of Appeal affirmed the ruling of the Federal High Court. The Supreme Court, however, held that NGOs such as the Centre have the requisite standi to sue in environmental matters. The court noted that the respondent, being a public authority, violated its constitutional and statutory obligations to ensure a safe and healthy environment, resulting in public injury. In the Supreme Court's opinion, it is in the interest of justice to allow the centre to pursue its case. Aka'ahs JSC concurs, noting the increasing concerns about environmental issues such as climate change, waste management,

---

[74]Obadina Ibrahim, 'Nigerian Supreme Court's stealth relaxation of Locus Standi in Environmental litigation: Redirecting judicial approach to Public Interest Litigation' (2021) Journal of Private and Business Law Vol. 2, No. 2, at 201
[75][2019] 5NWLR (Pt. 1666) 518

flooding, global warming, and pollution. He admonishes that those protecting the environment, such as the Centre, should be encouraged to check actions or omissions by government agencies or multinational oil companies that tend to pollute the environment.

Burden of proof and sufficient redress

The preponderance of the burden of proof or evidence is placed on victims who may not have the means to hire technical experts to testify on their behalf, while transnational companies (TNCs) can afford these costs and services to defend themselves and minimize damage. The burden of proof lies in the plaintiff succeeding in an action for negligence. The plaintiff may not have the financial resources to procure the services of experts, especially when the plaintiff does not possess the required knowledge to prove the defendant's non-compliance with environmental regulations and standards. While defendants in environmental litigation are often rich individuals or corporations, they can easily procure the services of experts to testify in a manner indicative of their non-negligence.

In *Shell Petroleum Development Company Nigeria Ltd v Chief G.B.A. Tiebo VII and others*,[76] the chiefs of the Perembiri community in their personal capacity and on behalf of the village community following a crude oil spill resulting from facilities belonging to the Shell Petroleum Development Company of Nigeria Limited. The company's equipment caused a spill of approximately 600 barrels of oil near Perembiri village and the Nun River in the Niger River Delta. The oil spill caused damage to farmland, fishing grounds, water sources, and religious

---

[76][1996] 4 NWLR 657; (2005) 9 NWLR (Pt.931) 439; [2005] 3-4 S.C 137

shrines and disrupted the livelihood of the Perembiri community, with a significant proportion of children. The community chiefs commenced legal proceedings for negligence against the company, seeking general and special damage to the harm caused. The plaintiffs were awarded only general damages by the court, as well as a sum, intended to cover their legal costs. The Perembiri community was dissatisfied with the amount of damages awarded and petitioned the Court of Appeals, which dismissed their actions. The Chief appealed to the Supreme Court.

The Supreme Court reviewed the damages awarded for harm to raffia palms and loss of water for drinking and domestic use. The lower court judge incorrectly classified the damages claim as general damages instead of special damages, which required strict proof of loss and causation. The lower court should have treated raffia palm and water loss claims as special damages, requiring specific evidence. As the plaintiffs failed to prove their entitlement to special damages, the lower court awarded general damages. However, this substitution is incorrect. The Supreme Court stated that it would only intervene in the amount of damages awarded if it was either 'manifestly too high' or 'manifestly too low', or if the judge used an incorrect principle for calculating damages. In this case, the plaintiffs provided evidence of significant damage to crops, land, waterways, and water sources, justifying the award for general damage. No order was made for environmental remediation, as the company's negligence was not considered.

However, in *Farah and Ors. v Shell*,[77] the Court of Appeals, reached a different conclusion regarding remediation. Five families who lived near an oil well in Nigeria operated by Shell sued the company seeking compensation for their damaged

---

[77][1995] 3 NWLR (Pt. 382) 148.

land. An oil blowout in 1970, meaning the uncontrolled release of oil following a pressure control system failure, caused extensive damage and prevented claimants from using the land for farming, hunting, and other farming activities similar in nature. The court observed that the damage the respondents suffered went beyond mere damage to crops and economic trees, as experts called on both sides to confirm that the respondents' arable land had been heavily polluted and rendered unproductive for many years. Consequently, it awarded compensation and rehabilitation to the damaged land, which is unusual, apparently as a result of the scale of the damage occasioned. This decision came in the wake of the international opprobrium that followed the federal government's killing of Ken Saro-wiwa. The courts apparently tried to distance themselves from the government on issues regarding oil pollution in the Niger Delta, which was championed by Ken Saro-wiwa.

Conversely, in *Shell v Isaiah*,[78] compensation was awarded, but no remediation order was made. Shell was sued to compensate for the damage and loss caused by extensive oil spillage and pollution. In defence, the company alleged that there was no spillage, but a minor splash of oil. Both the court of first instance and that court of appeal found that there was 'massive oil spillage' causing extensive damage to economic crops, economic trees, water resources, and hunting amenities.

Subject matter jurisdiction

Courts are established by certain rules that limit their ability to successfully determine the cases brought before them. Cases brought before courts must fall within their jurisdiction in order for them to decide on such cases. The scope of that jurisdiction,

---

[78][1997] 6 NWLR, 236.

however, is often a matter of disagreement.[79] Governmental bodies have raised objections to national and international courts accepting human rights cases with underlying environmental conditions or activities posing a risk of environmental harm. Furthermore, experiences of considerable backlash to some decisions related to economic development projects and environmental harm have occurred, with the government challenging the appropriateness of any judicial review of projects it is important to state' economic wellbeing. Often, both litigators and judges face pressure and sometimes threatens their personal safety.[80]

The commencement of an action for the enforcement of a right to the environment or a right related to environmental protection, a victim may bring an application to the court within the state where the infringement occurs or is likely to occur for redress. In an event that the infringement is outside the jurisdiction of the State High Court, the division of the Federal High Court administratively responsible for the State shall assume jurisdiction. In cases involving oil spillage, the law confers jurisdiction on the Federal High Court. The exclusive jurisdiction to entertain claims pertaining to mines and minerals, including oilfields, oil mining, geological surveys and natural gas rests on the Federal High Court.[81] In the case of *Shell Petroleum Development Company (Nigeria) Ltd v Abel Isaiah*,[82] massive spillage occurred while the defendants repaired their damaged pipeline. The High Court awarded 22-million-naira damages to the claimant. On appeal to the Supreme Court, the issue of jurisdiction was raised. It was held that the High Court

---

[79]Shelton n 2., at 99
[80]Ibid.
[81]See section 251 (1) (n) of the 1999 Constitution of the Federal Republic of Nigeria.
[82][2001] 5 S.C. (Pt.11) 1.

of Isiokpo, Rivers State, had no jurisdiction to entertain the matter at the time it gave judgment. In Supreme Court reasoning, the question of whether a court has jurisdiction to adjudicate can be raised at any stage of the trial, and it is always important to consider the issue of jurisdiction first.

The issue of jurisdiction was also raised in the case of *Shell v Tiebo VII,*[83] discussed above. While referring to the *Abel Isaiah case*, the Supreme Court had to determine whether the Court of Appeal acted *ultra vires* to uphold the jurisdiction of the High Court. It was reiterated that at the time the cause of action accrued, the suit commenced, and judgment was delivered, the State High Court had jurisdiction over cases of oil spills because the law applicable to an action is the law existing when the cause of action arose. The Supreme Court stated that it ventured into the case because the jurisdiction issue was raised. Due to a lack of jurisdiction, most environmental suits for oil pollution in the Niger Delta region of Nigeria filed in the High Courts of the state have been dismissed. From the above, State High Courts can exercise jurisdiction in environmental or pollution cases only when the subject matter is not related to oil and gas or is included within the scope of the jurisdiction of the Federal High Court stated in section 251.

---

[83]See, n 75.

Other Technical Impediments to Environmental Litigation in Nigeria

Limitation Period

The court made it clear in the case of *Akibu v Azeez*[84] that in the limitation of action, time began to run from the date the cause of action arose. The issue was raised by Shell when it asked the court to dismiss the case because too much time had passed before the second case was filed and their claim was barred by statutes in *Farah and ors. v Shell*.[85] The idea of the limitation period is to avoid a defendant having an indefinite claim threat.[86] It is very likely that a significant period of time can pass from the time a pollutant is introduced into the environment to when it is discovered to have impacted its victims. It is often a difficult challenge for potential litigants when they are faced with a statute of limitation. This is because time starts to run from the date the act or omission occurred and not the date of knowledge.[87]

Pre-action Notice

The law stipulates that before certain actions are commenced against certain agencies of the government or certain classes of defendants, a pre-action notice should be provided to them. The idea behind this requirement is to avoid embarrassing suits

---

[84][2003] 5 NWLR 643
[85]See, n 76.
[86]Olanrewaju Fagbohun, 'Mournful Remedies, Endless Conflicts and Inconsistencies in Nigeria's Quest for Environmental Governance: Rethinking the Legal Possibilities for Sustainability' (NIALS Press 2012), at 65
[87]Ibid.

and enable the statutory body to evaluate the facts to decide whether to contest them or settle amicably. Any case instituted without the service of such pre-action notice is incompetent and liable to be struck out.[88] In response to this argument, Fagbohun suggested that the nature of environmental risks is such that an injunction *quia timet* of ex parte nature may be required to avert the prospects of the imminent danger that loomed large. In his view, a provision requiring notice of one to three months, as the case may be, may result in harm of an irremediable nature.[89] Pre-action notice was treated as a condition precedent in *Mobile Producing (Nig) Unlimited v LASEPA, FEPA and Ors*[90]although the court held that the service of a pre-action notice is at best a procedural requirement and not an issue of substantive law. In the *Tiebo* case, the court held that it was merely a procedural irregularity.

Power of Regulatory Agencies to impose penalties

It is also important to discuss whether regulatory agencies have the power to impose fines without recourse to the courts. In *National Oil Spill Detection and Response Agency (NOSDRA) v Mobil Producing Nigeria Unlimited (Exxonmobil)*,[91] NOSDRA imposed a fine of Ten million naira on ExxonMobil Producing Unlimited (ExxonMobil) for the spillage of oil from its Qua Iboe facility, relying on its power to do so under the National Oil Spill Detection and Response Agency Act (Sections 6(2) and (3)). The agency instituted an action at the Federal High Court to recover the fine. In its defence, ExxonMobil argued that it took all the necessary steps, as provided under the

---

[88]*Bakare v NRC* [2007] 17 NWLR (Pt. 1064) 606
[89]Olanrewaju Fagbohun, n 55 at 64
[90][2002] 18 NWLR (Pt. 798) 1
[91][2018] LPELR-44210 (CA).

NOSDRA Act, for the remediation of the affected areas. ExxonMobil further argued that NOSDRA, as an administrative agency, lacked powers under the NOSDRA Act to impose fines/penalties. The Federal High Court, being the Court of First instance for such matters, granted judgment in favour of ExxonMobil, stating that the administrative agency acted ultra vires to its powers under the NOSDRA Act as such powers are vested in the courts. Dissatisfied with the FHC's Judgment, the Agency appealed to the Court of Appeal, where the Justices of the Court of Appeal upheld the decision of the lower court. They held that penalties or fines are imposed as punishment for an offence or violation of the law, and that the power as well as competence to establish that an offence has been committed belongs to the courts. However, in *Shell Nigeria Exploration And Production Company Limited (Shell) v National Oil Spill Detection And Response Agency (NOSDRA)*,[92] held that Sections 5, 6, and 7 of the NOSDRA Act, which empowers the agency to impose penalties, did not violate the provisions of the 1999 Constitution in terms of appropriating judicial powers vested in courts to issue sanctions in the form of fines. The Court further held that NOSDRA had acted in accordance with its powers under the NOSDRA Act by imposing a fine of USD$3.6 billion on Shell.

---

[92](Unreported) delivered on May 24, 2018. (9 July 2018) <https:// ng.andersen.com/federal-high-court-upholds-nosdras-powers-to-impose-sanctions-without-recourse-to-the-court/> accessed 18 August 2021

Drawing inspiration from the jurisprudence of the ECtHR

The European Court of Human Rights has made many important and innovative contributions to the corpus of international human rights law, including the interface between human rights and the environment. Strikingly, the Court has consistently held that it is not bound by the Framer's interpretation of the Convention terms.[93] Like the 1999 Constitution, the ECHR does not protect the environment or refer to any right to a healthy environment. Owing to the lack of an explicit environmental right in the European Convention on Human Rights (ECHR), the European Court of Human Rights (ECtHR) developed a substantial body of case law that effectively serves as a substitute for such a right.[94] Consequently, alleged breaches of environmental human rights are typically assessed in relation to other rights established within the framework of the convention.[95] Such rights as the right in Article 8 to privacy and family life, Article 2 protecting the right to life, Article 6 protecting the right to fair hearing in the determination of civil rights and

---

[93]Thomas Buergenthal, "The evolving International Human Rights System', (2006) 100 Am. J. Int'l L. 783,792-94 in Donald K. Anton and Dinah L. Shelton (eds), *Environmental Protection and Human Rights* (Cambridge University Press 2011), 338
[94]Ole W. Pedersen, 'The European Court of Human Rights and International Environmental Law' in John H. Knox and Ramin Pejan (eds), *The Human Right to a Healthy Environment*, (Cambridge University Press, 2018) 86
[95]Jonathan Verschuuren, 'Contribution of the case law of the European Court of Human Rights to sustainable development in Europe' in Werner Scholtz and Jonathan Verschuuren (eds), Regional Environmental Law: Transregional Comparative Lessons in Pursuit of Sustainable Development (Edward Elgar Publishing 2015) 366

obligations, Article 10 protecting the freedom of expression, and Article 1 of Protocol 1 protecting the right to property.

In light of recent developments, the Convention's provisions for environmental responsibility can now be triggered on the basis of potential harm, rather than only being applied after harm has occurred and been identified. The Court's readiness to permit societal realities to inform its interpretations has garnered significant esteem from the cognoscenti, who orbits the realms of international environmental law and human rights law.[96] While acknowledging the Court's progressive willingness to entertain environmental claims, it is important to note that the Court is significantly more likely to find against a state in which the responding state has failed to implement, apply, or adhere to its domestic environmental standards and rules. Essentially, the court is inclined to support an environmental claim founded on a rule-of-law rationale.[97] Furthermore, states enjoy a wide degree of discretion with regard to the court's self-imposed doctrine of the margin of appreciation in environmental decision-making. However, the Court is willing to extend the scope of the rights for the protection of the environment in the presence of proof of interference with the applicants' rights under the Convention.[98]

The Court, in its various decisions, has been able to establish the environmental responsibilities expected of contracting states in environmental decision-making processes. The most commonly used Article of the Convention to lodge such claims

---

[96]Ole W. Pedersen, n 93, 89.
[97]Ibid.
[98]Ibid.

has been Article 8,[99] the right to respect for private and family life provided for under Section 37 of the 1999 Constitution as amended.[100] It may be observed that the right to respect for private and family life of the ECHR guarantees rights that are not absolute, but qualified. The permissible limits for Article 8 have been set in Paragraph 2. Infringement of this article requires a two-step procedure. The first is the determination of whether there has been interference with the right contained in this article; the second is the determination of whether it was justified under Article 8, paragraph 2.[101] Interference with the right may be justified if it is (i) in accordance with law, (ii) necessary in a democratic society, and (iii) in furtherance of the legitimate aim identified in Article 8(2). In many cases before it,[102] the ECtHR explained that the test for necessity in 'democratic society' requires that 'the interference corresponds to a pressing social need and... is proportionate to the legitimate aim pursued'. The reasons given to justify the interference

---

[99]Article 8 on the Right to Respect for Private and Family Life, states: 'i. Everyone has the right to respect for his private and family life, his home, and his correspondence. ii. There shall be no interference by a public authority with the exercise of this right except such as is in accordance with the law and is necessary in a democratic society, in the interests of national security, public safety or the economic well-being of the country, for the prevention of disorder or crime, for the protection of health or morals, or for the protection of the rights and freedoms of others'. Article 8, *European Convention for the Protection of Human Rights and Fundamental Freedoms,* as amended by Protocols Nos. 11 and 14, 4 November 1950, ETS 5
[100]Section 37 provides that, 'The privacy of citizens, their homes, correspondence, telephone conversations and telegraphic communications is hereby guaranteed and protected.'
[101]Malgosia Fitzmaurice, *Contemporary Issues in International Environmental Law* (Edward Elgar 2009) 181.
[102]*Olsson v Sweden,* 11 EHRR [1988] 259

must be 'relevant' and 'sufficient'.[103] This is the so-called 'test of proportionality'. The tests of proportionality and the balancing of interests are at the heart of the jurisprudence of the ECtHR in cases that deal with human rights and the environment: that is, they involve, to a larger extent, the interpretation of Article 8 of the ECHR.[104]

A momentous decision was made to achieve harmony between economic prosperity and the preservation of inalienable rights. In the opinion of the court, severe environmental pollution can have a significant impact on an individual's well-being and ability to enjoy their home, which may negatively affect their private and family life.[105] However, such pollution does not pose a serious threat to human life. The Court found that the operation of the waste-treatment plant caused nuisance and serious health problems, and that the government of Spain had not adequately struck a balance between the economic interests of the town and the applicant's right to respect her home and private and family life.

The Court recognizes the duty of the state to take reasonable and adequate measures to safeguard private lives and homes, as well as the overall healthy and secure environment, of the affected individuals. In *Tătar v Romania*,[106] applicants, who lived near a gold ore extraction plant, raised concerns about the risks posed by the company's use of sodium cyanide. Despite assurances from the authorities of sufficient safety mechanisms, a large quantity of polluted water spilled into rivers in several countries in the year 2000. The Court found that there was no official documentation confirming the danger of the

---

[103]Ibid.
[104]Malgosia Fitzmaurice, n 100, 184
[105]*Lopez Ostra v Spain*, 20 EHRR 277, Judgment of 9 December 1994.
[106]Application No. 67021/01, Judgment of 27 January 2009

company's activities, and the applicants failed to prove a causal link between pollution and their health issues. However, the Court concluded that the spill posed a serious threat to applicants' well-being based on environmental impact studies submitted by the respondent state. As a result, the state had a legal obligation to implement appropriate and effective measures to safeguard the rights of the relevant parties to respect their private lives and homes, and an overall healthy, secure environment. This principle applied equally to the regulatory authorities both before and after the commencement of the plant's operations, as well as in the aftermath of the incident. The Court emphasized that the applicants must have experienced a state of constant anxiety and uncertainty, exacerbated by the inactive stance of the national authorities and compounded by the fear of a possible recurrence of the hazardous activity, which could result in another accident. Thus, the Court concluded that Article 8 of the Convention was breached.

It seems that the Court adopted a bifurcated approach to Article 8, as evidenced in the case of *Taşkin and Others v Turkey*.[107] The court was tasked with determining whether the national authorities had incorrectly extended the operating permit of a gold mine that employed a particular technique that could have detrimental effects on the environment and health of the applicant. In this instance, potential environmental damage should be deemed sufficiently severe to threaten the well-being and enjoyment of residents' homes. The court hesitates to engage in further examination of the nexus between pollution and its resulting negative consequences, as well as the severity of the impact on the individual.[108] The same holds true when the adverse consequences of an activity that the individuals involved are likely to encounter have been assessed in the con-

---

[107]Application No. 46117/99, judgment of 30 March 2005
[108]Ibid, paragraph 113

text of an environmental impact assessment process, such that a direct link with private and family life, as specified in Article 8 of the Convention, can be established. If this is not the case, the obligation of the state to take reasonable and appropriate measures to protect the applicant's rights, as outlined in paragraph 1 of Article 8, would be rendered ineffective.[109]

Article 8 primarily aims to shield individuals from arbitrary interference by public authorities. Additionally, public authorities may be required to take proactive measures to ensure the protection of the rights outlined in this article.[110] This responsibility is not limited to situations where environmental damage is directly caused by the state's actions, but also extends to instances where it arises from private sector activities.[111] Therefore, it is incumbent upon public authorities to ensure that necessary measures are implemented to safeguard the rights guaranteed under Article 8.[112] The Court emphasized that it is not only essential for the authorities to take proactive steps to avert environmental disturbances, including noise, as seen in the present case, but also to guarantee that these preventive measures are put into action and prove effective in safeguarding the rights of individuals as per Article 8.[113] Moreover, the Court has explicitly acknowledged that it is the responsibility of public authorities to inform the public about environmental risks.[114] In *Guerra's* case, the Court determined that the public authorities had failed to discharge their duty to ensure the ap-

---

[109]Ibid.
[110]*Guerra and Others v Italy*, Application No. 116/1996/735/932, 19 February 1998 paragraph 58
[111]*Hatton and Others v the United Kingdom,* paragraph 98; *Tătar v Romania*, paragraph 87.
[112]*Moreno Gómez v Spain*, paragraph 61.
[113]Ibid.
[114]*Guerra and Others v Italy*, n 109, paragraph 60; *Tătar v Romania*, n 110, paragraph 88.

plicants' right to respect their private and family life on account of the applicants' lack of crucial information from the public authorities, which would have enabled them to evaluate the potential hazards to themselves and their families if they remained in the area.

The positive obligation on states to take steps to safeguard the lives of those within their jurisdiction, even when threatened by other (private) persons or activities that are not directly connected with the State also applies to the right to life under Article 2 of the Convention.[115] The principal objective of Article 2 is to preclude the state from intentionally causing the death of an individual, except in situations explicitly defined.[116] This study intends to prohibit specific government actions and possesses an inherently negative nature. However, the court has developed the "doctrine of positive obligation" in its jurisprudence, which imposes on public authorities a duty to take steps to protect the right to life when it is threatened by individuals or activities not directly connected with the state. For example, the police have a duty to prevent individuals from carrying out life-threatening acts against others, and the legislature must make such actions criminal offenses. The court's case law demonstrates that this obligation is not limited to law enforcement agencies. Given the fundamental importance of the right to life and the irreversible nature of most infringements, this

---

[115]*Öneryildiz v Turkey*, Application No. 48939/99, Judgment of 30 November 2004, paragraph 71.

[116]Article 2(2) states that the deprivation of life shall not be regarded as inflicted in contravention of this article when it results from the use of force which is no more than absolutely necessary: (a) in defence of any person from unlawful violence; (b) in order to effect a lawful arrest or to prevent the escape of a person lawfully detained; (c) in action lawfully taken for the purpose of quelling a riot or insurrection.

positive obligation of protection can apply in situations where life is at risk. The court has also applied this provision in cases in which certain activities that endanger the environment pose a threat to human life.

In *Öneryildiz* case,[117] an incident involving an explosion occurred at a municipal rubbish tip, resulting in the loss of thirty-nine lives, including nine members of the applicant's family. Despite the fact that an expert report had brought the potential danger of a methane explosion at the tip to the attention of municipal authorities two years prior to the tragedy, no action was taken by the authorities. The Court found that there had been a violation of Article 2 of the Convention under its substantive limb, on account of the lack of appropriate steps to prevent the accidental death of nine of the applicant's close relatives. It also held that there had been a violation of Article 2 of the Convention under its procedural limb, on account of the lack of adequate protection by law safeguarding the right to life. The Court observed in particular that the Turkish Government had not provided slum inhabitants with information about the risks they ran by living there. Even if it had, it remained responsible, as it had not taken the necessary practical measures to avoid risks to people's lives. The regulatory framework proved defective, as the tip was allowed to open and operate without a coherent supervisory system. Likewise, the town- planning policy was inadequate and undoubtedly played a part in the sequence of events leading to the accident. Additionally, the Court mandates that states must fulfill their positive obligation to protect human life in instances of natural disasters, despite the fact that these events are beyond human control and differ from situations involving hazardous activities where states are obligated

---

[117]*Öneryildiz v Turkey*, n 114

to have prepared adequate warning and defence systems.[118] The Court's decision on an application stemming from a devastating mudslide caused by heavy rainfall, which resulted in numerous fatalities, established a causal connection between the applicants' deaths and the significant administrative shortcomings identified in this case.

In the *Öneryildiz and Budayeva* cases, the main responsibility stemming from the positive obligation outlined in Article 2 is to develop a legal and administrative system. Specifically, this involves creating regulations that consider the unique characteristics of a situation or activity, as well as the potential risk to human life. Hazardous activities require regulations that govern licensing, establishment, operation, safety, and supervision.[119] Moreover, it is crucial to emphasize the importance of ensuring public access to information regarding such activities. This is particularly significant in situations involving natural disasters, in which the maintenance of a robust defense and warning system is essential.[120] Finally, it is crucial to develop procedures for detecting any shortcomings in the technical processes and any errors committed by responsible individuals.[121] The disparity that is most pronounced between instances of natural disasters and hazardous activities lies in the fact that the Court typically accords a more extensive margin of appreciation to the former due to their unpredictable and uncontrollable characteristics that are beyond human influence.[122] Additionally, the Court stated that 'the scope of the positive obligations imputable to the State in the particular circumstances would

---

[118]*Budazeva and Others v Russia*, judgment of 22 March 2008, paragraph 135.
[119]*Öneryıldız v Turkey*, n 114, paragraph 89 - 90; *Budayeva and Others v Russia*, ibid, paragraph 129 and 132.
[120]Ibid.
[121]Ibid.
[122]*Budayeva and Others v Russia*, n 117 paragraphs 134-135.

depend on the origin of the threat and the extent to which one or the other risk is susceptible to mitigation.'[123]

Article 1 of Protocol No. 1 guarantees the right to the peaceful enjoyment of one's possessions. However, this right is not absolute and certain restrictions are permissible. Public authorities may order the deprivation of property, but it must be justified, based on law, and carried out in the public interest with a fair balance between the individual's interest and the public interest.[124] The payment of compensation to the individual concerned is also relevant in assessing whether a fair balance has been struck. Additionally, public authorities may impose restrictions on the right to the peaceful enjoyment of possessions, as long as they are lawful, in the public interest, and proportionate. The Court has applied these general features to environmental cases, but has noted that Article 1 of Protocol No. 1 does not guarantee the right to enjoy one's property in a pleasant environment. However, certain activities that could harm the environment could also reduce the value of the property, amounting to partial expropriation or limiting its use, creating a de facto expropriation situation. Therefore, the Court investigates the realities of the situation in question.[125] Safeguarding an individual's right to peacefully enjoy their property may require that public authorities guarantee specific environmental standards. This right's full exercise is not solely contingent upon the authorities' refraining from interference, but may instead demand positive measures to secure this right, particularly when there exists a direct correlation between the anticipated actions of the authorities and the individual's capacity to

---

[123]Ibid.

[124]*Brosset-Triboulet and Others v France*, paragraph 80.

[125]*Taşkın and Others v Turkey*, decision of 29 January 2004

effectively utilize their property.[126] The Court has determined that a duty of care may be imposed in instances involving hazardous activities, as well as, to a lesser extent, in circumstances of natural disasters.[127]

From a procedural perspective, Article 6 of the Convention guarantees the right to a fair trial, which, according to the court, encompasses the right of access to a court. Typically, the right of access to a court arises in instances where a ''civil right or obligation'' within the purview of the Convention is in dispute.[128] The Court has determined that the right to access a court is likewise among the constituent elements of the right to a fair trial, which is safeguarded by Article 6. This encompasses the right to enforce final and enforceable court judgments enforced, and implies that all parties, including public authorities, must respect the decisions of the court.[129] In matters pertaining to environmental pollution, applicants are entitled to assert their rights to safeguard their physical integrity and property rights. The Court acknowledged that the right to live in a healthy and balanced environment, as enshrined in national law, constitutes a "civil right" for the purpose of a fair trial.[130] Consequently, when this right is acknowledged in the national law, it is considered a civil right. In *Zander v Sweden*,[131] the European Court of Human Rights determined that the legal

---

[126]*Öneryıldız v Turkey*, paragraph 134; *Budayeva and Others v Russia*, paragraph 172.

[127]*Öneryıldız v Turkey*, paragraphs 134 and 135; *Budayeva and Others v Russia*, paragraphs 172-182.

[128]*Balmer-Schafroth and Others v Switzerland*, judgment of 26 August 1997, paragraph 32

[129]*Kyrtatos v Greece*, paragraph 32; *Taşkın v Turkey*, paragraph 134

[130]See *Balmer-Schafroth and Others v Switzerland*, paragraph 33; *Taşkın and Others v Turkey*, paragraph 90.

[131]Application No. 14282/88, Judgment of 25 November 1993.

protections provided to landowners in Sweden against the contamination of their well water constituted a "civil right" as defined by Article 6, paragraph 1 of the European Convention on
Human Rights. As the applicants were unable to have the government's decision reviewed by a court, the court ruled that
there had been a violation of this article. However, the right to
access a court under Article 6(1) is not absolute and can be restricted if the purpose is legitimate and proportionate. However, any legal or factual limitation may violate the Convention if
it hinders an applicant's effective access to a court.

Furthermore, the Court has emphasized that the right to the
execution of a judicial decision constitutes a vital component
of the right to a fair trial and the right of access to courts as
outlined in Article 6, paragraph 1. The ability to initiate legal
proceedings would be rendered meaningless and devoid of
practical significance if the domestic legal system permitted
final judicial decisions to remain ineffective.[132] The provision
of access to a court guaranteed by Article 6 is applicable in
cases where there exists a direct and substantial connection between the environmental issue at hand and the civil rights being
claimed; tenuous or indirect links, or consequences that are remote in nature, are insufficient to establish a valid
connection.[133] Article 6 may be invoked in the event of a severe, imminent, and specific environmental threat, provided
that the likelihood of harm has reached a level of certainty that
renders the outcome of the proceedings crucial to the rights of
affected individuals.[134]

Undoubtedly, it is essential that public authorities, when
faced with intricate questions of environmental and economic

---

[132]See *Hornsby v Greece*, judgment of 19 March 1997, paragraph
40; *Taşkın and Others v Turkey*, paragraphs 135 and 138.
[133]*Balmer-Schafroth and Others v Switzerland*, paragraph 40.
[134]Ibid; *Taşkın and Others v Turkey*, paragraph 130.

policy, ensure that the decision-making process considers the rights and interests of individuals whose rights under Articles 2 (right to life) and 8 (right to private and family life) may be impacted. In cases where such individuals believe that their interests have not been accorded adequate weight in the decision-making process, they ought to have the ability to seek recourse through the courts.[135]

Article 10 of the Convention guarantees the right to freedom of expression, another procedural safeguard.[136] The freedom to disseminate information and ideas, as protected by Article 10 of the Convention, is crucial in the context of the environment. The Court has acknowledged the significant public interest in allowing individuals and groups to participate in public discourse by sharing information and ideas on topics of widespread concern.[137] The limitations imposed by public authorities on the freedom to access and disseminate information and ideas, particularly regarding environmental issues, must be explicitly outlined in law and serve a legitimate aim. Any such restrictions must be proportionate to the intended purpose, and a balance must be established between the rights of the individual and the collective interests of the community.[138]

Articles 2 and 8 of the Convention may create a specific positive obligation on public authorities to guarantee the right to access information concerning environmental issues under cer-

---

[135]*Taşkın and Others v Turkey*, paragraph 119.
[136]Article 10 states that 'everyone has the right to freedom of expression. This right shall include freedom to hold opinions and to receive and impart informa- tion and ideas without interference by public authority and regardless of frontiers...'
[137]*Steel and Morris v the United Kingdom*, judgment of 15 February 2005, paragraph 89; *Vides Aizsardzības Klubs v Latvia*, judgment of 27 May 2004, paragraph 40.
[138]Ibid.

tain conditions.[139] This obligation to ensure access to information is generally complemented by the positive obligations of the public authorities to provide information to those persons whose right to life under Article 2 or whose right to respect for private and family life and the home under Article 8 are threatened. The Court has found that in the particular context of dangerous activities falling within the responsibility of the state, special emphasis should be placed on the public's right to information.[140] The Court has established that it is the duty of the states to inform the public in a timely and adequate manner about any life-threatening emergencies, including natural disasters, as mandated by Article 2.[141]

The Court, in *Guerra's* case, held that Article 10 was not applicable as it essentially prohibits public authorities from restricting an individual's access to information that others are willing or able to provide. Nevertheless, the Court determined that Article 8 had been breached due to the lack of information that would have allowed the applicants to evaluate the potential risks to themselves and their families if they continued to reside near the factory.[142] In Öneryıldız's case, the Court determined that a duty to inform exists in situations involving 'real and imminent dangers' to an individual's physical integrity or private life. The Court held that the applicant could assess some risks, such as health risks, and does not absolve public authorities from their proactive duty to inform. Therefore, the Court found a violation of Article 2. In this case, the Court concluded that the administrative authorities knew or should have known about the real and immediate risks to the inhabi-

---

[139]*Öneryıldız v Turkey*, paragraph 90; *Guerra and Others v Italy*, paragraph 60.
[140]Ibid.
[141]*Budayeva and Others v Russia*, paragraph 131.
[142]*Guerra and Others v Italy*, paragraph 60

tants of certain slum areas due to the deficiencies of the municipal rubbish tip. The authorities not only failed to remedy the situation but also failed to fulfill their duty to inform the inhabitants of potential health and environmental risks. Despite this, the Court found that respecting the right to information may not be sufficient to absolve the State of its responsibilities under Article 2, and practical measures must be taken to avoid risks.[143]

The decision rendered by the Court in *Budayeva's* case emphasizes the state's duty to safeguard the lives of individuals subject to its authority. This responsibility encompasses both substantive and procedural aspects, one of which is the obligation to implement regulatory measures and investigate any instances of fatalities arising during life-threatening emergencies. Furthermore, the State is required to promptly disseminate information about such emergencies to the public. In this instance, the authorities failed to provide the required information concerning the possibility of mudslides to the affected population.[144] The Court went further to formulate guidelines for the creation of procedures that were utilized to disseminate information. It has mandated that whenever public officials engage in actions that are harmful and known to pose potential health hazards, they must put in place a dependable and accessible system for individuals to gain access to all pertinent and crucial information.[145] Finally, it is imperative that the general public have access to the findings of environmental and health impact evaluations that are carried out.[146]

---

[143]*Öneryıldız v Turkey*, paragraphs 67 and 84-87

[144]*Budayeva and Others v Russia*, paragraphs 131-132.

[145]*McGinley and Egan v the United Kingdom*, judgment of 9 June 1998, paragraphs 97 and 101

[146]*Brânduşe v Romania*, judgment of 7 April 2009, paragraph 63.

It is evident from the case law of the European Court of Human Rights that the primary responsibility for environmental protection lies with the state. According to the Rio Declaration, the state is required to enact effective environmental laws, facilitate access for individuals to information, decision-making processes and judicial and administrative proceedings at national level, to apply the precautionary approach 'widely', and to undertake environmental impact assessment 'as a national instrument'.[147] These provisions echo the fact that the state has an obligation to deliver good environmental governance. In delivering good governance, one obligation that seems to encapsulate the desired outcome is the obligation to use due diligence, as Boyle and Redgwell opined.[148] The elements of this obligation as identified by case law include: 'an adoption of reasonably appropriate rules and measures; a certain level of vigilance in their enforcement; the exercise of administrative control applicable to public and private operators, such as the monitoring of activities undertaken by such operators; careful consideration of the technology to be used; and the standard of due diligence has to be more severe for the riskier activities'.[149] 'Although states are responsible only for their own failure to act diligently, not for any failure by the operator of a risky activity to do so, it is the state's responsibility to require the operator to follow national laws and regulations and enforce those laws. Failure to monitor compliance or to enforce the law is, in many respects, the simplest and most easily proven failure of

---

[147]Principles 11, 10, 15 and 17 of Rio Declaration respectively. See Alan Boyle and Catherine Redgwell, *Birnie, Boyle, and Redgwell's International Law and the Environment* (Fourth Edition, Oxford University Press 2021)., at 143
[148]Ibid, at 163
[149]Ibid.

due diligence'.[150] This is clear from terms such as 'best environmental practices'. In exercising power in relation to environmental challenges, the state cannot remain an abstract entity. Power is exercised through the institutional framework as mandated by law. Environmental laws have created new governance rules. This makes it an offence to pollute; trade in endangered species is banned, and a permit becomes necessary to carry out certain activities. If these laws are breached, the offender will face the consequences of levying fines or imprisonment in extreme cases.[151] The creation of new rules is not sufficient to ensure compliance because environmental challenges require the creation of new public institutions, especially administrative institutions. These administrative institutions of environmental law take many forms, including central government departments, independent regulatory agencies, scientific advisors, and committees. Generally, environmental laws provide a framework for action in which different administrative bodies pass delegated legislation or make individual decisions in accordance with that framework. Essentially, environmental law is administrative in nature, and vivid at all levels within a nation.[152]

According to Ogunkan, the success or failure of environmental governance is measured by the following indicators: governance effectiveness, policy implementation, legislation and enforcement, and institutional efficiency, of the existing environmental governance system.[153] Effective governance requires

---

[150]Ibid.

[151]Elizabeth Fisher, 'Environmental Law: A very Short Introduction' (Oxford University Press 2017) at 84

[152]Ibid, at 84-85

[153]David V. Ogunkan, 'Achieving sustainable environmental governance in Nigeria: A review for policy consideration' (2022) Urban Governance 2 at 217

engagement, accountability and transparency, and the rule of law as a precept for good governance, which in the Nigerian environmental governance space has been ignored. Public participation in environmental governance is still restricted by open access to environmental information, and public participation in environmental decision-making processes remains reluctantly progressive.[154]

As discussed above, the legislature although having enacted several environmental laws has allowed for several impermissible loopholes either intentionally or not which have caused and are still the cause of environmental injustices. The unwillingness at this time to resolve some of these issues as will be highlighted may mean that the legislative arm is complicit in these injustices. First, the NESREA Act which remains the leading environmental law has no authority in the oil and gas sector.[155] The NESREA Act established the Agency charged with the responsibility for the protection and development of the environment in Nigeria by enforcing compliance with laws, guidelines, policies and standards of environmental matters. The intention of the lawmakers is not clear in the outright removal of the petroleum industry from the perspective of NESREA. This is because the NOSDRA Act which created NOSDRA mandates the Agency in the preparedness, detection and response to all oil spills in Nigeria.

The primary aim of the National Oil Spill Detection and Response Agency (NOSDRA) is to monitor and detect oil spills that occur during oil production and exploration. It is suggested that the collaboration between the National Environmental Standards and Regulations Enforcement Agency (NESREA) and stakeholders in Nigeria on environmental standards, regu-

---

[154]Ibid.
[155]According to the NESREA (Establishment) (Amendment) Act, 2018.

lations, and enforcement would have been more effective if NESREA had been granted authority in the oil and gas sector. Despite having different mandates, cooperation between the two agencies would have been highly beneficial for the environment in Nigeria, particularly within the oil and gas sector. The new Petroleum Industry Act has failed to provide a solution to this challenge. The challenge is the general protection of the environment in the oil and gas sector through the enforcement of relevant environmental laws. The main objective of the Petroleum Industry Act is to ensure good governance and accountability, create a commercially oriented national petroleum company, and foster a conducive business environment for petroleum operations. Interestingly, the Act directs within the petroleum industry the need to promote healthy, safe, efficient and effective operational conduct in an environmentally acceptable and sustainable manner.[156] An environmental objective is absent from the general objectives of the Act,[157] however, in the general administration of the Act, petroleum operations are conducted in a manner that protects the health and safety of persons, property, and the environment.[158]

Thus, it is encouraging that Nigeria's environmental legislation has progressed from near-nothing to the current state of the environmental legal system, with the centralized power of environmental protection and management agencies. Nonetheless, legislation, as a component of environmental governance, continues to face several challenges and issues.[159] There is no denying that Nigerian environmental statutes are extensive, broad, and comprehensive, but the main issue is that enforcement is trivial: so much time elapses from noncompliance

---

[156]See section 6(d); 31(c) of the Petroleum Industry Act
[157]See section 2 of the Petroleum Industry Act.
[158]Section 66(1)(m), ibid.
[159]David V. Ogunkan, n 152, at 217

to enforcement, the punishment obtainable for noncompliance is grossly inadequate, and injured parties are not fairly recompensed. In addition, some environmental offenses are punished administratively rather than through corrective measures or criminal prosecutions.[160] Generally, the inability of administrative agencies to protect the environment through the implementation and enforcement of relevant regulations, standards, and provisions is a major contributing factor to Nigeria's continued degradation of the environment. This is attributable to factors such as gaps in the legal framework, institutional bottlenecks, corruption, insufficient funding, poor governance, intimidation, ignorance etc.[161]

Environmental litigation, a key indicator of environmental governance, is gaining grounds in Nigeria. Environmental litigation in Nigeria has been influenced mainly by British colonial rule, laws and common law principles in the legal and regulatory framework of Nigeria's environmental law. While a range of options exists, current mechanisms are based mainly on common law tort actions in trespass, nuisance, negligence, and strict liability. There are always challenges associated with the current mechanism, which justifies the need to explore other options in human rights law and administrative law as Nigeria continues to develop into an advanced democracy, that may deliver better outcomes in appropriate cases. Among other reasons, the dearth of environmental litigation is due in part to the difficulties in establishing liability as well as the very high cost of litigation, which the majority of victims could not afford, leaving them without a remedy. The technicalities and costs of litigating any of these actions are not only difficult for local people but also unaffordable, leaving the majority of those who suffer damage unable to sue and, therefore, without a remedy.

---

[160]Ibid.
[161]Ibid.

This may be the right time for legal and judicial remedies outside tort law for environmental pollution cases in Nigeria.

In the case of *Gbemri*, the Nigerian legal system witnessed a significant milestone in the realms of human rights and the environment. The judiciary acknowledged the interconnectedness of human rights and the environment and progressed from a confined approach to addressing environmental concerns through the court. This ruling empowered non-governmental organizations to seek legal recourse against government entities and multinational corporations. The Supreme Court's ruling in the *Centre for oil pollution watch* case further accentuated the importance of access to justice in cases of environmental degradation. Although the court may need to demonstrate greater assertiveness in awarding appropriate compensation, the Gbemri case signified a noteworthy advancement in the facilitation of litigation and integration of human rights into environmental protection in Nigeria.

In Isaiah's case, neither a remediation order nor a compensation order was issued for significant oil spillage at the court of the first instance and court of appeal. However, it is crucial to conduct clean-up activities to value compensation, as oil spills create hazards that cannot be adequately addressed by compensation alone. Environmental remediation, which involves the removal of all contaminants from the environment, is essential to restore the environment to its original state. Jurisdictional issues often arise within environmental litigation and can be raised at any stage of a trial. In Nigeria, human rights suits concerning the environment are typically brought before the State High Courts, whereas suits pertaining to mines and minerals are filed in the Federal High Courts. As a result, environmental matters outside extractive industries can be brought before the State High Courts, while matters involving mines and minerals, such as the oil and gas sector, must be brought before the Federal High Courts. To overcome the jurisdictional challenge, the establishment of a specialised environmental court with jurisdiction over all environmental suits using human rights law, administrative law, and tort law may be considered.

For this specialised environmental court, the judiciary may adopt an 'environmental administrative court' with jurisdiction to hear all environmental claims under torts, human rights, and administrative laws. This specialised court will have to be less expensive, less formal, easily accessible, and have fewer technicalities. Appeals from this court go to the court of appeal, giving the court the same status as both Federal and State High Courts. This court will address all the shortcomings of the judiciary regarding environmental litigation. Issues of jurisdiction leading to environmental injustice will be resolved as the court will have exclusive jurisdiction over all environmental cases. The doctrine of standing will be relaxed to enable not only those who have an interest, but also NGOs with environmental mandates, to seek redress.

Regulatory authorities are responsible for implementing environmental protection laws and policies in Nigeria, and the outcomes so far speak volumes. The impact of climate change in the Niger Delta region is compounded by the oil and gas industry. Consequently, the region is experiencing an additional layer of environmental degradation caused by oil extraction, which has led to frequent oil spills and numerous gas flare locations. This has become a recurring issue, and the people have learned to coexist with it. Continuous environmental problems imply the involvement of the Nigerian government. The underlying issue stems from inadequate environmental governance.

The results of this study indicate that policymakers must take steps to foster a comprehension of environmental governance by improving funding, refraining from interference, and implementing dynamic legislative frameworks that are suitable for the present circumstances. For instance, constitutionalizing the right to a clean and healthy environment. By making a clean and healthy environment a fundamental human right, it will to a large extent create awareness and consciousness among the regulated community regarding their right to a clean and healthy environment. People file complaints regarding environmental aberrations, such as the installation of telecom masts near residential buildings or the discharge of effluents from industries into water bodies. The absence of an explicit provision for the right to the environment as a fundamental right in the constitution leads these individuals to resort to filing complaints rather than pursuing legal action through the courts.

The findings of this study revealed that environmental education plays a significant role in environmental governance. However, many graduates and professionals lacked adequate knowledge of environmental protection. In Lagos, non-governmental organizations have taken up the responsibility of providing environmental education and enlightenment. Therefore, fundamental approaches are crucial for improving environmental governance. Additionally, the planners of Lagos identified certain areas as wetlands and took measures to plant trees and promote biodiversity. Unfortunately, the development of these areas has resulted in the natural habitat destruction and increased flooding. It is regrettable that these decisions are made by state officials who are responsible for environmental decision-making, and not by uneducated individuals.

In general, environmental governance in Nigeria is ineffective because of several key factors, including disregard for precepts of good governance, poor policy implementation, an incomprehensive legal framework, weak enforcement of environmental laws, weak institutional agency, incipient environmental litigation, and lack or inadequate public participation.

Environmental protection responsibilities are intertwined with environmental governance in a great deal. As previously argued, due diligence is a key aspect of environmental governance. In practical terms, environmental protection responsibilities, such as the obligation for due diligence, are state responsibilities that cannot be ignored or delegated to other key players in environmental governance, that is, the private sector or civil society who have their specific roles to play. Thus, weak environmental protection responsibilities may directly impact the right to a healthy environment because central to good environmental governance is transparent and accountable for decision-making. Commitment to environmental quality is a feature of advanced democracies that requires vesting power in unelected administrative institutions. This is where the role of the law, specifically administrative law, concerned with constituting, limiting, and holding public administration accountable to ensure that public administrative power is legitimately exercised is significant.[162]

Conclusion

This chapter attempted to answer the question of how present legal frameworks and judicial activism have affected the implementation of the right to a healthy environment in Nigeria. In doing so, this chapter draws from the provisions of environmental laws and judicial activism relevant to environmental protection in Nigeria with the aim of establishing a supportive idea for the prospects of a human rights-based approach to environmental protection. In this chapter, it was found that Nigeria is not deficient in environmental legislations generally and also in laws that are sector specific. The foremost of these laws

---

[162]Elizabeth Fisher, n 150 at 85

is the NESREA Act which created an Agency responsible for enforcing compliance with laws, guidelines, standards on environmental matters. The removal of the oil and gas sector was noted as a setback to the mandate given to the Agency for the enforcement of compliance with laws on environmental matters. For NESREA as the lead environmental enforcement agency, its mandate should strictly cover all environmental law enforcement efforts, including the petroleum sector. The agency should be involved in environmental permitting and monitoring of all new and existing projects, including the approval of strategic environmental impact assessment. It was found that generally, poor enforcement of environmental laws and policies is largely unwillingness from the government. Based on these llaws, there are mechanisms for enforcement, but there is a lack of enforcement strategies. For example, using the mechanisms of search and inspection, where financial strategies are lacking, carrying out searches and inspections becomes impossible.

Judicial decisions in relation to environmental matters have been progressive, especially the landmark decisions discussed earlier. First, the progressive attitude of the courts was in the liberalization of the right to sue. The liberalization was captured after the decision in the Oronto Douglas case, where the court held that the plaintiff, an environmental activist, failed to show that his right was affected or that any direct injury was caused to him. The decisions in Jonah Gbemri and the Centre for Oil Pollution case both reflect the relaxation of the right to sue. In the Centre for Oil Pollution case, the Supreme Court stated that it was in the interest of justice that the appellant was not shut out after showing that the appellant's interest was clear and not prompted by the mischief. It was noted that the issues connected to environmental degradation are contemporary, and public-spirited persons in the vanguard of protecting the environment should be encouraged to check actions or omissions that tend to pollute the environment. Second, the burden of proofing and obtaining sufficient redress is another aspect worthy of consideration. The burden of proof was found to lie within the plaintiff. The courts have been perceived as strict with the discharge of this duty on the plaintiff. It may be imperative to adopt a flexible approach, particularly for environmental cases in which human rights violations have been asserted. In addition, courts are often quick to award compensation without orders for remediation. The reason for the denial of an order for remediation in clear cases of environmental degradation is unknown, and perhaps advantageous to the environment and the enjoyment of human rights.

In conclusion, the present legal framework and judicial activism positively influence the implementation of the right to a healthy environment. It is clear that we are not yet there, but there is no denying that there is a progressive attitude towards the right to a healthy environment. It has been established that environmental protection responsibilities cannot be delineated from good environmental governance in the quest for a healthy environment. The idea of environmental governance generally relates to how and who decides, which often determines the type of decision made. The 'how' deals with the processes involved in conjunction with good governance precepts. The 'who' deals with those involved in the process, the state, private sector and civil society. According to Shelton, it may not be desirable for the judiciary to delve into legislative decisions in environmental matters, but 'a rights-based approach emphasizes that judicial oversight is necessary to protect the rights of those in marginalised and minority communities, who often bear a disproportionate burden of environmental harm'.[163] The

---

[163]Knox and Pejan, n 4, at 9.

need to seek redress through courts in Nigeria is vivid because the nation is fraught with balancing social, economic, cultural, and environmental imperatives.

Elections In West-Africa and the Challenges of Good Governance: Ghana and Nigeria as Case Studies

Oreoluwa Omotayo Oduniyi[1]

Introduction

Roger Gibbins in his article, Election, described an election as the formal process of selecting a person for public office or of accepting or rejecting a political proposition by voting. Elections are an important component of democracy, if not the most important aspect. It is considered the first step to a sustainable democracy.[2] Timothy Sisk classifies the importance of elections into three parts: First, as part of a democratic process; Second, as a determinant of change or continuity of leadership;

---

[1]LLB (Ife) BL(Lagos) LLM (Ife) Ph.D. Candidate (Ife), Lecturer, Department of Public Law, Faculty of Law, Obafemi Awolowo University, Ile-Ife, Nigeria. E-mail: oreoduniyi@oauife.edu.ng.
[2]Roger Gibbins and others, 'Election' (Britannica 2020) < https://www.britannica.comltopic/electionpolitical-science> accessed 5 April, 2023.

Third, as a way of institutionalizing electoral integrity.[3] Berouk Mesfin describes elections as the instrument that compels or encourages policy-makers to pay attention to citizens.[4] These policy-makers hold the mandate of the people to make political and economic decisions on their behalf. In other words, the people that elect public office holders during an election give such public officials the legitimacy to govern them.

However, there is a competitive side to elections that provides voters with the option of choosing their representatives among individuals, or parties. The most common is the multi-party system, where voters choose candidates presented by at least two political parties. According to Hazama Yasushi, it is when elections involve the true competition of political parties based on their ideologies and proposed policies, not the popularity of the candidates or voting based on special interests, that consolidation of democracy is achieved.[5] However, the competitiveness of the multi-party system has engendered two major election problems, namely; election fraud and election violence in the West African sub-region.

---

[3]Timothy Sisk, 'Election, Electoral Systems and Party Systems'(International Institute for Democracy and Electoral Assistance 2017)

[4]Berouk Mesfin, 'Democracy, Elections & Political Parties: A Conceptual Overview with Special Emphasis on Africa' (2008), Institute for Security Studies <https://www.files.ethz.ch/isn/98951/PAPER166.pdf> accessed 20 October, 2023.

[5]Hazama Yasushi, 'Political Parties and Elections: Minimal conditions for democracy' (Institute of Developing Economies Japan External Trade Organisation) <https://www.ide.go.jp/EnglishlResearchlTopics/PolfElections/overview.html> accessed 5 November 2023

Stephanie Burchard noted that African countries reintroduced multiparty politics in the early 1990s as the curtains came down on the Cold War era. She continued that by 1997.75% of countries in sub-Saharan Africa had adopted multiparty elections, except for Eritrea, which has not conducted presidential or national assembly elections since its independence referendum in 1993.[6] Many sub-Saharan African countries have made significant strides towards democratic development, but election-related violence has also increasingly become a common feature of the politics of alternation of power in Africa. Thus, while elections in sub-Saharan Africa have become ubiquitous, challenges around election management, particularly related to election fraud and election violence, are still present.[7]

In his submission, Sisk noted that in sub-Saharan Africa, competitive elections based on universal suffrage were introduced in three distinct periods. In the 1 950s and I 960s, several countries held elections following decolonization.[8] Although many of these countries reverted to authoritarian governments, there were exceptions. In the late 1 970s, elections were introduced in a few countries where military dictatorships were dissolved (Nigeria and Ghana are classical examples) and other countries in Southern Africa underwent decolonization.[9] Beginning in the early 1990s, the end of the Cold War and the reduction of military and economic aid from developed countries brought about democratization and competitive elections in more than a dozen African countries.[10]

---

[6]Stephanie Burchard, 'The Role of the Courts in Mitigating Election Violence in Nigeria' (2019)
38 Open Edition Journal
[7]Ibid
[8]Timothy Sisk (n 2)
[9]Ibid
[10]Ibid

Research shows that countries in the West-African sub-region are yet to rid their election process of election fraud and election violence. According to the International Peace Institute, "Democracy and stability have suffered from a culture of rigging and election remain challenged by a generation of leaders who refuse to see themselves out of office".[11] It is now a lingering problem, to which countries have no excuse for not being able to find a lasting solution in this day and age. This paper focuses on two leading countries in the West African Region and how they have fared with their election process in the last three decades. While Ghana seems to be getting some things right, judging by the success rate of their elections since 1992, Nigeria seems to have a long way to go when it comes to holding a free and fair election.

The relationship between democratization, elections, election fraud, and election violence is a complex one. This complexity may not be all that surprising, given the prevailing assumption that democracy and peace are, ideally, mutually reinforcing, with elections serving as the connecting cord between them.[12] Election fraud and election violence are fundamental problems that are rooted both in the constitutional setup and the political climate of the focus countries of this paper. We shall discuss these problems comprehensively in this paper and recommend possible solutions that will ensure a sustainable democracy in these focus countries and Africa as a whole.

---

[11]International Peace Institute, 'Elections and Stability in West Africa' (Relief Web 2011) <https://reliefweb.int/sites/reliefweb.int/ffles/resources/FullDocu2.pdf accessed 5 November 2023
[12]Bayo Adekanye, *Retired Military as an Emergent Power Factor in Nigeria* (Heinemann Ed. Books, 2005)

Elections in West Africa

The International Peace noted that from the 1950s through to the 1970s, decolonization swept across Africa. While freedom was greeted with euphoria in many places, it could not mask the deep political instability that comes with independence.[13] Violence and coercion became a common means of changing power. Coups, countercoups, and aborted coups littered the political landscape on the continent.[14] The post-Cold War period witnessed several positive changes with respect to democratization in Africa. Participatory politics grew in the 1990s and 2000s, as the percentage of African countries holding democratic elections increased from 7% to 40% and in 2010, Freedom House classified eighteen countries on the continent as electoral democracies.[15] During the past two decades, the general trend has been toward greater accountability of political leaders, whose legitimacy is largely linked to the means through which they attain and maintain power, yet progress has been uneven.[16]

Elections have facilitated the emergence of democratic governments in Benin, Cape Verde, Ghana, Mali, Nigeria, Senegal, and South Africa. Following autocratic regimes and protracted civil wars, more stable societies have emerged in Guinea, Liberia, Niger, and Sierra Leone. In some cases, however, elections have been manipulated in favour of legitimate autocratic regimes or to ensure dynastic successions on the continent. Vi-

---

[13]International Peace Institute, 'Elections and Stability in West Africa' (Relief Web 2011)
<https://reliefweb.intJsites/reliefeb.intJfiles/resourcesIFull_-Docu_2.pdf accessed 10 November 2023
[14]Ibid
[15]Ibid
[16]Ibid

olence still plagues approximately 20% to *25%* of elections in Africa.[17] In recent times, high-profile election crises in Kenya (2007–2008), Zimbabwe (2000 and 2008), and Côte d'Ivoire (2010-2011) have collectively led to at least four thousand deaths and hundreds of thousands displaced.[18] Electoral violence can erode a people's faith in the democratic processes. Additionally, countries with a history of election violence often experience a recurrence of such violence, as witnessed in Kenya, Nigeria, and Zimbabwe).[19] The spate of election fraud and election violence in Africa has increased in recent times, hence the desire to examine the nature of electoral processes in the sub-Saharan part of Africa.

The concept of election and democracy is no longer alien to all West African countries in this day and age, the problem over the years has been the total adoption of the tenets of a democratic government. Most political leaders and their regimes have been insincere about adopting democracy in their respective countries. There have been democratic deficits in the form of political authoritarianism, and regimes that are characterized mostly by their totalitarian tendency.[20] There have been reports of human rights violations that have led to political unrest and destabilizing tensions.[21] Most of this tension and resulting violence have been caused by distrust in the electoral process and the manifestation of election fraud by the candidates, political parties, and their loyalists. Be it clampdown on the opposition

---

[17]Ibid
[18]Ibid
[19]Ibid
[20]Mathias Hounkpe and Others, 'Electoral Commissions in West Africa: A Comparative Study' (2nd Friedrich-Ebert-Stiftung Regional Office 2011)
[21]United Nation Human Rights West African Regional Office, 'Elections in West Africa: Best Practises and Lessons Learned' (UN 2015)

political parties, elections without a choice, elections organized with results known well in advance, election fraud in favour of those in power, it has been a difficult ride to attain a perfect democracy in most West African countries.[22]

In the last decade, West African countries have achieved great strides when it comes to elections. However, the challenges of election fraud and election violence have not been completely eradicated.[23] There are still issues of pseudo-democratic regimes and unsuccessful electoral cycles.[24] Elections have been a conflict- generating tool for political players despite the existence of a functioning Electoral Commission and judicial system. Most of the Electoral bodies are oftentimes rubber stamps or sabotaged when carrying out their duties.[25]

While the above submission is the true state of things in most West African Countries, few countries have found a way to establish an effective Electoral Commission that will set up rules and modalities for a free and fair election.[26] We shall take a look at how two giants in the West African region, Ghana and Nigeria, have fared in their attempt to eradicate election fraud and election violence in their election process.

---

[22]NationaL Human Rights West African Regional Office, 'Elections in West Africa: Best Practises and Lessons Learned' (WESCA 2015) <hps://www.wesca.ohch.org/IMG/pdflelections_booklet-_en.pdf.> accessed 20 November 2023
[23]Ibid
[24]Mathias Hounkpe (n 19)
[25]Ibid
[26]Ibid

Election Rigging and Election Violence in West African

In most developing countries around the globe, elections have been often marred by malpractices and violent disputes. It engenders violence in situations where contestants or their supporters do not follow the rules or accept the outcome of the election as the legitimate expression of the will of the citizenry.[27]

Election Fraud

Election fraud can be described as the illegal interference of the election process to increase the vote count of the favourite or most powerful candidate.[28] It is done by reducing the votes of rival candidates or inflating the votes of the favoured candidates, and it also goes side by side with voter intimidation.[29] Election fraud varies depending on the prevailing method in every peculiar political climate, and it has been a veritable tool for political villains to inhibit the growth of democracy in their respective countries.

In West Africa, most countries have independent Electoral Bodies saddled with the responsibility of ensuring a free and

---

[27]West Africa Network for Peace building, Election Dispute Management for West Africa - A Training Manual, West Africa Network for Peace building 2013
[28]Ugwuala Ugwunna Donald, Kalu Uchechukwu Godson, "Electoral Fraud as A Major Challenge to Political Development in Nigeria" (2020) 13 (2) African Journal of Politics and Administrative Studies 5
[29]Ibid

fair election but, in reality, the independence is on paper.[30] There have been reported cases where heads of Electoral Bodies have been forced to resign, intimidated, or ordered to conduct the election in such a way that benefits the candidate with the most power.[31] The reason for election fraud in most West African countries is rooted in political leaders seeking to evade term limits, democratic resiliency in the face of armed conflict, and the increasingly overt efforts by external actors to shape election outcomes.[32]

Individuals that take part in election fraud, such as multiple voting, usually justify it by claiming loyalty to their preferred leader and their greed and personal interest.[33] The political leaders themselves also encourage election fraud using the citizens by giving cash to voters pre-election and during elections.[34] Sometimes this method is an effective rigging tool, other times, electorates take the money and either vote for another candidate or not vote at all. A good example is a perpetual presidential aspirant in Ghana named Alan John Kyerematen. He is known to always hand out money for election favour from the electorates, so much so he is now being referred to as

---

[30]Olusegun Victor Adesanya, 'Combating Electoral Fraud Using the Rights-Base Approach' (2020)11(2) Nnamdi Azikiwe University Journal of International Law and Jurisprudence 8
[31]Ibid.
[32]Joseph Siegie and Others, 'Assessing Africa's 2020 Elections' (Africa Centre for Strategic Studies 2020) <https://africacenter.org/spotlightlhighlights-africa-2020-elections/> accessed 29 September 2023.
[33]Adejuwon Soyinka, 'A Review of the Book - The Moral Economy of Elections in Africa' (*The Conversation* 2021) <https: lltheconversation.com/new-book-reveals-what-drives-election-riggingand-when-citizens-resist-it-i *56595*> accessed 10 August 2023.
[34]Ibid.

Alan Cash. However, he has not been able to fly his party's flag in a presidential election, let alone contest for the presidential election.

For politicians who are in power, election fraud is used in another dimension. The power of incumbency is used to the fullest, and one can say that election fraud is fairly easier for the incumbent. Democracies in West Africa are fragile and volatile, but most leaders cling to power by manipulating voters' lists, delineating voting rights, and amending the electoral rules to aid their continuity in power.[35] In Cameroon, the current president, Paul Biya, came into power in 1982 and has been in power ever since. He got to power through a democratic transition of power but has held on to power with different manipulations of the voting system and the electoral system as a whole.[36] There has been the circumvention of the country's multiparty system and repeated amendments of the constitution to secure his position as the president. The most notable amendment occurred in 2008 where Biya removed the presidential term limit.[37] Actions like that of Biya have inhibited the development of a sustainable democracy in West Africa.

---

[35]International IDEA Policy Dialogue, 'Emerging Trends and Challenges of Electoral Democracy in Africa' (Institute for Democracy and Electoral Assistance 2016) <https://www.idea.intlsites/defaultJfiles/publications/emerging-trends-and-challenges-of-electoraldemocracy-in-africa.pdf5' accessed 9 November 2023.

[36]Adejuwon Soyinka, 'Cameroon's Biya is Africa's Oldest President: Assessing us 38 Years of Power (2021) The Conversation <https://theconversation.comlcameroons-biya-is-africas-oldestpresident-assessing-his-3 8-years-in-power-i *56221*> accessed 20 August 2023.

[37]Ibid.

Election Violence

Election violence can be described as an arm of political violence that is distinguished by the timing, which is usually pre-election, during elections, and post-election.[38] It has been said that a competitive political system increases the prospects of election violence.[39] The relationship between political competition and election violence has been evident in West African countries like Kenya, Nigeria, and Cote d'Ivoire, where political actors have resorted to violence to manage electoral uncertainty and air their dissatisfaction with the election process.[40]

Election violence has can be categorized into 3 categories, namely: Physical election violence; Psychological election violence; and Structural election violence.[41] Physical election violence is characterized by the use of physical force on opposition candidates and their supporters, together with election officials, election observers, voters, security operatives, before, during, and after an election.[42] Psychological election violence is the use of threats of violence to instil fear and panic in the minds of political opponents, voters, and other electoral stakeholders. It could be carried out mostly during an election by attacking polling units, sporadic shootings, and harassment of officials and voters to discourage every stakeholder from par-

---

[38]Eldridge Adolfo and Others, 'Electoral Violence in Africa' (The Nordic Africa Institute 2012)
<https://www.diva-portal.org/smashlgetJdiva2:58 1 667/fulltexto1.pdf> accessed 10
October, 2023.
[39]Michael Wahman and Others, 'Pre-election violence and Territorial Control: Political Dominance and Subnational Election Violence in Polarised African Electoral Systems' (2020) 57 Journal of Peace Research
[40]Ibid
[41]Ibid
[42]Ibid

ticipating fully in the election.[43] While Structural election violence is carried out by establishing institutional or legal frameworks targeted at political opponents, to keep them away or disenfranchise them from the political space. This method is used to deny political opponents from political positions of authority.[44]

West Africa has come a long way in adopting the concept of democracy. From the years of western colonization to military rulers and authoritarian African leaders. In today's West Africa, multiparty elections are now a routine exercise, albeit with a lot of election fraud and election violence.[45] These routine elections have exposed the strengths and weaknesses of the democracies practiced in most West African States. Successful transition of power in countries like Guinea, Senegal, and Niger have shown that the region has made significant progress in the adoption of the concept of democracy.[46]

An Overview of Trajectory of Elections and Electoral Processes in Ghana

Ghana's post-independence history began in March 1957 with a civilian regime that soon degenerated into a quasi-dictator-

---

[43]Ibid
[44]Ibid
[45]International Peace Institute, 'Elections and Stability in West Africa: The Way Forward' (International Peace Institute 2012) <https://www.files.ethz.cbIisnJl439 I 5/ipi ej, ub_elections_in_west_africa.pdf5> accessed 12 October, 2023
[46]Ibid

ship, and as a result, the first military coup of 1966.[47] From then on, there were switches between democratic governments and military governments.[48] At a point in 1964, Kwame Nkrumah, the then president, in the midst of stiff opposition, pushed for a constitutional amendment that made Ghana a one-party state and made him the life president before he was over-thrown in 1966.[49] After the military coup in 1966, there was a democratic election in 1969 that ushered in Edward Akufo-Addo until 1972 when he was overthrown by the military.[50] The military government then proposed a fused government of military and civilian to which an election was held in 1979 which brought in a government that lasted until 1981 when an-other coup took place.[51] There was a hiatus of democratic gov-ernment from 1981 to 1992 when a referendum was held to bring back democracy. The then military Head of State, Jerry Rawlings, contested in the election, which was boycotted by the opposition and won under the National Democratic Con-gress Party.[52] Rawlings won the 1996 election and then handed over to John Kufour in 2000 in an election that symbolized the maturity of Ghana's democracy.[53] Elections were held in 2004,

---

[47]B Gyimah, *Six Years of Constitutional Rule in Ghana 1993-1999: An Assessment and Prospects of the Executive and Legislature* (Gold type Ltd 2000)
[48]Voice of America, 'Ghana's Experiences at Democracy Since Independence' (*VOA* 2009) <https://www.voanews.comlarchive/ghanas-experiences_democracy-independence> accessed 12 October 2023.
[49]Angela Thopsefi, 'A Brief History of Ghana Since indepen-dence' (*Thought Co.* 2019) <https:/www.thoughtco.comlbrief-history-of-ghana-3996070> accessed 12 October 2023
[50]Ibid
[51]Ibid
[52]Ibid
[53]Ibid

2008, and in 2012, the then president, John Atta Mills died in office and there was a smooth transmission to his Vice, John Mahama, as provided by the constitution.[54] As of today, Ghana has a total of 29 political parties which suggest that they run a multiparty system.[55]

The first 3 decades after independence saw the desire for a continuous democratic government short-lived by military interruptions.[56] This trend changed in 1992, which witnessed the return of a democratic government. With 8 successful general elections that have seen three changes of governments between two major political parties, Ghana is now viewed as a beacon of thriving democracy not only in West Africa but across the continent.[57]

1992 and 1996 Elections in Ghana

The last time Ghana had an election before 1992 was in 1979 and there were a lot of high expectations after an extended military rule. The incumbent military head of state, Jerry Rawlings, was also part of the contest under the auspices of NDC.[58] With voter turnout pegged at *50.2%,* NDC won with *55.4%* of votes. The opposition accused Jerry Rawlings and his supporters of rigging, which prompted them to boycott the parliamen-

---

[54]Ibid
[55]A Osei, 'Party System Institutionalization in Ghana and Senegal' (2012) 48(5) Journal of Asian and African Studies 577–593
[56]Richard Kweitsu, 'Ghana, 61 Years After Independence: Challenges and Prospects' (Mo Ibrahim Foundation 2018) <https://mo.ibrahim.foundationlnews/20 1 8/ghana-6 1-years-independence- challenges-prospects> accessed 30 October, 2023
[57]Ibid
[58]Richard Jeffries and Clare Thomas, 'The Ghanaian Elections of 1992' (1993) 92(368) African Affairs 331,366

tary elections.[59] The outcome of the 1992 election left a sour taste in the mouth of those hoping to see the re-democratisation of Africa.[60] The 1992 Commonwealth Observer Group noted that the reputation of Jerry Rawlings and the way he came to power created an atmosphere of distrust among the opposition.[61] Rawlings, on the other hand, based his campaign on the fact that the opposition was seeking power in order to reverse the revolutionary process.[62]

In the election proper, there were complaints of multiple voters' registers, both of the 1992 referendum and the updated presidential election register. Many prospective voters could not find some of their information used in the old list, while others who did not participate in the referendum found themselves excluded from the 1992 elections.[63] However, with the reports of irregularities with the voters' lists, observers noted that the election process was free and fair.[64]

1996 saw the return of Jerry Rawlings as the president of Ghana and the election process was not without some irregular-

---

[59]Ibid

[60]Ibid

[61]Commonwealth Observer Group, 'Ghana Presidential and Parliamentary Elections' (2012) Commonwealth Secretariat <https://theconimonwealth.org/sites/defaultJfiles/inline/Ghana-Elections-FinalReport2012.pdI accessed 13 October 2023

[62]Mike Oquaye. "The Ghanian Elections of 1992 – A Dissenting View' (1995) Volume 94 African Affairs

[63]Carter Centre Ghana Election Mission, 'Report of The Carter Centre Ghana Election Mission ' (1992) The Carter Centre of Emory University

[64]Commonwealth Observer Group, 'Ghana Presidential and Parliamentary Elections' (2012) Commonwealth Secretariat <https://thecommonwealth.org/sites/default/files/inline/Ghana-Eiections-FinalReport20 12.pdf> accessed 10 January 2023

ities. There were reports of inadequate election materials, poor visibility during the vote counting, a few reports of election malpractices.[65] Major election irregularities were recorded in Tamale, Salaga, Bimbilla, Kpandai, and Wulensi regions where it was reported that there were child voters with ID cards and names on the voters' lists.[66] Some other observer groups noted that there were issues such as delays in getting results from some polling stations, the lack of political parties' code of conduct.[67]

There were some positives from the 1996 election as noted by observers. Some of the positives include a revamped Electoral Commission and election process engendered by a new Constitution; an independent Electoral Commission that put in place frameworks that assured the electorates of a smooth election process and the successful concurrent holding of Presidential and Parliamentary elections.[68] As for the election process itself, it was reported that polling stations opened on time; security was adequate in most places; party agents were present at most of the stations visited, and electoral officers performed their duties with diligence.[69] Overall, the conditions of the

---

[65]Maame Gyekye-Jandoh, 'Civic Election Observation and General Elections in Ghana Under the Fourth Republic: Enhancing Government Legitimacy and Democratisation Process' https: J/codesri&org/IMG/pdf/2-Issues_in_ghana_s_electoraimaame-civic electionobservation_and_general_elections.pdf accessed 13 October 2023.
[66]Ibid
[67]Commonwealth Observer Group (n 63)
[68]Ibid
[69]Maame Gyekye-Jandoh (n 64)

1996 elections allowed Ghanaians to choose their representatives in a free and fair.[70]

2000 Elections

The 1996 election was an encouraging indication that Ghana was serious about having a working democracy with a seamless election process. The 2000 election was of great significance to Ghanaians because it was going to mark the first peaceful transition of power via the ballot box.[71] It was a keenly contested Presidential race between the incumbent Vice President, John Atta-Mills, and John Kufour. There was no victor in the first round of the election, as neither candidate met the 50% majority criteria provided for in the constitution. A run-off election was held and John Kufour emerged as the winner.[72] The then UN Secretary General, Kofi Annan, noted that

---

[70]Commonwealth Observer Group, 'Ghana Presidential and Parliamentary Elections' (2012) Commonwealth Secretariat < https://thecommonwealth.org/news/commonwealth-observer-group-issues-final-report-2012-elections-ghana> accessed 10 January 2023.

[71]Kwame Boafo-Arthur, 'Democracy and Stability in West Africa: The Ghanaian Experience' (Claude Ake Memorial Papers No. 4, Department of Peace and Conflict Research Uppsala University and Nordic Africa Institute 2008)

[72]Ghana Parliamentary Chamber: Parliament, 'Election Held in 2000' (IPU 2000) <http://archive.ipu.org!parline-e/reports/arc/2 1 23_00.html> accessed 12 January 2022

Ghana had demonstrated that democracy and its institutions are taking root in Africa.[73]

Even though the election was largely a success, there were some downsides observed by domestic and international monitoring groups. Sporadic clashes were reported between supporters of the two major parties, which led to a dusk-to-dawn curfew order in the northern town of Bawku. Thirteen people were reportedly killed on election day.[74] There were also reported cases of impersonation, multiple voting, under-aged voters, and inadequate supply of voting materials. These problems were, however, not significant enough to dent the credibility of the general election in 2000.[75] Both rounds of elections that produced John Kufour as the president of Ghana were declared free and fair by domestic and international observers.[76]

2004 Elections

In 2004, the two main contenders of the previous election had a go at it again, and John Kufour emerged as the winner without a runoff this time around. In the parliament, NPP won the

---

[73]Felix Anebo, 'The Ghana 2000 Elections: Voter Choice and Electoral Decisions' (2001) 6 *African Journal of Political Science*
12 January 2023.
[74]Ghana Parliamentary Chamber (n 71)
[75]AM Amoako, 'The Dominance of Two Parties in the Politics of Ghana's 4th Republic: The Electoral System a
Factor?' (2019)8(3) International Journal of Science and Research (IJSR)
[76]Observer Group, 'Ghana Presidential and Parliamentary Elections' (Commonwealth Secretariat 2012)

majority seats, taking 128 out of 230 seats.[77] The 2004 elections caught the eye of the international community, the Electoral Body, and Ghana as a whole were commended for their conduct at the polls.[78] This was the election that produced the first non-military individual as president that will complete a full 8-year tenure.[79]

Even though there were reports of political tension, unrest, and other irregularities, the 2004 election was declared free and fair by both local and international observers.[80] Even though it was not significant enough to put a dent in the credibility of the election, the major negative report of the 2004 election was that there was a high number of rejected votes. This was due to a lack of voters' education. Rejected votes accounted for 2.14% of the total votes, which was more than the votes some of the Presidential candidates had in the election.[81]

The 2000 and 2004 elections were a success with minimal election-related issues. It put Ghana on the world map as the leading nation in the crusade for democracy in Africa. The Electoral Commission was growing into its role as the umpire of elections, and the citizens were also becoming aware of the

---

[77]Michael Amoako Addae, 'Party's Presidential Primaries and the Consolidation of Democracy in Ghana's 4th Republic' (2021)7(1) Cogent Social Sciences
[78]Ben Gun, 'Report on Ghana 2004 Election' (KAS-Landerber-itchte) <https://www.kas.de/c/document_library/get_file?uuid89 I 5402f-ee7d-OfSf-c14b8- 569bfc9b9442&groupId=252038> accessed 13 January 2023.
[79]Commonwealth Observer Group, 'Ghana Presidential and Parliamentary Elections' (Commonwealth Secretariat 2012) <https:Jlthecommonwealth.orgsites/defaultlfilesinline/Ghana-Elections-FinalReport201 2.pdf> accessed 13 January 2023
[80]Ibid
[81]Ibid

reputation the country was building for itself in terms of elections and democracy. Therefore, they always conducted themselves in an impressive manner to ensure that the country lives up to the expectations.

2008 Elections

In 2008, it was time for John Kufour to hand over to a democratically elected government. John Atta Mills emerged as the winner, and it marked the second time that there will be a transition of power to the opposition party. This election showed how far Ghana had come and how matured the politicians and the electorates had become as everyone acted in good faith and according to the provisions of the constitution.[82] The 2008 election was a test of how strong Ghana's burgeoning democracy had become. The two major parties had both enjoyed a full term of 8 years prior to the election, and there was no doubt that it was going to be keenly contested.[83]

There were concerns in the build-up to the elections because of the Electoral Commission's delay in the updating of the voters' lists to capture new or relocated voters and remove deceased voters. The Electoral Commission blamed it on the difficulty in procuring new registration equipment and a delayed start to voters' registration. This proved costly as there were

---

[82]The Carter Centre, 'Observation Mission to Ghana's 2008 Presidential and Parliamentary Elections - Final Report' (The Carter Centre 2009) <https://www.cartercenter.org/resources/pdfs/news/peacej,ublications/election> accessed 11 November, 2023.

[83]AM Amoako (n 74)

some incidents of violence in some areas.[84] The election was generally peaceful and there were some agitations as the two major parties were already celebrating their win before the official announcement. This was short-lived, as the official result revealed that there had to be a run-off election to determine the winner of the presidential election.[85] There were some tensions in the build-up to the run-off election, but the election itself was generally peaceful amidst extensive security operations. Voting was cancelled and rescheduled in Tam District due to security challenges.[86] The re-vote was boycotted by agents of NPP, but other than that, it was deemed free and fair.[87] The 2008 general election was deemed a success, even with the complications of having to hold a run-off election. It confirmed Ghana's maturing democracy and made it a point of reference for other African countries. The electoral commission played a significant role in the success of the elections.[88]

2012 Elections

The 2012 election was another watershed in Ghana's election history. It marked the first time that an election outcome will be challenged by the opposition. It also tested the independence of

[84]Commonwealth Observer Group, 'Ghana Presidential and Parliamentary Elections' (Commonwealth Secretariat 2012) <https://thecommonwealth.org/sites/default/files/inline/Ghana-Elections-FinalReport20 I 2.pdf'> accessed 20 January 2023
[85]Kathrin Meissner, 'Elections and Conflict in Ghana — Country Analysis' (Friedrich Ebert Stiftung 2010) <https://library.fes.de/pdf-files/iez/07676.pdf> accessed 20 January 2023.
[86]Ibid.
[87]The Carter Centre (n 81)
[88]Commonwealth Observer Group, 'Ghana Presidential and Parliamentary Elections' (Commonwealth Secretariat 2012) <https://thecommonwealth.org/sites/defaultJfiles/inline/Ghana-Elections-FinalReport2o 1 2.pdf> accessed 23 January 2023.

the Electoral Commission (EC) which it passed in flying colours.[89] The 2012 elections also witnessed the introduction of biometric verification machines, which caused some setbacks as voting was suspended in some polling stations across the country.[90]

Coming off the heels of the death of the incumbent president, John Atta Mills, and the transmission of power to his Vice, John Mahama, and coupled with the internal politics of the ruling party, the 2012 election was arguably the most delicate of all Ghanaian general elections.[91] John Mahama was declared as the winner of the elections and days later, the battleground shifted from the polling stations to the Supreme Court when the NPP filed a petition challenging the outcome of the election.[92] The Supreme Court gave its ruling in August 2013 and upheld the election result.

The president, John Mahama, was lauded for not resorting to violence giving that he had only been in office for 5 months, following the death of John Atta Mills. His respect for the constitution and the judicial system was commended and once

---

[89]Benjamin Agyekum, 'Newspaper Coverage of the 2012 Presidential Election Petition: A Content Analysis of the Daily Graphic' (MA Communications Dissertation, University of Ghana 2014)
[90]Ibid
[91]Commonwealth Observer Group, 'Ghana Presidential and Parliamentary Elections' (Commonwealth Secretariat 2012) <https://thecommonwealth.orglsites/defaultlfiles/inline/Ghana-Elections-FinalReport20 12.pdf> accessed 23 January 2023.
[92]Benjamin Agyekum, 'Newspaper Coverage of the 2012 Presidential Election Petition: A Content Analysis of the Daily Graphic' (MA Communications Dissertation, University of Ghana 2014)

again showed how far Ghana's democracy had come.[93] The opposition was also commended for respecting the ruling of the Supreme Court on the matter.[94] It was argued that the election petition in the 2012 election was an indictment on the neutrality of the Electoral Commission. It also raised the question of why election officers were not included in the proceedings, let alone punishing any erring election officer.[95] The petition of the election outcome was a stain on the almost perfect track record of general elections in Ghana. It exposed the loopholes in the election administration of Ghana. Some of the loopholes include irregularities in ballot accounting, result tallying, non-compliance with electoral rules by some election officials, and poor capacity of some election officials.[96]

2016 Elections

The 2016 election saw the defeat of the incumbent President and the party after just one term. It was similar to the 2000 and 2008 elections when the incumbent party lost to the opposition.[97] It was reported that over 15 million Ghanaians participated in the 2016 general elections to vote for their lawmakers and choose a president. It was a shift from the norm where the incumbent president enjoys the full tenure of 8 years.

---

[93]Ishaq Alhassan, 'Accountability, Contract Officers and the Integrity of the 2012 Election Outcome in Ghana' (2016) 15 Journal of African Elections
[94]Ibid
[95]Ibid
[96]Ibid.
[97]Joseph Ayee, 'Ghana's Elections of 7 December 2016. A post Mortem' (2017) 24 *South African Journal of International Affairs.*

It was a landslide victory for the NPP.[98] This election further strengthened the four prominent democratic trends, namely: The embrace of elections; The acceptance of Constitutional norms; The emergence of free media and active civil society; and The establishment of regional pro-democratic conventions and protocols.[99]

The 2016 elections witnessed the appointment of a new Electoral Commission chairperson. There was a perception that her inexperience in the role may affect the election process and the overall outcome. The political stakes were also higher than the previous 6 elections because the incumbent president had been in office for just one term and the opposition candidate pursued his final run for office. There was also the petition of the 2012 election result, which dented the electorates' confidence in the Electoral Commission and the election process.[100] After votes were cast, the incumbent lost and was magnanimous in defeat. He congratulated Akufo-Addo and stated that each victory belonged to the people. He also admitted that there were some irregularities during the election, but it was in the best interest of the nation for him to concede victory and ensure the sustenance of democracy in Ghana.[101]

---

[98]Isaac Nsiah, 'Ghana's 2016 Elections: An Overview of Selected Relevant Background Themes' (2020) 19 Journal of African Elections

[99]Ransford Van Gyampo and Others, 'Ghana's 2016 General Election: Accounting for the Monumental Defeat of the National Democratic Congress (NDC)' (2017)16 Journal of African Elections

[100]Joseph Ayee, 'Ghana's Elections of 7 December 2016: A post Mortem' (2017) 24 South African Journal of International Affairs

[101]John Mbaku, 'The Ghanian Elections: 2016' (African in Focus 2016) <https://www.brookings.edu/blog/africa-in-focus/20 16/12/1 5/the-ghanaian-elections-20 16/> accessed 23 January, 2023.

Generally, it was believed that the Electoral Commission and its chairperson did a poor job in overseeing the election, due to the launch of a 5-year plan to make the Commission the benchmark in Africa. It portrayed the commission as unserious and not ready for the election.[102] It is widely believed that the presidential candidates were the lifeline of the election. They believed in the will of the people and they respected it. While John Mahama was magnanimous in victory, Akufo Addo was humble in victory.[103]

How Has Ghana Faired Over the Years

Perhaps, the position of Ghana as a beacon of democracy in Africa is a fitting one. It is the first country in sub-Saharan Africa to attain independence from a colonial power, and it has managed to build a sustainable democracy that serves as a point of reference for other African countries.[104] Election is a major key to achieving democracy. Democracy has two elements: participation and competition.[105] It can be said that Ghana's 4 republic has these two elements as it has witnessed

---

[102]Joseph Ayee (n 99)

[103]Policy & Practice Brief, 'Ghana, A Beacon of Hope in Africa' (Accord) <https://www.accord.org.zalpublicationlghana/> accessed 5 September, 2023

[104]Policy & Practice Brief, 'Ghana, A Beacon of Hope in Africa' (Accord) <https://www.accord.org.zalpublicationlghana/> accessed 5 September, 2023.

[105]Baffour l3oakye, 'Electoral Politics in Ghana's 4th Republic (1992-2016) and its Implications on Future Elections' (2018) SSRN Electronic Journal <https://www.researchgate.net/publicationI326756749_Electoral_Politics_in_Ghana's_4th_Republ ic_1992-201 6_andjt-s_Implications_onFuture_Elections> accessed 5 September, 2023

three peaceful transitions of power between major political parties as well as improving the performance of its Electoral Commission and Judiciary to guarantee a sustainable democracy.[106] The 2012 election was a true test of Ghana's formal democratic institutions saddled with the responsibility of ensuring a sustainable democracy. From the conduct at the polls to the verdict of the Supreme Court, stakeholders hailed Ghana's multi-party democracy and noted that it should be adopted as a model by other African countries.[107]

The journey for a sustainable democracy began in 1992 when the Fourth republic's constitution was passed into law. This constitution had provisions that catered for modem liberal democracy which protected Fundamental Human Rights — civil, political, social, economic, and cultural rights.[108] Chapter 18 of the constitution established a Commission on Human Rights and Administrative Justice that handles issues that bother on fundamental rights and freedom, injustice, corruption, and the abuse of power by political officeholders.[109] What has distinguished Ghana from other West African countries and ensured that they have a sustainable democracy is the fact that all citizens, including public officeholders, respect and act according to the provisions of the constitution.[110]

The 1992 constitution also established the Electoral Commission to manage and conduct all public elections and to handle all matters directly relating to the conduct of elections in

---

[106]Ibid
[107]Ibid
[108]Policy & Practice Brief, 'Ghana, A Beacon of Hope in Africa' (Accord) <https://www.accord.org.zalpublicationlghanal> accessed 5 November 2023.
[109]Ibid
[110]Ibid

Ghana.[111] The Commission has conducted the presidential and parliamentary elections from 1992 to 2016, and it can be said that it gained the confidence and trust of the public because of the independence, professionalism, and neutrality it exuded when conducting elections over the years.[112] However, this reputation was achieved over time. The first election in 1992 was fraught with irregularities and accusations of election fraud, so much so the opposition boycotted the parliamentary election.[113] Since the conduct of the 1992 elections, there have been progressive improvements in how the Electoral Commission and other formal democratic institutions have conducted themselves during elections. A testament to these improvements can be seen in the 2000, 2008, and 2016 elections, which saw the incumbent party lose the presidential elections and all stakeholders, including the candidates, accepted the outcome of the election.[114]

---

[111]The Electoral Knowledge Network, 'Electoral Commission of Ghana' (ACE) <chttpsj/aceproject.org/ero_en/regions/africalGHlelectoral-commission-of-ghana> accessed 5 November, 2021
[112]Shola Omotola, 'The Electoral Commission of Ghana and the Administration of the 2010 Elections' (2023) 12(2) Journal of African Elections

[113]Baffour Boakye, 'Electoral Politics in Ghana's 4th Republic (1992-2016) and its Implications on Future Elections' (2018) SSRN Electronic Journal <https://www.researchgate.net/publicationl326756749_Electoral_Politics_in_Ghana's_4th_Republ ic_i 992-2016_and_its_Implications_on_Future_Elections> accessed 5 November, 2023.
[114]Felix Kumah-Abiwu and Others, 'Elections and Democratic Developments in Ghana: A Critical Analysis' (2020) 11 Journal of Economics and Sustainable Development

Democracy is a fragile institution that has to be constantly guarded and strengthened to ensure it is sustained.[115] The year 2012 put Ghana's democracy to the test and the world watched whether it will break under some unprecedented political occurrences. The first was the death of the incumbent president, John Atta Mills. The public was informed of his death immediately it was confirmed by doctors and within hours, there was a smooth transition of power to his Vice, John Mahama, as provided by the constitution.[116] The respect for the constitution was commended by both local and international stakeholders, and it showed Ghana as a country that respected its constitution and formal institutions that were established to ensure a robust and sustainable democracy.[117] Another test for Ghana's electoral and democratic legitimacy was the 2012 elections, which were rejected by the opposition. There were allegations of irregularities that led to the opposition filing a petition to upturn the election result.[118] The Supreme Court in its ruling upheld the election result, and this was viewed as another major step in the consolidation of Ghana's democratic institution. The accolades were majorly based on the fact that the opposition did not

---

[115]Ghana Election Watch, 'December 2020 General Elections' (International Republic Institute 2020) <https:Jwww.ndi.org/sitesJdefaultJfiles/ Ghana%20Election%20Watch%20V4.pdf' access
[116]Policy & Practice Brief, 'Ghana, A Beacon of Hope in Africa' (Accord) <https://www.accord.org.zalpublication/ghana/> accessed 5 October, 2023.
[117]Anyway Sithole, 'Ghana: A Beacon of Hope in Africa' Policy & Practice Brief— Knowledge For Durable Peace <https://www.files.ethz.ch/isnll 54807/AC-CORD-policy-practice-brief- 18.pdf' accessed 5 October, 2023.
[118]Shola Omotola (n 111)

resort to violence both after the election and after the Supreme Court's ruling.[119]

Overall, it is clear that Ghana's democracy has been founded on the establishment and respect for its formal democratic institutions, that is; A strong adherence to the rule of law by political actors; The independence and integrity of the legal system[120] and A highly effective election management system. However, with the success and accolades of Ghana's election process and democracy, it also has its flaws which have reared its ugly head in every election, albeit not in a significant way to affect the credibility of these elections. Some of these illiberal practices include monetized politics, vote-buying, election frauds, violence, political vigilantism, selective justice, and lack of punishment of politically connected corrupt persons.[121]

---

[119]Baffour Boakye, 'Electoral Politics in Ghana's 4th Republic (1992-2016) and its Implications on Future Elections' (2018) SSRN Electronic Journal <https://www.researchgate.net/publicatio-nJ326756749 Electoral politics in Ghana's 4th Republic

[120]Kwame Boafo-Arthur, 'Democracy and Accountability in West Africa: The Ghanian Experience' (Claude Ake Memorial Papers No. 4 Department of Peace and Conflict Research Uppsala University & Nordic Africa Institute 2008)

[121]Kofi Nsia-Pepra, 'Flawed Democracy the Bane of Ghana's Success in Curbing Corruption' (2017) 8 ASPJ Africa & Francophonie <https: /www.airuniversity.afedu!Portals/l O/ASPJFrenchljournalsE/Volume-O8lssue-2/nsia- pepra_e.pdf' accessed 5 October, 2023.

These problems have prevented Ghana's democracy from further developing into a global beacon for democracy.[122]

An Overview of the Trajectory of Elections and Electoral Processes in Nigeria

Nigeria's democracy journey began after its independence in 1960. Three years into the independence, tension began to brew, and it was largely blamed on the controversial 1962-1963 census.[123] Nigeria experienced its first military coup in 1966, followed by a civil war that lasted until 1970.[124] Lieut. Col Yakubu Gowon, who was the Head of State from 1966, was ousted by Brig. Gen Murtala Ramat Mohammed in 1975. Murtala Mohammed promised to return power to a democratically elected government after 4 years. He made significant changes to the Nigerian polity, which showed his seriousness to fulfil his promise.[125] It is worthy to note that Nigeria's vast heterogeneity (specifically its ethnic, linguistic, religious, and region-

---

[122]Kai Brima, 'Democracy in Ghana: lesson For Africa' (A dissertation -presented to the Faculty of Arts in the University of Malta for the degree of Master in Contemporary Diplomacy 2012) <https:/www.diplomacy.edulsystemlfiles/dissertations/03 1220131 60535_Brima%2528Library% 2529.pdf accessed 5 October, 2023.

[123]Adeyinka Theresa Ajayi and Emmanuel Oladipo Ojo, 'Democracy in Nigeria: Practice, Problems and Prospects' (2014)4(2) Developing Country Studies

[124]Idris Ahmed Jamo, 'Democracy and Development in Nigeria-Is There a Link? (2013)3(3) Arabian Journal of Business and Management Review (OMAN Chapter) 6

[125]Adeyinka Theresa Ajayi and Emmanuel Oladipo Ojo (n 127)

al diversity) has always been an abiding source of societal tensions and conflicts. It is one of the major reasons why Nigeria is finding it hard to establish a true democratic government set-up like that of Ghana.[126]

Murtala Mohammed was assassinated in 1976 and his trusted Lieutenant, Olusegun Obasanjo, completed his tenure and handed over power to a democratically elected civilian government in 1979 as promised by his former boss)[127] Shehu Shagari emerged as the president of Nigeria in 1979 and was re-elected in 1983 amidst allegations of Election fraud and election irregularities. Tensions were high and crisis broke out. The military, led by Maj. Gen. Muhammed Buhari, felt obligated to step in to take control of the political crisis and failing economy. Hence, another coup took place in 1983 which was uninterrupted until 1999.[128]

It is noteworthy to mention that there was an election in 1993 that was critically acclaimed as the freest, fair, and most peaceful in the history of Nigeria to date. However, it was annulled by the then Head of State, Gen. Ibrahim Babangida. This put paid to the dream of a return to a civilian government. Gen. Babangida was later overthrown by Gen. Sani Abacha.[129] Abacha's sudden death in 1998 saw the appointment of Gen. Abdulsalam Abubakar, who promised to hand over power to a democratically elected government in 1999.[130]

Nigeria has since been enjoying successive democratic governments, but the elections that have ushered in these democratic governments have been fraught with different forms of elec-

---

[126]Daniel Egiegba Agbiboa, 'The Evolution of Democratic Politics and Current Security Challenges in Nigeria: Retrospect and Prospect' (2013) Democracy and Security
[127]Ibid
[128]Ibid
[129]Ibid
[130]Ibid

tion irregularities, which have engendered various postelection recriminations and dissatisfaction from oppositions and stakeholders.[131] Olusegun Obasanjo, a former military Head of state, emerged as the president in 1999 and was re-elected in 2003. Umaru Yaradua won in 2007 but died in office and his term was completed by his vice, Goodluck Jonathan, who contested the 2011 elections and won amidst allegations of election irregularities.[132]

Nigeria attained a milestone of some sort in the 2015 elections as it saw an opposition party win the election for the first time in the 4th republic and also a president not completing his full 8-year tenure. The 2015 elections were commended by both local and international observers as it was seen to have broken the election fraud pattern since 1999.[133] Muhammed Buhari became president and contested for a second term in 2019 in what is considered the worst election in the history of elections in the 4th republic.[134]

---

[131]Osita Agbu, 'Elections and Governance in Nigeria's Fourth Republic' (Council for the
Development of Social Science research in Africa 2016) <https://codesria.org/IMG/pdfl0-
elections_and_governance_in_nigeriaprelim_intro.pdf5' accessed 16 October, 2023.
[132]Ibid
[133]John Campbell, 'The Legacy of Nigeria's 199 transition to Democracy' (Council For
Foreign Relations 2019) <https://www.cfr.org!blog/legacy-nigerias- 1999-transition-democracy>
accessed 16 October, 2023.
[134]Ibid

1999 and 2003 Elections

The 1999 general elections were the first in the 4th republic and the first election after the 1993 coup. It was a landslide victory for Olusegun Obasanjo of the People's Democratic Party.[135] The party also won the majority in the National assembly with a 42.1% voters' turnout for the parliamentary elections.[136] Nigerians were grateful to have another shot at a democratic government, so much so they were willing to ignore all the democratic contradictions that bedevilled previous democratic experiments in Nigeria. Contradictions like divided loyalties, corruption, election malpractices, and lack of political discipline.[137]

While there was little or no report of election violence, the election process was fraught with election fraud. The registration process and the election process itself were marred with varying degrees of irregularities and outright fraud.[138] There were reports of inflated vote returns, ballot box stuffing, altered results, and disenfranchisement of voters, as well as administrative problems on the part of the electoral body, INEC.[139] Observers reported a worrying level of arbitrariness in the application of the voting regulations. Elections did not hold in some parts of the country, especially in Bayelsa State, where there was no election in the whole state) The reported turnout figures

---

[135]Michael M Ogbeidi, 'A Culture of Failed Elections: Revisiting Democratic Elections in Nigeria, 1959-2003' (2010) 21 *Historia Actual Online*
[136]Ibid
[137]Julius Ihonvbere, 'The 1999 Presidential Elections in Nigeria: The Unresolved issues' Vol. 27
[138]The Carter Centre, 'Observing The 1998-99 Nigeria Elections — Final Report' (1999) Special
[139]Human Rights Watch, 'Elections in The Delta' (HRW) <https://www.hrw.org/reports/1 999/nigeria2! Nigeria993-06.html> accessed 16 August, 2023.

for the 1999 elections were not plausible in many states. It was most prominent in the South-South region of the country. Observers who were present throughout the whole day noted that turnout was extremely low in States like Rivers and Delta, yet a turnout of 71% and *45%* were reported in the election result.[140] Also, the 1999 elections and transition to a civilian government occurred without a constitutional framework or genuine public debate about the nation's constitutional future and how it will affect its democracy.[141] This has been considered by many as the root cause of the poor electoral process of the 1999 elections and even subsequent elections.

2003 Elections

The 2003 elections saw the incumbent president, Olusegun Obasanjo return to power for a second term, defeating his opponent, Muhammed Buhari by over 11 million votes. Voter turnout was pegged at 69.1%. Unlike the 1999 elections, the rate of election violence in the 2003 elections was higher, leaving scores of people dead and many others injured.[142] There were also reports of gross election fraud in parts of the country. The Lagos police command uncovered five million false ballots. There were reports of multiple voting, pre-field ballots, or altered results.[143]

---

[140]Ibid.
[141]David U Enweremadu, 'The Judiciary and The Survival of Democracy in Nigeria Analysis of the 2003 and 2007 Elections' (2011) 10(1) Journal of African Elections
[142]Ibid
[143]Amaramiro A Steve, Matthew Enya Nwocha, Igwe Onyebuchi Igwe, 'An Appraisal of Electoral Malpractice and Violence as an Albatross in Nigerian's Democratic Consolidation' (2019)10(1) Beijing Law Review 10

The electoral body, 1NEC, failed in its responsibilities to effectively manage the election and the outcome. There was a flawed voter registration process, and controversies pertaining to the certification of candidates.[144] Election-related logistical preparations were nothing to write home about, as most of the voting stations were unprepared for the elections.[145] Observers noted that while the electorates were eager to decide who their leaders will be, the political class was eager to corrupt the election process and rig its way into office.[146] In the city of Warri, there were *135,739* registered voters and INEC claimed that *133,529* voted for the parliamentary election. Observers reported that only a few polling stations opened on election day and there could have been no way the number of votes could be up to what was announced by INEC.[147]

One week before the parliamentary election, the incumbent president and leaders of his party met with NEC officials without the presence of representatives of the opposition parties. This raised a lot of questions as to the credibility of the election process and results.[148] It was reported that supporters of the ruling party were responsible for inciting violence around the country, causing the death of at least 100 people. There were also reports of voters' intimidation at the polling units by party supporters in order to falsify votes.[149] The 2003 elections were marred by violence, election malpractice, and the ineptitude of the electoral body, INEC.

---

[144]Ibid
[145]Ibid
[146]Festus Iyayi, 'Elections and Electoral Practices in Nigeria: Dynamics and Implications' (2005)5(2) Sabinet African Journals <https://journals.co.za/doi/pdf/10.10520/AJA15955753_129> accessed 15 September, 2023
[147]Ibid
[148]Ibid
[149]Ibid.

2007 Elections

The 2007 general election was a significant milestone in the history of elections and democracy in Nigeria because it was the first time there will be a change of civilian governments.[150] Before this election, Nigeria had not held a free and fair election since the transition from military to civilian government. The previous two elections were characterized by widespread violence, intimidation, bribery, election fraud, vote rigging, and corruption).[151] The formal democratic institutions failed to carry out their responsibilities as expected. The National Assembly failed to review the constitution in order to give real autonomy to INEC, who had also failed to fully prepare for the elections. Voters' registration and the issuance of voters' cards had not been completed days to the election.[152]

The lack of preparation on all fronts of government institutions meant that the flaws associated with the 2003 elections reached unprecedented heights in the 2007 elections.[153] The discord between the incumbent, Olusegun Obasanjo, and his

---

[150]Hakeem Onapajo and Dele Babalola, 'Nigeria's 2019 General Elections – A Shattered Hope?' (2020)109(4) The Commonwealth Journal of International Affairs 10

[151]Isah Musa Yusuf, 'Electoral Violence in Nigeria: Disentangling the Causes' (2019) 9(10) Research on Humanities and Social Sciences 8

[152]Jibrin Ibrahim, 'Nigeria's 2007 Elections — The Fifth Path to Democratic Citizenship' (2020) United States Institute of Peace Special Report <https://www.usip.orgJsites/defaultlfiles/resources/srl 82.pdf' accessed 25 January, 2023.

[153]Yusuf Isma'ila and Zaheruddin Othman, 'Challenges of Electoral Processes in Nigeria's Quest for Democratic Governance in the Fourth Republic' (2015)5(22) Research on Humanities and Social Sciences <https://core.ac.uk/download/pdf/234674783.pdf> accessed 20 April, 2023.

vice, Atiku Abubakar which led to the disqualification of Atiku by NEC and the overturn of that decision by the Federal High Court five days to the election proved to be a logistical nightmare for NEC.[154] There were reports of late delivery of voting materials, late opening of polling stations in most states, ballot box stuffing, falsification of votes amongst other election malpractices.[155] In States such as Rivers, Ogun, Oyo, and Ekiti, the total number of votes recorded far exceeded the number of registered voters.[156]

Interethnic and regional tensions and conflicts were also on the rise. These stemmed from the friction between the southern politicians and northern politicians caused by the debate on which region should be in power come 2007).[157] There were violent clashes between party supporters which led to the death of over 70 people. There was no adequate response to the violence by the Federal government, neither were the sponsors and perpetrators of the violence. Amid the violence and election malpractice, Umaru Yaradua, the chosen candidate of the incumbent president, was announced by INEC as the winner of the election.'65 All players of Nigeria's democratic institution failed woefully to deliver a free and fair election in 2007.

2011 Elections

There was a slight improvement in the election process of the 2011 elections compared to the previous elections. It was therefore considered as a milestone in Nigeria's democratic devel-

---

[154]Ibid
[155]Ibid
[156]Jibrin Ibrahim (n 156)
[157]Ibid

opment.[158] TM The incumbent president, Goodluck Jonathan, who took over after the death of the 2007 winner, Umaru Yaradua emerged as the winner of the 2011 election, while his party, PDP went on to win majority seats in the parliamentary and governorship elections.[159] The 2011 election also came off the heels of the amendments to the Electoral Act and the 1999 constitution in 2010 and early 2011. These modifications addressed the flaws of the election frameworks that led to the failure of the 2007 polls. All these and the appointment of a new INEC Chairman, Professor Attahiru Jega[160], increased public confidence in the success of the 2011 election process.[161]

The National Assembly elections were reported to have been free and fair with a sprinkle of allegations of vote-rigging, ballot-box stuffing, and snatching, but were at a reduced level compared to the 2007 elections.[162] The presidential election was also commended as very well organized since the begin-

---

[158]Kelvin Ashindorbe and Nathaniel Danjibo, 'Two Decades of Democracy in Nigeria Between Consolidation and Regression' (2022)21(2) Journal of African Elections

[159]Jibrin Ibrahim, 'Nigeria's 2007 Elections — The Fifth Path to Democratic Citizenship' (United States Institute of Peace Special Report 2020) <https://www.usip.orglsites/defaultlfiles/resources/srl 82.pdf> accessed 25 January, 2023.

[160]Professor Attahiru Jega is a renowned scholar and a former President of the Academic Staff Union of Universities (ASUU) and a human right activist.

[161]Ibid

[162]Sam Egwu and Others, 'Nigerian Elections Since 1999 — What does Democracy Mean?' 8 Journal of African Elections

ning of the fourth republic).[163] While the electoral body managed the 2011 elections better than the previous elections, there was still post-election violence by. supporters of the main opposition, Muhammadu Buhari, who believed a northerner should be in power. The violence claimed over 800 lives in 3 days and displaced over 65,000 people, majorly in the northern part of the country.[164] There were reports of voter's intimidation, using bomb attacks, to ensure a low turnout. The new voting system which required voters to be certified in the morning of the election before voting in the afternoon discouraged many voters from casting their votes).[165] Observers noted that out of the 74 million registered voters in the country, only 39 million participated in the elections. There were reports of underage voting, mostly in the north, and over 1 million votes were disqualified by 1NEC, which showed poor voter's education.[166]

---

[163]Ogaba Oche, 'Presidential and Gubernatorial Elections in the Fourth Republic' (CODESRIA)
<https:/codesria.org/IMG/pdf/7-elections_and_govemancein-nigeria_oche.pdf" accessed 21
October 2023.
[164]Democratic Institute for International Affairs, 'Final Report on the 2011 Nigerian
General Elections' (DIIA 2012)
<https://www.ndi.org/sites/defaultlfiles/ND1%2OFinal%2oReport%2Oon%20the%20Nigeria%202> accessed 16 November, 2023.
[165]International Republican Institute, 'Election Observation Report: Nigeria April 2011 National Elections' (International Republican Institute 2014)
[166]National Democratic Institute for International Affairs, 'Final Report on the 2011 Nigerian
General Elections' (2012)
<https:/fwww.ndi.org! sites/defaultlfiles/NDI%2OFinal%2oReport%2Oon%2othe%20Nigeria%202> accessed 16 November, 2023.

Despite the violence, especially in the northern parts and election malpractices, the 2011 elections were considered the benchmark for future elections in Nigeria because it was believed to have expanded democratic participation and raising the standard for electoral fairness.[167]

2015 Elections

The 2015 election saw a rematch between the main contenders of the 2011 elections. It was a contest between an incumbent and a retired General. It was also a test of the incumbent's ability to retain power after losing the support of the people and there were questions of whether there will be regional friction which was witnessed in the last election.[168] Overall, the 2015 elections were deemed an improvement on the 2011 elections, especially in the voting process.[169] The success of the election in the middle of a precarious political and security environment of the country during the period was particularly commended.[170] The innovations of the Anti-Electoral Fraud Procedures (AEFP) such as smart card reader and permanent voter's card with microchips set the 2015 elections a cut above the previous elections).[171] Despite these positives, there were

---

[167]Ibid.
[168]Uduak-Obong I. Ekanem and Ole J. Forsberg, "An Analysis of the 2015 Nigerian Presidential Election" (2018)1(2) <https://www.pvamu.edu/pursue/wp-content/uploads/sites/155/2018/06/2015-nigerian-presidential-election.pdf> accessed 24 September, 2023.
[169]Ibid.
[170]Ibid.
[171]Gani Yoroms, 'Electoral Violence, Arms Proliferations and Electoral Security In Nigeria: Lessons From The Twenty-Fifteen Elections For Emerging Democracies' (Conference paper 2019) <https://inecnigeria.org/wp-content/uploads/2019/02/Conference-Paper-by-Gani-Yoroms1.pdf> accessed 9 September,2023.

reports of violence in some polling stations. It was reported that Boko Haram, a terrorist organization, attacked several polling stations in the north, killing over 39 people.[172] There were allegations of voting irregularities across the country, states like Rivers and Akwa Ibom witnessed a flurry of election petition cases Cost-election.[173] However, it was widely believed that the level of violence and election irregularities did not affect the credibility and overall outcome of the election.

The takeaways from the 2015 elections were generally positive ones. It was the first time an incumbent president and his party will lose to the opposition. This was a break from what could have been a trend of the incumbent always winning re-elections.[174] Some also argued that it was the first time that candidates of the presidential election were elected on issue-based politics rather than region-based, which has been the norm since 1999.[175] The icing on the cake was the peaceful transition of power by Goodluck Jonathan to the winner, Muhammed Buhari. President Jonathan placed a phone call to the President-elect, Buhari, a few hours before the official results were announced to concede defeat and congratulate the

---

[172]Ibid
[173]Babayo Sule and Others, 'Nigerian 2015 General Election: The Successes, Challenges, and
Implications for Future general Elections' (2018) 1 Journal of Social and Political Sciences
[174]Nwachukwu Orji, 'The 2015 Nigerian general Elections' (2015) 50 Afrika Spectrum:
Deutsche Zeitcbrift fur Gegenwartsbezogene Afrikaforschung
[175]Aremu Fatai Ayinde and Others, 'Nigeria's 2015 Elections: Permanent Voter's Card, Smart Card Readers and Security Challenges' (2016) 15 Journal of African Elections
<https://www.eisa.org/pdfYJAE 1 5.2Ayinde.pdf accessed 25 April 2023.

winner.[176] This singular act doused the political tension already brewing around the country amidst allegations of election fraud and irregularities between supporters of both candidates. It also set a new benchmark for elections in the country and showed that meritocracy is gradually taking its root in the polity of Nigeria.[177]

2019 Elections

The 2019 elections were one of the most keenly and closely contested elections in the history of Nigerian Presidential elections. The outcome saw the incumbent president, Muhammed Buhari, re-elected for another term of four years.[178] The 2019 elections deepened democratic practice in Nigeria and kept the hope of continuous civilian rule in the country.[179] Judging by the standards set in the 2015 elections, stakeholders were expecting a consolidation of these standards in the 2019 elections. It was not to be so, as the 2019 elections were fraught with serious shortcomings that questioned the credibility of the election.[180]

Elections were postponed hours to voting without any prior notice. INEC based this decision on its inability to meet up with logistical obligations for the elections.[181] The resultant effect of the postponement was confusion over the appropriate duration of candidate and party campaigns, low voter's turnout and apathy on the new date, and ultimately, loss of confidence

---

[176]Ibid
[177]Ibid
[178]Ibid
[179]Ibid
[180]Nwachukwu Orji (n 177)
[181]Ibid

in the electoral body.[182] There were allegations of insincerity on the part of the incumbent president when he suspended the Chief Justice of the Federation, weeks before the election. This was deemed as a political move.[183] The president also refused to give assent to the bill that sought to amend vital aspects of the 2019 Electoral Act months before the Elections, on the ground that the timeframe was too short for INEC to implement the amendments.[184] This increased tension among stakeholders, as many felt the amendment will enhance transparency and accountability in the electoral process.[185]

The security situation of the country contributed to the issue of low turnout, which gave room for election malpractices in major parts of the country. It was reported that 11 out of the 36 states were in potential security threat risk, while 22 were in the red zone.[186] There were issues of godfatherism, money politics, violent campaigns, hate speech, insurgency, ethno-religious conflicts, political thuggery, and an unprepared electoral

---

[182]Babayo Sule, 'The 2019 Presidential Election in Nigeria: An Analysis of the Voting pattern,
Issues and Impact' (2019) 15 Malaysian Journal of Society and Space

[183]Babayo Sule and Others, 'The 2019 General Election in Nigeria: Examining the Issues, Challenges,
Successes and Lessons for Future General Elections' (2020) 6 International Journal of Social Sciences Perspectives

[184]Nigeria Civil Society Situation Room, 'Report of Nigeria's 2019 General Elections' (2019) <https://situationroomng.org/wp-content/uploads/20 I 9/09/Report-on-Nigerias-20 19-General-E l ections.pdf accessed 25 April 2023.

[185]Olu Awofeso, 'Observers Report and the 2019 General Elections in Nigeria: A Focus On
Electoral Violence and Lessons for Future Elections' (2020) Vol. 8 Global Journal of Political Science and Administration

[186]Ibid

body.[187] All these marred the 2019 elections, which was the most expensive in the history of the country, costing N374 billion, and it also set a low bar compared to the previous two elections.[188]

2023 Elections

The 2023 presidential election was the most competitive and contentious in Nigeria's history. The election was a three-way race between Bola Tinubu of the All Progressive Congress (APC), Atiku Abubakar of the People's Democratic Party (PDP) and Peter Obi of the Labour Party (LP). Tinubu, a former governor of Lagos state and a political godfather in the south-west region, emerged as the winner with 37% of the vote, followed by Abubakar with 29% and Obi with 25%. Tinubu met the constitutional requirement of winning at least 25% of the vote in two-thirds of Nigeria's 36 states and the capital, Abuja. He also won the most votes nationwide, despite losing some key states to his rivals, such as Kano, Rivers and Adamawa. Tinubu's victory was greeted with jubilation by his supporters in his strongholds in the south-west, where he is widely credited with transforming Lagos into a modern megacity. His campaign slogan "*Emi Lokan*", which translates to "it's my turn [to be president]" in Yoruba, resonated with many voters who felt that he deserved to lead the country after years of political struggle and sacrifice. Tinubu also promised to tackle

---

[187]EU Election Observation Mission, 'Nigeria General Elections 2019 Final Report' (2019) "Olu Awofeso, 'Observers Report and the 2019 General Elections in Nigeria: A Focus On Electoral Violence and Lessons for Future Elections' (2020) Vol. 8 Global Journal of Political Science and Administration
[188]Ibid.

Nigeria's security and economic challenges, such as the insurgency by Islamist militants Boko Haram, the separatist agitation by pro-Biafra activists, the farmer-herder clashes, the high unemployment rate and the inflation.

However, Tinubu's victory was not without controversy. His main rival, Abubakar, a former vice-president and a wealthy businessman, rejected the results and called for a rerun, alleging widespread rigging and manipulation by the electoral commission and security agencies. He also accused Tinubu of being unfit to rule due to his poor health and corruption scandals. Abubakar filed a petition at the presidential election tribunal, seeking to overturn Tinubu's victory. The tribunal dismissed his petition for lack of evidence and upheld Tinubu's election. The third candidate, Obi, a former governor of Anambra state and a successful entrepreneur, also challenged Tinubu's victory at the tribunal, claiming that he was robbed of millions of votes due to irregularities and intimidation. He argued that he was the only candidate with integrity and a clear vision for Nigeria's development. He enjoyed massive support on social media and among young and educated voters, especially in the south-east region where he hails from. However, he failed to win any state outside his region and could not match Tinubu's or Abubakar's political clout and resources. The tribunal also dismissed his petition for lack of merit.

Both Alhaji Atiku Abubakar and Peter Obi appealed the decision of the Presidential Election Petition. However, in a unanimous decision, the Supreme Court dismissed all the Appeals for lacking merit and upheld the decision of the Presidential

Election Petition Tribunal.[189] This decision finally laid to rest the legal battle on the 2023 Presidential elections. However, there has been divergent views on the decision of the Supreme Court. Femi Falana SAN,[190] while commenting on the Supreme Court judgement, stated that the Judiciary should not be determining election results.[191] He opined that the Independent National Electoral Commission (INEC) should be the sole organ responsible for determination of winners in an election. Despite the judgement delivered by the apex court's seven-man panel led by Justice John Okoro, Falana stressed that the nation is yet to maintain a strong footing on the conduct of elections that are devoid of acrimony. This author disagrees with the learned silk on his position. The Judiciary is the arm of government responsible for determination of disputes, and thus has the power to determine issues on elections brought before it. Even in developed countries, there are situations where electoral disputes are settled by the Court. This position does not in any way downplay the obvious shortcomings and inadequacies of INEC in the presidential elections.

---

[189]The Supreme Court on October, 23, 2023 delivered a unanimous judgment on the Appeal filed by the Alhaji Atiku Abubakar and Peter Obi challenging the results of the 2023 presidential elections. The Court dismissed the two Appeals for lack of merit and upheld the earlier decision of the Presidential Election Petition Tribunal.

[190]Femi Falana is Senior Advocate of Nigeria and Human Rights Activist.

[191]Judiciary shouldn't determine election winners, says Falana punch news October 27, 2023 <https://punchng.com/judiciary-shouldnt-determine-election-winners-says-falana/> accessed 20 November, 2023.

On his part, Ebun Adegboruwa SAN[192] argued that though the judgement of the Supreme Court has laid to rest the legal battle on the results of the 2023 presidential elections, it does not remove the fact that INEC failed in the discharge of her duties during the conduct of the elections.[193] He stated that the judgement of the Supreme Court which affirms the failure to upload election results in real-time on IREV[194] does not nullify the outcome is sound. According to him, this is an indication that the Independent National Electoral Commission (INEC) has failed Nigerians. Adegboruwa however wondered what the penalty would be for INEC, who failed Nigerians in its constitutional duty. He suggested that the National Assembly should set up a special committee to scrutinize the judgement of the Court of Appeal and Supreme Court for the purpose of amending the Electoral Act 2022 for future polls.

According to him, "The Supreme Court held that failure by INEC to upload election results on IREV leads to loss of public confidence in the electoral process." The Court, however, held that such failure will not lead to the nullification of election results. The judgement is sound in law and accords with the relevant statues on the issue. He stated that the use of technology is to prevent manipulation of election results. He urged INEC to help Nigeria by keeping it its guidelines and public

[192]Ebun Adegboruwa is a Human Rights Activist and Senior Advocate of Nigeria

[193]Iwok Iniobong, Business Day, 'Supreme Court judgement sound but INEC failed Nigerians — Ebun Adegboruwa' (*Business Day*) <https://businessday.ng/politics/article/supreme-court-judgement-sound-but-inec-failed-nigerians-ebun-adegboruwa/> accessed 20 November, 2023.

[194]IREV is the INEC Result Viewing Portal. It is a platform created by the Independent National Electoral Commission (INEC) in Nigeria to provide real-time transmission of election results from polling units to the central collation centre.

statements and undertakings. These two views by are apt and timely, it is however unfortunate that INEC failed to redeem her image in during the conduct of off-cycle governorship elections in Bayelsa, Imo and Kogi States.[195] The elections were characterised by vote buying, abduction and holding of poll officials' hostage in some communities such as Brass Local Government Area in Bayelsa State.[196] There was the death of George Sibo, which allegedly occurred at a collation centre in Twon Brass, also in Bayelsa. Furthermore, is the reported bypass of Bimodal Voter Accreditation System Device, better known as BVAS by some unscrupulous INEC poll officials. The ugly incidents include the discovery of pre-filled result sheets in some LGs in Kogi. According to INEC, reports indicate that the incidents occurred in Adavi, Ajaokuta, Ogori/Magongo, Okehi and Okene Local Government Areas.[197] The most serious incidents occurred in Ogori/Magongo, affecting nine of the 10 registration areas.

Another shocking revelation came from a press statement issued by YIAGA Africa[198] on Sunday, November 12, 2023. According to the civil society organisation which was accredited to observe the polls, reports from some Watching the Vote observers in Imo State indicate elections did not take place in 12 per cent of YIAGA Africa-sampled polling units. These cases were prevalent in Orsu, Okigwe, Oru East, and Orlu LGs.

---

[195]INEC conducted off-cycle governorship elections in three states on Saturday, November 11, 2023.

[196]Jide Ojo, 'Musings on Imo, Kogi and Bayelsa States Off-Cycle Elections' (*Punch News*, 15 November, 2023 <https://punchng.com/musings-on-imo-kogi-bayelsa-off-cycle-elections/> accessed 20 November, 2023.

[197]Ibid

[198]Yiaga Africa is a non-profit civic hub of change makers committed to the promotion of democratic governance, human rights and civic engagement.

YIAGA Africa also monitored the upload of results on the IREV, especially those from polling units where elections did not hold. The group gave a breakdown of about 40 of such polling units where elections did not hold in Imo State, yet results were uploaded on the IREV Portal.[199] There were cases of inflated results where the number of voters is higher than the figures of those who were accredited in the polling unit. This is clear evidence of result manipulation. This happened because the integrity measures put in place in Section 64 subsections 1 – 9 of the Electoral Act 2022 were ignored by the presiding officers as well as the collation and Returning Officers.

The presidential elections trend in Nigeria since 1999 shows that Nigeria has made some progress in consolidating its democracy and conducting peaceful transitions of power. However, it also reveals some challenges and problems that need to be addressed, such as electoral malpractice, violence, regional polarization, ethnic and religious divisions, corruption, insecurity and underdevelopment. Nigeria needs to strengthen its institutions, promote national unity and inclusiveness, enhance accountability and transparency, improve security and welfare, and foster a culture of tolerance and dialogue among its diverse people. Nigeria will be able to achieve her full potential as a great nation, when all these issues are deliberately addressed and given priority.

Conclusion

It is a known fact that elections in most African countries are unpredictable due to several social, economic, ethnic, and religious factors.[200] However, from the discussions in this paper, it

---

[199]Ibid
[200]Ibid

is evident that Ghana has found a way to structure its election process to guarantee a sustainable democracy and an election process that has been regarded as a beacon for other African countries. Between 1992 and 2016, Ghana has been able to alternate power peacefully between two major political parties; namely New Patriotic Party and the National Democratic Congress.[201] In contrast, Nigeria has been phased with a myriad of election problems varying from election violence, election fraud, incompetent electoral body, ethnic diversity, and so many others. It is yet to find a way to conduct its elections in a free and fair manner devoid of all these problems. A major difference in the democratic structure of Ghana and Nigeria is the foundation on which their democracy is built. Ghana held a referendum before the return of democracy and the citizens were actively involved in the drafting of the constitution on which its democracy was founded.204 Nigeria, on the other hand, based its fourth republic democracy structure on the 1979 constitution with few amendments. Worst of all, it was a select few appointed by the then Head of State, Gen. Abdulsalam Abubakar, that decided that it was the best for the country. While Ghana's constitution establishes different formal democratic institutions to handle its election process and these institutions are conferred with absolute autonomy when carrying out their duties, that of Nigeria only establishes these institutions on paper as they are not independent of the interference from political players in power.

The secret to Ghana's election success rate which the other West African States including Nigeria can take a cue from is the independence of its formal democratic institutions concerned with the organization and execution of a successful election. These institutions include the Election Commission,

---

[201]Ibid

the Judiciary, and the Media. All these institutions are truly independent and are not interfered with by the government of the day. They are allowed to function seamlessly during and after an election cycle. Political actors must also put the democratic institutions of the country above their thirst for power. Any aggrieved party should seek redress in the Courts rather than inciting violence and discrediting the entire election process. An election should not be a 'do-or-die' affair.

About the Publisher

Sulis International Press publishes select fiction and nonfiction in a variety of genres under four imprints:

- Riversong Books (fiction)
- Sulis Press (general nonfiction)
- Keledei Publications (spirituality)
- Sulis Academic Press (academic works)

For more, visit the website at
https://sulisinternational.com

Subscribe to the newsletter at
https://sulisinternational.com/subscribe/

Follow on social media
https://www.facebook.com/SulisInternational
https://twitter.com/Sulis_Intl
https://www.pinterest.com/Sulis_Intl/
https://www.instagram.com/sulis_international/